W9-BNP-564

THE SOCIAL MISSION OF THE U.S. CATHOLIC CHURCH

The Social Mission

OF THE

U.S. Catholic Church

~

A Theological Perspective

CHARLES E. CURRAN

GEORGETOWN UNIVERSITY PRESS
Washington, D.C.

© 2011 Georgetown University Press. All rights reserved. No part of this book may be reproduced or utilized in any form or by any means, electronic or mechanical, including photocopying and recording, or by any information storage and retrieval system, without permission in writing from the publisher.

Library of Congress Cataloging-in-Publication Data

Curran, Charles E.
    The social mission of the U.S. Catholic Church : a theological perspective / Charles E. Curran.
        p.   cm.
    Includes bibliographical references and index.
    ISBN 978-1-58901-743-6 (pbk. : alk. paper)
    1. Church work—United States—History.   2. Christian sociology—United States—History.   3. Church work—Catholic Church—History.   4. Christian sociology—Catholic Church—History.   5. Catholic Church—United States—History. 6. United States—Church history.   I. Title.
BX2347.C87   2011
253.088′2820904—dc22

                        2010012974

∞ This book is printed on acid-free paper meeting the requirements of the American National Standard for Permanence in Paper for Printed Library Materials.

15   14   13   12   11   10   9   8   7   6   5   4   3   2
First printing

Printed in the United States of America

To Colleen and David Wallace

CONTENTS

T his book deals with the social mission of the U.S. Catholic Church from a theological perspective, and treats four significant aspects of that mission—its importance, who carries it out, how it is carried out, and the roles that the Church and individual Catholics play in supporting it.

Post–Vatican II theology has insisted on the importance of the social mission of the Church as a constitutive dimension of the Gospel and the Church's mission. Simply stated, without a social mission there is no Church. The daunting task facing the Church is to ensure that all its baptized understand that the social mission is fundamental and necessary.

Who carries out the social mission of the Church? The basic answer is quite simple—all baptized members of the Church. Catholic theology recognizes the bishops' oversight and teaching role in the Church and its social mission. As overseers the bishops have a responsibility to make the whole Church recognize the theoretical and practical importance of the social mission. But individual Catholics, various movements, and institutions also exercise important leadership functions as regards the social mission of the Church. The pope and bishops have proposed a body of teaching—often called Catholic social teaching—which contributes to the Church's social mission but cannot be identified with the social mission as such. Like all good teachers, the pope and bishops must also be learners. Most of this teaching focuses on the need to work to effect public policies and changes in political and economic structure. This call for transformation constitutes a definite part—but only a part—of the total social mission of the Church.

Theology before Vatican II saw the laity as carrying out the temporal mission of the Church, but post–Vatican II theology recognizes the laity's role in the internal life of the Church as well as in its social mission. There has been a controversy in the U.S. Church about the role of religious and clergy related to lay people in the social mission of the Church. Religious and clergy can and should have a role but the primary role belongs to the laity who carry out the social mission in family, neighborhood, work, social, professional, cultural, and recreational milieux and in their role as citizens in the community.

How is the social mission of the laity carried out? Institutions such as Catholic health care facilities and Catholic Charities have a long history of caring for the sick and needy. Movements such as the Catholic Worker have contributed much to the social mission of the Church. These two institutions and the Catholic Worker movement have undergone great change over the years. In the pre–Vatican II Church in light of the understanding of Catholic action, Catholics joined together to work for a particular cause (such as peace or racial integration) or to influence a particular milieu (such as the Catholic Family Movement). However, after Vatican II movements involving only Catholics gradually declined, and Catholics carried out the social mission in their daily life and in conjunction with all other people of goodwill.

What are the various roles the Church and its members play in supporting the social mission? The primary role is the formation and education of the baptized to understand the centrality of the social mission and put it into practice within the Church and in the lives of the baptized. In addition to teaching and formation, the Church and its members serve, advocate for, and empower the poor; and in their lives strive to bear witness and serve as role models. Bishops, as leaders of the Church, support or oppose particular policies, but ordinarily not particular political candidates and parties. In the United States bishops' efforts to overturn existing abortion laws have been especially fraught. This book will devote many pages to this controversial issue, but will also demonstrate that the support of particular policies by Church leaders constitutes a comparatively small aspect of the total social mission.

The social mission of the Church depends on three historically changing factors—the theological understanding of the Church and its social mission, the sociological situation of the Church and its members in relationship to U.S. society and ethos, and the changing historical circumstances affecting U.S. society.

This book is not meant to be a history of the social mission of the Church in the United States. The premier historian of public Catholicism in this country is David J. O'Brien, whose work will often be cited in the following pages. This volume is a work of theology, which includes ethical and pastoral dimensions. In light of historical developments affecting the social mission of the Church, historical examples and illustrations are necessary, but some significant instances—such as Central Verein, National Catholic Rural Life Conference, the Sodality, the Grail, and the cooperative movement—are not treated herein.

Catholic social ethics and Catholic social teaching detail the specific content of the social mission. What is proposed in this book is in my judgment in accord with acceptable understandings of the Constitution and First Amendment—although the volume does not deal directly with the First Amendment questions.

Writing this book from a theological perspective, I have come to appreciate the many who in daily life have tried to live out the social mission of the Church. The book has as its primary focus a theological and therefore somewhat theoretical understanding of the social mission of the Church, but it is hoped that such a perspective will also provide insight as to how the Church and individual Catholics can live out the social mission of the Church as a constitutive dimension of the Gospel.

Finally, I want to recognize my debts and express my thanks to all who have helped me in the research and writing of this book. Above all I am grateful to my institution, Southern Methodist University (SMU), for providing me the opportunity and support for my research. My students, faculty colleagues, the librarians at Bridwell Library, and the administration of the university have made SMU a very congenial, hospitable, and challenging academic home for me. Since coming to SMU in 1991 I have been privileged to hold the Elizabeth Scurlock University Professorship of Human Values, established by Jack and Laura Lee Blanton in memory of Laura Lee Blanton's mother. Laura Lee Blanton died in 1999, but she continues to influence the life of SMU thanks to the major and significant benefactions of the Blantons. Richard Brown, the director of Georgetown University Press, and James F. Keenan, the editor of its Moral Traditions series—together with the most cooperative staff of the press—have been most helpful and supportive. I am appreciative to those who critically read the manuscript and gave me helpful suggestions: Ken Himes, Marv Mich, Bill Donnelly, and John Gargan read the entire manuscript; Chuck Fahey and Ron Hamel read particular chapters. This volume would never have seen the light of day without the help of those who worked with me in preparing the manuscript—Carol Swartz, Josh Mauldin, and especially Chris Dowdy.

1

Early Historical Context and
Taking Care of Our Own

An overview of the social mission of the Catholic Church in the United
States before the Second Vatican Council (1962–65) will provide important building blocks for developing a contemporary systematic understanding of the social mission of the Church. Three factors heavily influence
the social mission of the Church—the understanding of the Church (ecclesiology), the changing sociological relationship of the Catholic Church to U.S.
society and ethos, and the changing circumstances affecting life in the United
States.

Catholic ecclesiology as a separate discipline came into existence after the
Protestant Reformation. In this context of defensiveness Catholic ecclesiology
emphasized almost exclusively the institutional aspects of the Church, especially the hierarchical structure. These were the aspects that had been denied
by the Protestant reformers. But there were also developments in the understanding of ecclesiology in the nineteenth and twentieth centuries. There is no
doubt that the Catholic Church became more centralized and more authoritar-
ian than ever before in the period before the Second Vatican Council. The First
Vatican Council in 1870 dealt only with the papal office and contributed to the
emphasis on the ultimate and all-embracing authority of the papacy in the
Church. The role of the papacy in terms of the teaching and ruling aspect of
the Church only increased as it entered the twentieth century. Vatican II's
ecclesiology, while recognizing the role of the papal office in the Church,
insisted that the Church is the people of God and not just the hierarchy. In
addition, Vatican II's teaching on the collegiality of all bishops together with
the bishop of Rome opposed a monarchical vision of the Church that was
associated with what was often called the ultramontane approach, which in

the nineteenth and subsequent centuries stressed papal prerogatives above all else.[1]

Life in the United States has changed dramatically since the seventeenth century, and the relationship of the Church to the surrounding culture profoundly affected its social mission. Three different situations emerged in the United States: the early colonies, especially Maryland; the growing immigrant Church that characterized the Catholic Church in the United States from the 1830s onward; and the growth of the immigrant Church in the twentieth century as the second and third generations of immigrants assimilated into the U.S. middle class.[2]

MARYLAND AND THE EARLY CATHOLIC CHURCH

The earliest Catholic settlement in the United States was in Maryland. Some Catholics, including two Jesuit priests, made the original voyage under the leadership of Lord Baltimore in 1634. Catholics were never the majority, but the colony was originally conceived to be a place where Catholics were accepted. Over time Puritans became more powerful in Maryland and restricted Catholic worship. Catholics, however, regained their right to practice their religion in the Maryland colony. After the American Revolution, Catholics constituted a small population in Maryland—15,000 out of 319,700 persons. Charles Carroll of Carrollton was the only Catholic among the 56 who signed the Declaration of Independence. His cousin, John Carroll (1735–1815), became the first Catholic bishop in the United States.[3]

Catholics in the Maryland colony were far removed from Rome and consequently had to work out many of their early approaches themselves. Carroll, the first bishop in the United States, was elected by the clergy. Liturgies were often celebrated in English because the Catholic leaders thought this was what should be done in the new world. However, over time Rome's authority grew in importance as the American Catholic Church also experienced the ultramontane emphasis on the papal office.

The first Catholic settlers in Maryland belonged to the landed classes and were associated with the conservative and royalist sympathies of the Calverts, who founded and led the colony. They lived on plantations and accepted the social realities of their circumstances—land tenure, indentured servants, and slavery. They also fought to maintain the right to practice their faith and strongly supported the need for religious tolerance in Maryland. These Catholic families had both agricultural and merchant interests, like so many of their compatriots. They generally supported the American Revolution, the Federalist view of government as a strong central authority, and the role of the propertied classes.

C. Joseph Nuesse, whose work I draw upon in this book, in his study of the social thought of American Catholics before 1829, concludes that Catholics in Maryland strongly echoed the political and social ideas of their compatriots. American Catholics maintained a social outlook best described as conformist. Factors other than their religious tenets most affected their social thought and action. The faith of the Catholics in Maryland was strong in its own way, but it had little or no effect on their attitudes toward public and societal life and political institutions.[4]

One early-eighteenth-century American Catholic who was a strong advocate of social reform was Matthew Carey (1760–1839). An Irish immigrant who had supported Irish independence and the repeal of the penal code, Carey was also acquainted with and helped by both Benjamin Franklin and the Marquis de Lafayette. As a publisher and pamphleteer he gained a reputation as a reformer. He opposed laissez-faire economic policies and advocated a living wage, relief for the poor and unemployed, good education for all, and penal reform. But he did not appeal to his Catholic faith or any Christian motivation in support of institutional reforms; his staunch Catholicism did not affect his public stance. He was a humanitarian.[5]

One significant instance of conformism in the period before the Civil War concerns the issue of slavery.[6] In 1785, John Carroll—then the Church superior in this country—wrote to Rome explaining that in Maryland there were 9,000 Catholic adults and 3,000 Catholic slaves. The Jesuit province in Maryland were slaveholders. After arguments back and forth the Jesuits in Maryland finally sold their remaining slaves to Louisianans in 1837. The Vincentians south of St. Louis, Missouri, were major slaveholders. The Ursuline Sisters had slaves from their arrival in New Orleans in 1727.[7]

In a long series of published letters John England, the bishop of Charleston, justified the U.S. practice of slavery on the basis of history, scripture, and natural law. He later admitted he was not personally amenable to slavery but recognized the impossibility of abolishing it at that time. It was up to the legislature, not him, to determine how slavery should be abolished.[8]

Francis P. Kenrick, who in 1851 became the Archbishop of Baltimore, discussed slavery in his 1840s textbook on moral theology for seminarians and priests. Kenrick maintained that slavery was not counter to natural law; nor did scripture condemn slavery. Although the ancestors of U.S. slaves were brought to this country unjustly, he justified the continuance of slavery in the

United States on the basis of prescription and longevity. Concern for the good order of society justified limiting the freedom of the slaves in the United States in the 1840s.[9] Before 1861 no American bishop spoke out publicly on the evils of slavery.[10]

The acceptance of slavery by U.S. Catholic bishops and other leaders such as Orestes Brownson was based on several factors—racial prejudice, tolerance of slavery by past Catholic authorities, fear of social upheaval were the slaves to be freed, and a perception of slavery as just one of many miseries to be endured in this world. John T. McGreevy proposes another very significant reason: Many American abolitionists viewed both slavery and Catholicism as despotic institutions.[11]

The Catholic leaders' acceptance of slavery indicates once again the conformist attitude of U.S. Catholics. Robert Emmett Curran concludes his study of the Catholic attitudes toward slavery by saying that the survival of the Church dictated silence and conformity: "This strategy worked but one can today wonder at the price that was paid."[12]

THE IMMIGRANT CHURCH

From the 1830s, the Catholic Church in the United States was primarily a church of immigrants. As the nineteenth century progressed there were great influxes from Ireland and Germany. In 1827 there were twenty thousand Irish Catholic immigrants; by mid-century there were nearly a million. Total nineteenth-century growth was phenomenal: in 1800 there were 318,000 Catholics in the United States, or 3 percent of the population; in 1900 there were more than 12 million Catholics (16 percent); and by 1965 Catholics numbered 46 million—24 percent of the total population.[13]

In the nineteenth century the Catholic Church was overwhelmed by immigrants who were generally poor and uneducated. But another problem arose —anti-Catholicism. Anti-immigration and anti-Catholicism came in three different waves in the nineteenth century. Nativist prejudices against immigrants and Catholics arose in the 1830s. Provoked by anti-Catholic speakers and publications, violence soon ensued. Catholic convents and churches were burned in some areas. In the 1850s the Know-Nothing Party was formed; the party strongly opposed Catholics and foreigners. In 1887 a third wave of anti-Catholic prejudice came in the form of the American Protective Association.[14]

Historical realities influenced the response of the U.S. Catholic bishops, whose primary concern was to care for the spiritual and, to a degree, the material needs of incoming Catholic immigrants. A secondary agenda related to the problem of anti-Catholicism was that bishops as leaders of the Catholic community attempted to prove that Catholics were good, loyal, patriotic American citizens, in hopes of overcoming the prejudices and discrimination to which they were often subjected.[15]

A good illustration of this strategy was the founding of the national association of bishops in the United States in 1917, occasioned by World War I. There was a need to coordinate the activities of individual Catholic groups—such as the Knights of Columbus and Chaplains' Aide Associates—and especially to show that the Catholic Church as a whole was 100 percent behind the war effort. Thus, the National Catholic War Council (NCWC) came into existence. Only after Vatican II did national bishops' conferences come into existence in the rest of the Catholic world.[16]

After the war the bishops decided to maintain their national body, giving it the title National Catholic Welfare Council. Rome was fearful that this was a type of church authority with power and jurisdiction over individual bishops; U.S. bishops pointed out that the body was a voluntary association based on the free support of the bishops and had no church authority or jurisdiction. Rome allowed the organization to continue, but insisted that it could not use the word "council" since it implied some type of church power and authority. The acronym NCWC was kept, but the name was changed to the National Catholic Welfare Conference. This organization ultimately played a significant role in structuring the social mission of the Church in the United States.

Inevitably, there were and always will be tensions between being Catholic and being American. One such tension that arose in the nineteenth century regarded the growth of a separate Catholic school system. Catholics complained that public schools really were Protestant, and thus established their own schools. As time went on questions arose about public funding for Catholic schools. Many Americans saw the separate Catholic school system as divisive, which further fueled views of Catholicism as an alien religion.[17]

The greatest problem many Americans had with the Catholic Church was its failure to accept religious freedom and the basic principles of the U.S. Constitution. This tension continued in the twentieth century, came to the fore during Al Smith's 1928 presidential campaign, and was a major factor in John F. Kennedy's 1960 campaign. Only at Vatican II in 1965 did the Catholic Church finally accept religious freedom for all.[18]

There were also tensions on the Catholic side. Many, especially in Rome, were fearful that the U.S. Catholic Church would become too American. Since the United States was primarily a Protestant country, they worried that Catholics would lose their faith and become Protestant if they Americanized. Some—such as Isaac Hecker (1819–88), the founder of the Paulist Fathers—saw the U.S. ethos as open to and very appreciative of Catholic views. The Catholic faith affirmed the goodness of humans and of human reason and the acceptance of religious freedom and democratic values in the United States. In his view, Catholics should shed some of their defensiveness and authoritarianism, but Catholic humanism is most appealing to the American spirit.[19]

In the late nineteenth century, Archbishop John Ireland of St. Paul and Bishop John Keane, the first rector of the Catholic University of America, were at the forefront of what was called American Catholic liberalism. They urged the Americanization of immigrants and the Church's greater accommodation of U.S. culture. Conservative bishops, especially Michael A. Corrigan of New York City and Bernard J. McQuaid of Rochester, opposed such accommodation but Cardinal James Gibbons of Baltimore, the leader of the U.S. hierarchy, generally sided with the progressives.[20]

In 1899, however, Pope Leo XIII, in his apostolic letter *Testem benevolentiae*, condemned Americanism as accommodation in the name of gaining converts, and for emphasizing natural and active virtues associated with democracy over such supernatural and passive virtues as humility and obedience. Liberal American bishops replied they agreed with everything in the document but that it better represented French ideas about the U.S. situation than the reality found in the United States.[21]

Even as Catholics mainstreamed more fully into U.S. life and culture after the World War II, tensions continued to some degree—as illustrated by debates over public aid to Catholic schools and sending an ambassador to the Vatican. Paul Blanshard's *American Freedom and Catholic Power* developed the thesis that Catholic power was a threat to American freedom and democracy.[22] However, the election of John F. Kennedy in 1960, the papacy of John XXIII (1958–63), the writings of John Courtney Murray, and the acceptance of religious freedom at Vatican II helped to ease most of these tensions.

This strategy of defending and promoting the faith of hordes of Catholic immigrants to this country and presenting them as good Americans meant that the Catholic Church did not have time or inclination to consider reform of U.S. social institutions. Until the last decades of the nineteenth century Catholic social thought was conservative, cautious, and individually oriented. There may have been great concern about charity and taking care of the poor—especially the Catholic poor—but there was little talk of justice or the reform of economic institutions.[23]

CONTINUED GROWTH AND SOME ASSIMILATION

The overlapping third historical stage came with the greater number of Catholics and their gradual assimilation into the American ethos, resulting in growing concern about U.S. political and social institutions. A very early indication of an interest in social structures involved upholding the right of poor workers, many of whom were Catholic, to form unions. U.S. bishops—and especially their leader, Cardinal Gibbons—supported the Knights of Labor, a union founded in 1869 by Catholic Terence Powderly. In 1886 the Vatican reaffirmed the earlier condemnation of the Knights in the ecclesiastical province of Quebec, Canada. Gibbons submitted an 1887 memorial to the Vatican arguing against the condemnation of the Knights in the United States. The Vatican was concerned in the main because this was not a union composed only of Catholics. Gibbons made a number of arguments against condemnation: there was a real social problem behind the formation of the Knights; the Catholic faith of the workers was strong and there was no possibility for a strictly Catholic association; a condemnation could very easily occasion many working people to leave the Church; and the organization probably would not last very long. Gibbons's concern was the Church and not the broader society.[24] Gibbons was successful and the Knights were not condemned.

The social problems created by the Industrial Revolution grew. Pope Leo XIII's 1891 encyclical *Rerum novarum* addressed the rights of workers and the need for legislation to protect their rights. John A. Ryan was the most vocal Catholic defending the rights of labor and the need for government intervention to protect these rights in the early twentieth century. Ryan was a Minnesota priest who published his Catholic University doctoral dissertation on a living wage in 1906. He later came back to teach at Catholic University, and became the first director of the Social Action Department of the National Catholic Welfare Council.[25]

A significant early document concerning social justice was the "Bishops' Program of Social Reconstruction," issued by the Administrative Committee of the National Catholic War Council. This document expressed the Catholic bishops' belief that the Church should address areas of social justice affecting the political and social institutions of the United States in the aftermath of World War I. The bishops proposed a number of short-term reforms—including a legal living wage and state provision for insurance against illness, unemployment, and old age. Three long-term systemic defects that needed to be changed were inefficiency and waste in production and distribution, insufficient incomes for the majority of workers, and unnecessarily large incomes for a small minority of privileged capitalists. John A. Ryan wrote the first draft of this document.[26] The 1919 "Bishops' Program" indicated that the U.S. Catholic Church was now in a position to address in a more systematic and consistent way the issues of justice and peace facing the United States as a whole. Throughout the twentieth century, and into the twenty-first, bishops continued to speak out on such issues.

Taking Care of Our Own

The most obvious social mission of the ever-growing immigrant Catholic Church in the United States in the nineteenth and early twentieth centuries was to take care of the material needs of those they viewed as their own. The St. Vincent de Paul Society—founded in France in 1833 by Antoine Fréderic Ozanam to allow lay people to serve the poor—played a significant role. From the 1840s the society had a presence in most large dioceses in the United States. At first the society existed primarily on the parish level. After 1860 it expanded its efforts and established orphanages and care for delinquent children in many dioceses. Other activities included foster home programs, libraries, and cultural and recreational programs for youth. The society was organized at different levels: the local level of the parish, intermediate councils, and a national general council. National meetings began in 1864.[27]

Catholic Charities

Dorothy M. Brown and Elizabeth McKeown, in their very well-received history of Catholic Charities, see the New York situation as paradigmatic of what ultimately happened nationwide.[28] One of the primary problems of fighting poverty in the nineteenth century was taking care of poor children in orphanages and detention homes. The St. Vincent de Paul Society was a leader in caring for poor Catholics in general, and included some institutional care for children. Many women's religious orders started foundling homes and orphanages but most residents were children whose parents could not take care of them, not true orphans who no longer had parents. Many Catholic lay volunteers, especially women, shared in the work of providing and caring for these poor Catholic children.

Their motives were obviously to take care of their own but also to keep Protestants from winning over these children. The existing New York City policy was to give public money to Anglo-Protestant groups who cared for children in institutions. Thanks to Catholic ties to Democratic Tammany Hall, children could be cared for in Catholic institutions and with the help of public funds. This approach differed diametrically from the case of religious schools. New York State also passed a "Children's Law" with a clause guaranteeing that children would be placed in private institutions in accordance with the religion of their parents.

In New York City some social work professionals and Protestants began to oppose the provision of public funds for religious—and especially Catholic—children's institutions. John Purroy Mitchel, who was elected mayor of New York City in 1914 as an anti-Tammany candidate, opposed the system and tried unsuccessfully to change it. Reports indicated many Catholic institutions were poorly run and should be taken over by public authorities; public monies would be saved in this manner. Catholics fought back and were able to keep their existing systems, but Archbishop Patrick Hayes recognized problems in many Catholic institutions and worked to get more central control over institutions that had previously been independent. His purpose was to ensure compliance with public regulations and to guarantee that Catholic institutions would still be supported by public funds in addition to an annual diocesan-wide collection for these institutions. Thus a greater professionalization and centralization came to characterize many Catholic efforts to care for poor children, necessitating trained social workers.[29]

Thousands of religious women, some religious men, and many lay volunteers (mostly women) were to take care of their own Catholic children and build the largest private social work system in the United States. The drive toward centralization, coordination, and professionalism meant that the leadership of Catholic Charities fell to bishops, clerics, and professional social workers. Most of the professional social workers were lay women who faced a glass ceiling and could not advance to positions of leadership in Catholic Charities. A good number left Catholic Charities and assumed leadership positions in local, state, and federal agencies.[30]

The National Conference of Catholic Charities was founded in 1910; for its first ten years it was an informal association of lay volunteers and a few professional social workers under the leadership of the St. Vincent de Paul Society, and supplemented by a large number of Catholic women and a handful of clerics. Father John O'Grady, who became executive secretary in 1920, pushed for greater professionalization and greater centralization, with ultimate control of the organization in the hands of diocesan directors. These priest diocesan directors became powerful as a result of the centralization of Catholic Charities on the diocesan level.[31]

By the middle of the twentieth century the National Conference did advocate for some structural change, but it was only after Vatican II that this advocacy became more prominent. The move to professionalism meant that Catholic Charities was dominated primarily by social workers. In many dioceses Catholic Charities agencies were called Catholic Social Service Agencies, and provided professional counseling and help to families, adoption services, group homes, institutional care for the elderly, and provision for the needy. These agencies were usually run by priest directors; boards of directors, where they existed, were Church controlled.[32] The emphasis on professionalism had the downside of eliminating the work of volunteers who had played prominent roles in the early provision of social service.

Catholic Hospitals

Another important part of the social mission of the Church to "our own" was Catholic hospitals.[33] The Catholic Church had traditionally been associated with care for the sick and hospitals—primitive as those were up until a few centuries ago. In the United States, Catholic religious women (with some help from religious brothers) started Catholic hospitals. It was only in France during the seventeenth century that St. Vincent de Paul and St. Louise de Marillac started the first noncloistered women's religious community with a ministry outside the cloister. Descendents of this community were the first sisters to start hospitals in the United States in the early nineteenth century. They were quickly joined by many other orders of religious women. By 1910 religious congregations had established more than three hundred acute Catholic hospitals in the United States.[34] Many of these Catholic hospitals also developed nursing schools to provide more professionalized nursing in their institutions. In 1915 over thirty communities of religious women sponsored about 220 nursing schools in their hospitals.[35]

Growing professionalization, modernization of hospitals, and the need for coordinated approaches led to the founding of the Catholic Hospital Association (now called the Catholic Health Association) in 1915. Catholic hospitals had to keep up with the introduction of modern equipment, greater professionalization of the staff, and the need to meet the accreditation standards developed by the American Medical Association and the American College of Surgeons. Just as the religious life of women (which meant, among other things, limited travel and no night meetings) kept many religious women from active participation in the National Conference of Catholic Charities in its early years, such problems faced the Catholic Hospital Association (CHA). The organizing force and first president of CHA was Charles Moulinier, a Jesuit priest of Milwaukee, who had the support of women's religious communities and the encouragement of Sebastian G. Messmer, the archbishop of Milwaukee. Messmer urged his fellow bishops to support the CHA. From the very beginning, however, CHA was primarily a sisters' organization. Moulinier himself thought a sister should be the head of CHA, but their religious lifestyle at the time meant that they could not fulfill officers' roles. Only in the 1960s did religious women take leadership roles in the CHA.[36]

From the very beginning the CHA and communities of sisters and brothers worked closely with bishops, who held no direct administrative or financial roles in the hospitals. Anti-Catholic movements affected Catholic hospitals less than other Catholic institutions, perhaps because the sisters attended to Catholics and non-Catholics alike—especially in times of war, deprivation, and epidemics. Thus, in the early twentieth century Catholic Charities and Catholic hospitals were the two most significant examples of Catholic social mission especially, but not only, to its own. These two institutions exist today in very different circumstances and contexts, but they were begun to meet the needs of the immigrant Catholic Church in the United States. The next chapter considers some theoretical underpinnings and practical illustrations of the social mission in the early twentieth century.

NOTES

1. For an evaluation of the developments in ecclesiology and a very significant contemporary approach, see Richard P. McBrien, *The Church: The Evolution of Catholicism* (New York: HarperCollins, 2008).

2. On Catholics in the colonial period and especially in Maryland, see James Hennesey, "Catholicism in an American Environment: The Early Years," *Theological Studies* 50 (1989): 657–75; Jay P. Dolan, *The American Catholic Experience: A History from Colonial Times to the Present* (Notre Dame, Ind.: University of Notre Dame Press, 1992), 69–124.

3. In synthesizing this history, I rely heavily on James M. O'Toole, *The Faithful: A History of Catholics in America* (Cambridge, Mass.: Belknap Press of Harvard University Press, 2008); Chester Gillis, *Roman Catholicism in America* (New York: Columbia University Press, 1999); Dolan, *American Catholic Experience*. None of these authors use the threefold division I have used here, but their own divisions are in accord with my work.

4. C. Joseph Nuesse, *The Social Thought of American Catholics, 1634–1829* (Washington, D.C.: Catholic University of America Press, 1945), 283–86.

5. Nuesse, *Social Thought*, 227–49.

6. Robert Emmett Curran, "Rome, the American Church, and Slavery," in *Building the Church in America: Studies in Honor of Monsignor Robert F. Trisco on the Occasion of His 70th*

Birthday, ed. Joseph C. Linck and Raymond J. Kupke (Washington, D.C.: Catholic University of America Press, 1999), 30–49.

7. Cyprian Davis, *The History of Black Catholics in the United States* (New York: Crossroad, 1990), 35–39; Robert Emmett Curran, "'Spiritual Poverty': Jesuit Slave Holding in America, 1800–1838," in *Catholics in the Old South: Essays on Church and Culture*, ed. Randall M. Miller and Jon L. Wakelyn (Macon, Ga.: Mercer University Press, 1983), 125–46.

8. Davis, *History of Black Catholics*, 46–48.

9. Joseph D. Brokhage, *Francis Patrick Kenrick's Opinion on Slavery* (Washington, D.C.: Catholic University of America Press, 1955); John T. Noonan Jr., *A Church That Can and Cannot Change: The Development of Catholic Moral Theology* (Notre Dame, Ind.: University of Notre Dame Press, 2005), 108–9.

10. Curran, "Rome, the American Church, and Slavery," 48.

11. John T. McGreevy, "Catholics in America: Antipathy and Assimilation," in *American Catholics, American Culture, Tradition and Resistance*, ed. Margaret O'Brien Steinfels (Lanham, Md.: Rowman and Littlefield, 2004), 7–8.

12. Curran, "Rome, the American Church, and Slavery," 49.

13. John Tracy Ellis, "United States of America," *New Catholic Encyclopedia*, vol. 14, 425–48. This article provides statistics on the growth of Catholicism in the United States.

14. Dolan, *American Catholic Experience*, 201–3.

15. For a fuller development of the strategy of the U.S. bishops, see works cited in note 3.

16. Douglas J. Slawson, *The Foundation and First Decade of the National Catholic Welfare Council* (Washington, D.C.: Catholic University of America Press, 1992).

17. David J. O'Brien, *Public Catholicism* (New York: MacMillan, 1989), 103–12.

18. In an earlier monograph I analyzed Catholic social ethics in the United States in the light of this tension between being Catholic and being American. See Charles E. Curran, *American Catholic Social Ethics: Twentieth Century Approaches* (Notre Dame, Ind.: University of Notre Dame Press, 1982).

19. An acclaimed biography of Hecker is David J. O'Brien's *Isaac Hecker: An American Catholic* (New York: Paulist, 1992).

20. O'Brien, *Public Catholicism*, 95–123.

21. For the classical study of Americanism, see Thomas E. McAvoy, *Americanist Heresy in Roman Catholicism* (Notre Dame, Ind.: University of Notre Dame Press, 1963); also Margaret Mary Reher, "Pope Leo XIII and Americanism," *Theological Studies* 34 (1973): 678–89. The entire issue of *U.S. Catholic Historian* 11 (Summer 1993) is dedicated to Americanism.

22. Paul Blanshard, *American Freedom and Catholic Power* (Boston: Beacon, 1949). For John Courtney Murray's response, see John Courtney Murray, "Paul Blanshard and the New Nativism," *The Month*, n.s., 5 (1951): 214–25.

23. Aaron I. Abell, *American Catholicism and Social Action: A Search for Social Justice* (Garden City, N.Y.: Doubleday, 1960), 27–53.

24. Henry J. Browne, *The Catholic Church and the Knights of Labor* (Washington, D.C.: Catholic University of America Press, 1949).

25. Francis L. Broderick, *Right Reverend New Dealer: John A. Ryan* (New York: Macmillan, 1963). See also John A. Ryan, *Social Doctrine in Action: A Personal History* (New York: Harper and Brothers, 1941).

26. Joseph M. McShane, *Sufficiently Radical: Catholicism, Progressivism, and the Bishops' Program of 1919* (Washington, D.C.: Catholic University of America Press, 1986). For Ryan's own commentary on the document, see John A. Ryan, *Social Reconstruction* (New York: Macmillan, 1920).

27. Daniel P. McColgan, *A Century of Charity: The First 100 years of the Society of St. Vincent de Paul in the United States*, 2 vols. (Milwaukee, Wisc.: Bruce, 1951).

28. Dorothy M. Brown and Elizabeth McKeown, *The Poor Belong to Us: Catholic Charities and American Welfare* (Cambridge, Mass.: Harvard University Press, 1977). I am closely following this book in the subsequent paragraphs.

29. Brown and McKeown, *The Poor Belong to Us*, 13–50.

30. Brown and McKeown, *The Poor Belong to Us*, 51–85. For O'Grady's contributions, see Thomas W. Tifft, "Toward a More Humane Social Policy: the Work and Influence of Monsignor John O'Grady" (PhD diss., Catholic University of America, 1979).

31. Brown and McKeown, 193–94.

32. Jack Balinsky, "Introduction: The Evolution of Catholic Charities in the United States," in *A History of Catholic Charities of the Diocese of Rochester*, www.dor.org/Charities/AHistorybyJackBalinsky.htm.

33. In this section on hospitals I rely on Christopher J. Kauffman, *Ministry and Meaning: A Religious History of Catholic Health Care in the United States* (New York: Crossroad, 1995); and Ursula Stepsis and Dolores Liptak, eds., *Pioneer Healers: The History of Women Religious in American Health Care* (New York: Crossroad, 1989).

34. Stepsis and Liptak, *Pioneer Healers*, 287.

35. Kauffman, *Ministry and Mission*, 167.

36. Kauffman, *Ministry and Mission*, 168–92.

2

The Social Mission of the Church in the First Part of the Twentieth Century

The concerns of the immigrant Church in the nineteenth century left little place for the social mission of the Church in the broader U.S. society. American Catholics assimilated into American society as immigration declined and they could pay more theoretical and practical attention to the social mission of the Church. The writings of John A. Ryan and the bishops' 1919 "Program of Social Reconstruction" illustrate the first attempts by the U.S. Catholic Church to develop its social mission. This chapter discusses the theory behind the social mission in the first part of the twentieth century and the ways in which the social mission was carried out.

THEORETICAL UNDERSTANDING OF THE SOCIAL MISSION

In keeping with the U.S. Catholic emphasis on practice rather than theory, little has been written about the theoretical underpinnings of the social mission of the Church. The two most important figures before Vatican II in Catholic social ethics were John A. Ryan and John Courtney Murray; each to some extent discussed the social mission of the Church.

John A. Ryan, a professor of moral theology at the Catholic University of America (1915–39) and the director of the Social Action Department of the NCWC (1920–45), was the leading expert on both the theory and practice of Catholic social justice in the United States in the first half of the twentieth century. His work in the area of economic justice, aptly called "economic democracy," developed in three stages—social reform by legislation, a new status for workers, and the occupational group system.[1]

Occasionally, and comparatively briefly, he wrote explicitly on the social mission of the Church. Ryan cites Leo XIII to emphasize that social questions are not merely economic matters but moral and religious issues that need the input of the Church.[2] His justification of the social mission of the Church fits with the characteristic neo-scholastic distinction between the natural and supernatural. The Church's primary mission is the salvation of souls. Compared with supernatural realities, temporal goods such as education, wealth, and fame are insignificant. The soul lives righteously and comes to its eternal reward through right conduct. It is the duty of the Church to teach the moral law of right conduct to help people save their souls. For this reason the Church has always had a social mission.[3]

To Ryan, like his contemporaries, the Church is primarily the hierarchical Church. The Church inculcates the virtues of charity and justice that should permeate all aspects of life. The authoritative teaching of the pope and bishops exists on three levels—teaching moral principles such as the right to a living wage, condemning certain systems such as socialism, and advocating certain methods or approaches as illustrated in the "Bishops' Program of Reconstruction." But these three levels do not have the same authoritative force because the third level involves issues of practical expediency. Here Ryan distinguishes different levels of Church teaching and the response that is due each.[4] Ryan recognizes that Catholic laity must become involved in different aspects of social reform either by working to change certain policies or by participating in institutions such as labor unions. However, bishops and priests have to lead social work and action by assisting and directing cooperative associations of all kinds, settlement houses, and consumer leagues—not just orphanages and schools. Seminaries must train priests in Catholic social thought and action including courses in sociology and economics.[5]

In his early writings Ryan contrasts his understanding of the social mission of the Church with that of many Protestants who tend to identify religion with humanitarianism. The mission of the Church is not to realize the kingdom of God on earth but to save individual souls by teaching moral law and thus making them fit for the kingdom of God in heaven.[6]

Ryan's understanding of the social mission of the Church depended on a number of factors—his understanding of the Church as primarily a hierarchical institution; the neoscholastic distinction between the supernatural and the natural orders; the Catholic recognition of the role of works in gaining salvation; and the emphasis on influencing and changing legislation as the best way to bring about social justice and reform.

John Courtney Murray is best known for his celebrated defense of religious freedom, which played a decisive role in Vatican II's acceptance of it. But in the process of defending religious freedom he saw the social mission of the Church primarily as the work of the laity. Murray staunchly defended the separation of church and state—meaning the Church has no direct power over the state and its institutions—but he also strongly opposed Continental liberalism that reduced the role of the Church to the sphere of the personal and the private. How could he hold both positions? The Church primarily influences the public and temporal world via the layperson, who is at the same time a Christian and a citizen. The Church as such has no power over the state, but it can and should influence and affect the temporal order through the works of Christian lay people. The specific finality of the laity consists in their mediation of the spiritual to the temporal.[7]

In the early and mid-1940s Murray had explained the role of the laity and the social mission of the Church in terms of the discussion then taking place in many parts of the Catholic world about Catholic Action. Murray points out that Pope Pius XI (d. 1939) desired that Catholic Action ideally involve the organized participation of the laity in the apostolate of the hierarchy. This, however, implies a broader sense of the role of laity that does not involve a juridical organization under the hierarchy. Murray emphasizes this approach, which he calls Catholic action (as opposed to Action), or the lay apostolate. In light of the separation today between the spiritual and the temporal and the growing secularization of society the Church cannot retreat into the private and personal realms. The saving message of the Church includes a necessary but secondary task of furthering the common good of humankind.[8]

Murray gives two justifications for social mission. First, the external conditions in which Christians live in this world should favor their salvation, even though this is not absolutely necessary. Second, human life in this world depends on God's will and God desires a world of unity, justice, and peace.[9] The ministerial and hierarchical priesthood mediates grace and the Holy Spirit to human beings; this is the divinizing mission of the Church. The laity mediate the Christian spirit to the institutions of civil society; this is the humanizing mission of the Church. Murray thus sharpens the distinction between spiritual and temporal orders so as to unite them more organically, but without danger of confusion.[10]

Murray insists on one important characteristic of lay action in contemporary times—its social nature. As Pope Pius XI pointed out the personal one-on-one apostolate will not be able to change a milieu or an ethos or an institution. In light of this Murray strongly defended the need for Catholic laity to be involved in intercreedal cooperation with other Christians working for a more peaceful and just world. His opponents in the 1940s claimed that intercreedal cooperation involved the forbidden *communicatio in sacris*—sharing spiritual realities with non-Catholics. Murray defends this type of intercreedal cooperation by adding another layer to the meditation process. What he calls "Religio-Civic Action" involves the participation of all people of goodwill, including Catholic laity. Such an involvement is a type of Catholic action twice removed— removed from any roots in the organic unity of the Catholic Church and removed from organic relationship to the pastoral authority of the hierarchy.[11]

Murray, who came after Ryan and was influenced by the theology of Catholic action, saw the social mission of the Church as a secondary mission based on the distinction between the supernatural and the natural orders. Murray went beyond Ryan in his understanding the social mission of humanization as the work of the laity bringing the spiritual to the temporal.

SPECIFIC INVOLVEMENTS

This section discusses significant social involvements on the part of the Church before Vatican II. The approach is primarily chronological, although some types of involvement continue to the present day.

Industrial Relations

For a number of reasons, industrial relations became the first and the primary area of the Catholic social mission in the first part of the twentieth century. Modern papal social teaching (often called Catholic social teaching) is generally recognized to have its beginnings in the encyclical *Rerum novarum*, Pope Leo XIII's 1891 response to problems created by the Industrial Revolution. Pope Pius XI's 1931 encyclical *Quadragesimo anno* is an extension of this approach. Owing to the growing emphasis on the papacy and papal teaching in Catholic life as the twentieth century progressed, these documents had a significant influence in the United States.[12] The issue of industrial relations was pertinent to U.S. Catholics, since most of them were immigrants, poor, or lower-middle-class people who were primarily laborers. Recall Cardinal Gibbons's successful efforts to prevent Roman condemnation of the Knights of Labor in the 1880s. The issue of the rights of workers and the role of the state in protecting workers became even more prominent during the Depression and throughout the 1930s. Since 1919 U.S. Catholic bishops met yearly as the National Catholic

Welfare Conference and, through its administrative board and through the body itself, issued more statements and teaching documents on industrial relations than on any other area. Without a doubt this was their primary social concern.[13]

The 1940 statement of the administrative board of the NCWC, "Church and Social Order," summarizes the approach taken by U.S. bishops. The document insists that the Church is the teacher of moral law in general, and particularly as it applies to economic and social conduct in business, industry, and trade. In this the bishops follow closely the teachings of Pope Pius XI. The principles proposed in this document include the workers' right to organize; the need for a living wage; government intervention to help and protect those made vulnerable by problems created in the industrial order; and a more equitable sharing of the goods of creation among all God's people. Following the teaching of Pope Pius XI, the document calls for a more organic society in which owners, workers, and consumers cooperate in occupational or vocational groups for the good of all. The document also points out the need for the United States to respond to the Depression in accord with the principles of papal teaching in order to avoid a radical takeover by atheistic communists.[14]

Another factor behind the emphasis on industrial relations was the structure of the NCWC itself, which was divided into six departments—education, press, general secretary, social action, lay activities, and legislation. Each department was headed by a bishop from the administrative committee but run on a day-to-day basis by a director and small staff in Washington, D.C. The general secretary (the first was Paulist John J. Burke) supervised the overall operation, but the directors of each department basically reported directly to the administrative bishop in charge of that department.[15] John A. Ryan was one of the first two codirectors and soon became the director of the Social Action Department; he served until 1945 and was ably assisted by Raymond A. McGowan, who eventually succeeded him.[16] George G. Higgins, a Chicago priest who worked in the office, became director in 1954.[17]

Ryan's theoretical expertise and practical area of social action lay in industrial relations. He and his very small staff sought to make Catholic social teaching known to people in the Church and the broader public. The department ran conferences, short courses, and lectures to train priests to work in the labor apostolate. Later the department issued the monthly bulletin *Social Action Notes for Priests*. As other issues came to the fore they were initially addressed by the Social Action Department, but ultimately led to the creation of additional departments: rural life, family life, health and hospitals, and international relations.[18] In keeping with the institutional ecclesiology at that time a top-down approach was taken—from pope to bishops to priests to Catholic lay people, especially those who were workers or involved in industrial relations.

According to its legal incorporation the NCWC's purpose was "to unify, coordinate, encourage, promote, and carry on all Catholic activities in the United States; to organize and conduct social welfare work at home and abroad; to aid in education; to care for immigrants and generally to promote . . . the objects of its being."[19] The Lay Activities Department included the National Council of Catholic Men and the National Council of Catholic Women, which brought many different associations of Catholic men and women under the authority of the bishops. In the area of industrial relations the National Council of Catholic Women, for example, organized to provide a voice for Catholic women and to address problems of unemployment and other injustices. They also fought for a living wage for working mothers.[20] The major project of the National Conference of Catholic Women, under the leadership of Agnes Regan, was to finance and conduct their own school of social work—the National Catholic School of Social Service.[21]

Three specific aspects of the U.S. Catholic social mission in the pre–Vatican II Church have origins in the dissemination of Catholic social teaching and the work of the Social Action Department of the NCWC. First, many dioceses and Catholic institutions of higher learning established labor schools with the two-fold purpose of disseminating the principles of Catholic social teaching and training Catholic workers for participation and leadership in their unions. In 1948 over forty dioceses had labor schools or related projects.[22]

Second, individual priests in many areas throughout the country involved themselves in support of workers and unions. In the early part of the century Peter Dietz strongly supported the American Federation of Labor (AFL) and other unions, but his attempt to found a national organization of Catholic workers did not succeed.[23] Pro-labor priests not only involved themselves in supporting unions and workers but also became involved in works of mediation and arbitration.[24]

Third, in 1937 the Association of Catholic Trade Unionists was founded in New York City to help Catholics imbue their unions with Catholic social principles and thereby overcome the dangers of communist influence in American labor. The group published *Labor Leader* and had eleven chapters throughout the United States in its heyday.[25] By the 1950s, none of these social actions remained vital.

Catholic social teaching also influenced the formation of two intellectual associations in which NCWC played no direct role, but principles of Catholic action were significant. The American Catholic Sociological Society was founded in 1938. The society was five hundred strong and published a journal, *The American Catholic Sociological Review*; it sought not to cut itself off from academic sociology but to apply Catholic social principles as found in the encyclicals to the realities of the United States.[26] A few years later Catholic academics founded the Catholic Economic Association, and its journal, *Review of Social Economy*; the association had the same basic purpose as its sister organization.[27] Both societies and their journals have ceased to exist in their original form. Now called the Association for the Sociology of Religion and the Association for Social Economics, theirs are much broader religious and humanistic approaches.

Cleaning Up the Movies

A concerted effort to support decent, wholesome films and to prevent indecent and exploitive motion pictures was a goal of the pre–Vatican II Catholic Church. The effort involved bishops acting as a group and as individuals; as well as individual Catholics associated with the movie industry; members of the International Federation of Catholic Alumnae (IFCA), a group that had come into existence in 1914; and, above all, all Catholics as a unit.

However, this action took place within a much broader context.[28] In the early twentieth century many throughout the United States came out against what they considered to be an increasing number of immoral films. In 1915 the Supreme Court ruled that the motion picture industry was not covered by the freedom of speech clause in the First Amendment. Already there were state and local censors, and the movie industry feared the prospect of federal censorship and licensing. As early as the 1920s some Catholic groups, including the International Federation of Catholic Alumnae under the leadership of Rita McGoldrick, sanctioned and produced lists of what they called good movies. Fearful of censorship by government authorities and others, the movie industry set up a self-policing mechanism under the leadership of Will Hays, a well-connected politician and a Presbyterian.

Martin Quigley, a lay Catholic who published significant trade journals for the movie industry, worked for a more forceful self-policing policy. Quigley asked Jesuit Daniel Lord to provide a better industry code, which Hays ultimately accepted. This was the Motion Picture Production Code, or simply the "Hays Code." Catholics shied away from taking credit because they did not want it to be known publicly as a Catholic code. But the code had no teeth and was not well enforced. In 1934 the movie industry established the Production Code Administration (PCA) under the leadership of a Catholic, Joseph

Breen. Every movie shown in the major theater chains in the United States needed to have the seal of the PCA. Breen and his staff often called for changes before a movie could receive approval.

Also in 1934 U.S. bishops—advised by Quigley, Breen, and others—established the Legion of Decency. The Legion classified films in three categories: A, morally unobjectionable; B, morally objectionable in part; and C, condemned. The Legion reviewers relied heavily on sixty to one hundred members of the IFCA who went through a lengthy preparatory process. These reviewers prescreened all films. Favorable depictions of illicit sex, divorce, adultery, criminality, communism, as well as scanty costumes could earn a film a condemned rating. Legion officials met with individual producers to make changes to circumvent such a rating. Breen at the PCA worked hand in hand with the Legion, but they had occasional differences over particular films. The movie industry went along with the PCA and even the Legion of Decency both for economic reasons and to avoid further restrictions.

At the time Catholics assumed that going to a C movie was a mortal sin. Once a year in church Catholics "voluntarily" took a pledge condemning indecent and immoral pictures and promised to stay away from them and the movie theaters that showed them as a matter of policy. Furthermore, individual bishops occasionally urged Catholics to boycott a particular movie or even a particular theater.

In the 1950s both the Production Code and the Legion faced difficulties. The domestic industry was competing with foreign films that did not need the seal of approval; even more important, television was taking a significant share of movie audiences. American mores and tastes also were changing. Catholics themselves were becoming better educated, and many resented being treated like children. Boycotts called by individual bishops were not always successful. Catholic intellectuals such as John Courtney Murray and Harold C. Gardiner opposed coercive methods in the public sphere but pointed out that for the most part the Legion did not engage in boycotts and coercion.[29] Faced with these changing realities, the movie industry itself came up with a new rating system and the Legion of Decency declined in influence. Catholics no longer took pledges. Today the Catholic bishops' organization still rates movies but in a less doctrinaire way and without much sway even in Catholic Church circles.

Influenced by the success of the Legion of Decency, Catholic bishops established the National Office for Decent Literature (NODL) in 1938. This group, which focused on youth and which also gathered some non-Catholic support, provided a monthly list of magazines and pocketbooks judged to be injurious to youth. Volunteers then went to local newsstands to urge that these objectionable materials be removed. Sometimes local boycotts were organized, and local law enforcement agencies used the NODL list to enforce the law. This organization never had the influence of the Legion of Decency either in society at large or in the Catholic Church, and what influence it had waned greatly in the 1950s.[30]

In retrospect, the most unique aspect of the Legion of Decency as a form of Catholic social action was that it effectively involved the whole Church—bishops, the IFCA, committed Catholic laymen who were connected with the movie industry, and especially the Catholic community who were its foot soldiers. Movie industry leaders knew that the majority of Catholics faithfully attended the classifications of the Legion, especially with regard to condemned movies. One reason for the declining influence of the Legion was the fact that members of a more educated and assimilated Catholic Church would not always agree with the prudential moral judgments of others. Never again would Catholics be united in social action based on a prudential moral judgment accepted by all. Today the very complexity of moral judgments makes near unanimous agreement within the Church a nigh impossibility. The Legion of Decency was the only example of a monolithic U.S. Catholic Church acting on the basis of a prudential moral judgment promulgated by bishops.

Catholic Association for International Peace

The pre–Vatican II Catholic Church in the United States undertook some social movements for peace.[31] A very early example was the Catholic Association for International Peace (CAIP), started under the auspices of the Social Action Department of NCWC in 1927 and led by John A. Ryan and his associate Father Raymond McGowan.[32] As part of the NCWC the association worked primarily toward education and not social action. Its members were Catholic intellectuals and other leaders who issued statements and wrote pamphlets on specific issues and tried to disseminate them to the Catholic public, especially in existing fora in Catholic colleges. Their proposals included a federated Europe, a world police force, and a world bill of rights. As early as 1931 they condemned the threat of world communism and also insisted on the need to halt Japanese aggression against Manchuria in 1932. The CAIP was not pacifist but adhered to the theory of just war. In the late 1930s they opposed isolationism and the call for the United States to be neutral in the upcoming European struggle. As war became imminent they strongly supported the use of military force to oppose Hitler.

After World War II this group of Catholic scholars and people interested in government policy addressed such issues as the peacetime draft and foreign aid and supported the Vietnam War and nuclear deterrence based on just war principles. John Courtney Murray was an important figure in this group. CAIP participated in off-the-record meetings with the U.S. State Department and had observer status at the UN. In the late 1950s the most significant subcommittee in the CAIP was one that called for arms limitation using just war principles and that did not embrace total nuclear pacifism. The group informally sent their proposals for consideration at Vatican II. By definition the work of the CAIP was limited to education and proposals for public policy, but it did not have much effect on the daily life of the Church, and in 1968 it was discontinued.

The Catholic Worker

The Catholic Worker Movement, founded in 1933 by Dorothy Day and Peter Maurin, had a profound effect on U.S. Catholicism in advocating the cause of pacifism, conscientious objection to war, and nonviolent resistance. The movement differs from previous approaches because it was entirely a lay movement and involved a more radical approach to Christian life.

The Worker program as developed in the early 1930s involved three aspects.[33] The first element is the clarification of thought, brought about especially by the publication of the paper the *Catholic Worker*, which began in 1933 and continues to the present day. Roundtable discussions also furthered the clarification of thought. The program as enunciated in the paper calls for a Gospel radicalness of heroic love exercised through corporal works of mercy, with a special emphasis on voluntary poverty. The paper opposes the present economic order—with its emphasis on profit, wealth, and materialism—and insists on a Christian personalism. This personalism takes a more concrete form in anarchism or in Christian utopian communities in which there is no coercive government. The second part of the program calls for houses of hospitality, which the Worker wanted to see in all Catholic parishes but which for all practical purposes existed only under the auspices of the Worker. In these houses the poor were fed, clothed, and sheltered by people committed to voluntary poverty and other volunteers. The third part of the program involves farming communes where people live together and take care of the needs of one another in a life close to God and the soil.

The anthropology of Christian personalism definitely influenced many of the positions and practices adopted by the Catholic Worker.[34] Personalism is committed to the primacy of the person as a free and spiritual being and is opposed to any coercion, and advocates moving away from self-centered individualism toward the good of others. This is accomplished by taking personal responsibility for changing conditions rather than looking to the state or other institutions to provide impersonal charity.

The Catholic Worker movement quickly spread beyond New York. By 1941 there were thirty-two houses of hospitality in twenty-seven cities, and twelve additional Catholic Worker cells that functioned in some lesser way. There were no officers and no specific set of rules. Christian personalism could not accept bureaucracy, and Dorothy Day was opposed to any such organizations.[35] However, in February 1940 and at other times the *Catholic Worker* occasionally did publish articles detailing the aims of the movement.[36]

Each Worker house was independent and functioned on its own. Since they operated autonomously, each Worker group developed its own character and interests to some degree. Some were relatively intellectual; some were involved in labor organizing, rent strikes, and similar forms of direct social action in the midst of the Depression. Some emphasized liturgical concerns. Some had a strong core of stable leadership over the years; others experienced rapid turnover. At the insistence of local groups Dorothy Day often appointed leaders, but she insisted that the local group deal with its own problems and development.[37] Its minimal structure gave the movement the flexibility to grow and develop, and today there is ever more pluralism in the diverse Catholic Worker movement. But the spirit and basic approach of Dorothy Day guides the general movement.

Christian personalism also influenced the ways in which houses of hospitality operated. Respect for the person demands at a minimum no coercion of the poor and no proselytizing—quite a departure from most other Christian houses serving the poor. "Hospitality" comes from the Latin word for guest, and according to the Worker philosophy it expresses an equal relationship between host and guest. The Worker gives the poor the material goods they need but also compassion, dignity, and respect as children of God. Christ comes to us in the person of the poor and the needy. As time went on Workers realized that one cannot expect gratitude from the poor: they are not only materially poor but also poor in kindness, gratitude, and charity.[38] William D. Miller titled his study of the Catholic Worker movement *A Harsh and Dreadful Love*, recalling Dorothy Day's frequent reference to a passage in Dostoevsky's *The Brothers Karamazov*. A woman confides to the monk Zossima that she needs to experience gratitude and immediate repayment for the kindness and love she gives to others. The monk responds that the radicalness of Christian love ignores time and does not need immediate results: "Love in action is a harsh and dreadful thing compared to love in dreams."[39]

Government by its very nature tends to be depersonalizing and coercive, but the *Worker* distinguished between different levels of government. The *Worker* opposed paying federal income taxes, but not local taxes that support hospitals and fire departments that serve all in the community. The paper frequently reiterated its position that people in the movement should not vote because this only contributes to the perpetuation of the state.[40]

One incident struck even some of the loyal supporters of the Worker as hard to understand. The September 1960 issue of the *Catholic Worker* printed a copy of a letter Dorothy Day had written to the city of New York. The city had sent her a check for $3,579.39—interest on the payment of $68,000 that the Worker was given for their property on Christie Street. Dorothy Day returned the money because Catholic Workers do not believe in lending money at interest; Christian charity calls for lending freely. Despite its poverty and its needs the Catholic Worker was not going to accept interest.[41]

There can be no doubt that the Catholic Worker vision and practice were radical. Many significant Catholic figures in the Worker movement—such as Michael Harrington (author of *The Other America*), John Cort and Ed Marciniak (both strong advocates of labor unions), and John Cogley and Jim O'Gara (both subsequent editors of *Commonweal*)—left to adopt more liberal approaches to social reform, trying to transform existing institutions such as labor movements and government itself to bring about such reform. However, these people continued to be appreciative of Dorothy Day and the Worker.[42]

Dorothy Day was committed to pacifism, but in the beginning she did not provide any in-depth defense of this position in the *Catholic Worker*. Fathers Paul Hanly Furfey and John Hugo developed the Gospel basis for pacifism in the pages of the *Catholic Worker*.[43] Dorothy Day staunchly defended her pacifism even during World War II, but many people associated with the movement (such as the Chicago Catholic Worker) disagreed with her and rejected pacifism. The movement and the paper were at their lowest ebb during the war years precisely because of her staunch commitment to pacifism. Dorothy Day opposed the draft, urged noncooperation, and offered assistance to individuals who conscientiously opposed the war. Bill Callahan, managing editor of the paper in the 1930s, organized Pax, a Catholic group opposed to the war and the draft. In 1940 the group changed its name to the Association of Catholic Conscientious Objectors (ACCO). The highest estimate of the number of Catholic conscientious objectors during World War II was 135.[44]

In the postwar period from 1948 to 1955, editor Robert Ludlow's writings in the *Catholic Worker* introduced the Gandhian theory of nonviolence and proposed this as the position that should be adopted by the Catholic Church. In the mid-1950s Ammon Hennacy succeeded Ludlow as editor and introduced into the *Worker* the theoretical concept of Catholic anarchism and the practical tactic of civil disobedience. The Civil Defense Act required participation in New York's air raid drill so that people would know how to protect themselves against the possibility of nuclear attack. In 1954, Dorothy Day, Ammon Hennacy, and some others refused to take shelter during the drill, and were sentenced to jail for five days. These protests continued in subsequent years and demonstrated the Worker's willingness to work with non-Catholic peace groups.[45] The Trappist monk Thomas Merton often wrote for the *Catholic Worker* and was a leading figure in the Catholic peace movement.[46]

In the early 1960s, Catholic Workers, especially under the leadership of Eileen Egan, organized a special Catholic group dedicated to peace and pacifism, and resurrected the name of Pax. Some from this group—especially Egan, James W. Douglass, and Gordon Zahn—lobbied the fathers of Vatican II about pacifism and conscientious objection. This group later became Pax Christi USA.[47]

A unique aspect of the Catholic Worker is the fact that it was a lay movement without any direct connection with the hierarchical or institutional Church. In fact, many Catholics strongly opposed the movement and some objected to the use of the name Catholic. The New York Archdiocese accepted Dorothy Day's explanation that the name Catholic did not signify official Church approval of herself, the paper, or the movement. In this regard it was no different from the Catholic Library Association, the Catholic War Veterans, and similar groups. The Worker was a group of individual Catholics involved in lay action and they were not a part of Catholic Action under the hierarchy.[48]

The somewhat paradoxical nature of Dorothy Day's Catholicism is illustrated by her relationship with Cardinal Spellman. In 1949 the gravediggers at the Catholic Calvary Cemetery in New York City went on strike against Cardinal Spellman and the New York Archdiocese. The *Catholic Worker* supported the strike, and members provided food and support for picketing workers. But Dorothy Day said on another occasion that if Cardinal Spellman asked her to close down the Worker tomorrow she would. Dorothy Day strongly opposed Spellman's position on the Vietnam War, but to its credit the archdiocese of New York neither spoke nor acted against the Catholic Worker.[49]

This group had a most profound effect on the Catholic Church in the United States, for it was the forerunner of the Catholic peace movement, which, under the Berrigans and others, strongly opposed the Vietnam War through the use of nonviolent civil disobedience. In their 1983 pastoral letter, U.S. bishops recognized pacifism as a legitimate position in the Catholic Church for individuals but not for nations.[50] No lay movement in U.S. Catholicism has ever had the effect on the Church that the Catholic Worker has had.

Anti-Communism

The strongest Catholic social movement in the twentieth century before Vatican II was anti-communism. Charles R. Morris, in his recent sympathetic history of U.S. Catholicism, refers to "the Church's obsessive anti-communism."[51] Anti-communism touched U.S. Catholicism in many different dimensions of its life, including in liturgy and devotional life. Prayers were said at the end of every mass for the conversion of Russia. The Blessed Mother appeared to children in Fatima in 1917 and asked that Russia be consecrated to her immaculate heart. Catholics were urged to attend mass and receive Holy Communion (to use the phrase then in vogue) on the first Saturdays of each month for the conversion of Russia. Catholic social teaching strongly condemned socialism and later communism. Worldwide, the Catholic Church was obsessed with the Bolshevist threat to religion. Communism, in the Catholic understanding, was a religious and a philosophical heresy because of its atheism and materialism.

This theoretical opposition to communism had broad and deep pastoral and social applications. Catholic support for unions and the rights of workers had the partial aim of diminishing the influence of communism. In the 1920s Catholics were appalled by the anti-clericalism and Church persecution in Mexico by what Catholics perceived to be a leftist and communist-inspired regime. William F. Buckley, father of the founder of the *National Review*, collected funds to overthrow the communists in Mexico while the Knights of Columbus, the largest fraternal Catholic association, urged U.S. intervention to overthrow the Mexican government.

In the next decade, anti-communism was a very important factor behind the international Catholic Church support of Francisco Franco and the Nationalist cause against the communist-influenced Republicans in Spain. Horrible atrocities were committed by both sides in this civil war, but probably many more by Franco than the Republicans. Catholic clergy and the Catholic press in 1938 generally rallied to defend the Spanish arms embargo and prevent arms going to the Republicans. Russia strongly identified with and helped the Republicans, which obviously fueled Catholic anxieties, but the vast majority of Catholics did not seem that troubled by Fascist and Nazi support for Franco. The different attitudes toward communist influence in Mexico and during the Spanish Civil War created a great friction between Catholics and secular liberals and many Jews. In the 1930s the pope had condemned Nazism and Fascism, but the condemnation of communism was the more basic Catholic position. Papal actions and statements during World War II were heavily influenced by opposition to and fear of communism and atheistic Russia.

But a dramatic change occurred with the Cold War. Now the Vatican and the Catholic Church were the two great opponents of communism and Russia and often worked together in various ways. Karl Barth, the eminent Swiss reformed theologian, was asked why he had not condemned communism when he had so strongly stood up to Hitler and Nazism in the 1930s. Barth replied that everybody knew that communism was wrong thanks to Harry Truman and the pope.[52]

All-embracing Catholic anti-communism was a predominant feature in the Catholic press and radio and television programs by such Catholic speakers as Fulton J. Sheen. Thanks to his writings and reports of the late 1940s and early 1950s Father John F. Cronin of the Social Action Department of the National Catholic Welfare Conference became known as the Catholic expert on communism, and was especially trusted by the U.S. bishops. Some of his anti-communist pamphlets were published by the U.S. Chamber of Commerce, but anonymously so that people would not know they were authored by a Catholic priest. Cronin was in close contact with the FBI, and shared with congressman Richard Nixon and others his knowledge about communist activity and possible spying, even naming Alger Hiss.[53] Cronin himself opposed the witch-hunting tactics of the Catholic senator from Wisconsin, Joseph B. McCarthy. Other leaders and clerics were generally quite supportive of McCarthy but Catholic laity were not as staunchly pro-McCarthy.[54]

By the 1950s the whole world and every single Catholic knew that the Catholic Church was opposed to communism. Unfortunately, this was primarily a negative opposition. The average Catholic in the pew remained oblivious to the social teaching of the Church, which condemned communism but also individualism and laissez-faire capitalism. Without a doubt the anti-communist movement penetrated U.S. Catholicism more deeply than any other social movement.

Race Relations

An earlier section pointed out the failure of the Catholic Church in the United States to condemn slavery in the pre–Civil War years. The number of Catholic

African Americans was comparatively small—not more than 800,000 in 1965.[55] Internally the Catholic Church willingly practiced segregation even into the twentieth century. Catholic seminaries and Catholic colleges and universities were unwilling to accept Catholic African Americans.[56] One bright spot was the organized efforts of black lay Catholics, beginning with their first congress in 1889. Thomas Wyatt Turner (1877–1978), who held a doctoral degree in biology from Cornell University, was a leader in lay black Catholic movements of the 1920s and 1930s. These groups fought for their rights as Catholics (to education and black priests, for example) and opposed racism in the Church. The lay leadership here was exemplary but, of course, there were almost no black Catholic priests. Turner was the president of The Federated Colored Catholics, which primarily aimed to improve the lot of blacks in the Catholic Church. Two white Jesuits and black leaders, who wanted to make the movement concerned primarily with interracial justice in both the Church and society, took over the organization in 1932. A leading figure was the patrician Jesuit John LaFarge, who earned a name for himself as the best-known Catholic working for interracial justice.[57]

LaFarge started the Catholic Interracial Council of New York, composed of whites and blacks to work for social justice for African Americans. LaFarge, who had worked in black pastoral missions in southern Maryland, guided the group to educate themselves and try to bring about change by putting Catholic teaching on racial justice into practice. Their publication, the *Interracial Review*, helped to carry out the mission. LaFarge also received support from influential non-Catholic blacks such as Roy Wilkins and Walter White, who was then director of the NAACP. The LaFarge approach was primarily to disseminate Catholic teachings on racial justice and motivate people to work to attain such justice based on the Catholic understanding of the role of the laity. Several interracial councils sprang up in other cities, especially Chicago, but the movement faced an uphill battle in the Catholic Church and remained a small if somewhat influential minority trying to move Church and society forward. Some Catholics who were sympathetic to the cause criticized it for being a top-down organization with narrow leadership that had little or no effect on black Catholics in the pew.[58] Unfortunately, LaFarge had taken over the leadership of a black Catholic organization geared to achieve justice for black Catholics in the Church.

LaFarge, who among other activities also served as an editor of the Jesuit weekly *America*, published *Interracial Justice: A Study of the Catholic Doctrine of Race Relations* in 1937.[59] The book was far too generous in its praise of the Catholic Church and what it had done for racial justice in the United States, but it did set out in scholastic language the teachings of the Church on racial equality and justice for all God's people, and exerted a positive influence on some Catholics. The book came to the attention of Pope Pius XI, who in 1938 asked LaFarge to collaborate with others to draft an encyclical on fascism and racism. Working especially closely with German Jesuit Gustav Gundlach, he produced a draft that was given to the Jesuit General and ultimately to the pope. But Pius XI died in 1939 before the encyclical could be released. LaFarge's contribution condemned Nazism, totalitarian statism, racism, and anti-Semitism, but could have been more forthright and decisive. Despite strong condemnation of anti-Semitism there were remarks that would offend Jewish people and many Catholics today (such as calling Jews "misguided souls"). On balance, however, the Catholic Church would have been much the richer if the encyclical had been published.[60]

Catherine de Hueck and her movement, Friendship House, encouraged a few of the Catholic action oriented to work for interracial justice. A Russian aristocrat immigrant and convert, de Hueck started Friendship Houses in Canada and came to Harlem in 1938. She and her mostly white followers lived in voluntary poverty, celebrated liturgy and prayed together, gave assistance to blacks in the area, and criticized discrimination and segregation in the Church and society. The movement spread to other cities, including Chicago, where it was headquartered in the 1950s. By 1960 the Chicago house was the only one left; it joined with the Catholic Interracial Council to work for racial justice in the city.[61]

The institutional leadership of the Catholic Church was hesitant to address issues of integration, segregation, and racial justice. Some courageous bishops in the late 1940s and early 1950s integrated Catholic schools in their dioceses despite local opposition.[62] There was some reluctance among the bishops to issue a statement, but in 1958 they wrote "Discrimination and the Catholic Conscience," which insisted that race was a moral and religious issue and opposed enforced segregation as irreconcilable with the Christian understanding.[63] The primary drafter of the letter was John F. Cronin, who had been prodding the bishops on this matter for a number of years.[64]

The most significant racial development during and after World War II was the mass migration of African Americans to the industrial cities of the north. Here, as described by John T. McGreevy, African Americans ran into the Catholic parishes, whose religious, cultural, and social aspects dominated their neighborhoods. Some Catholic parishes with inner-city schools began losing parishioners. Catholic schools became a magnet for many of the newly arrived African American families. A number of African Americans became Catholic precisely because their children were in Catholic schools. This way of operating built on the older notion of national parishes that had been in existence and were at least tolerated by the American bishops in dealing with earlier waves of immigrants.[65]

The biggest racial problem in the northern cities was that of housing and white flight to the suburbs, aided by real estate agents who played on prejudices and hoped to make a quick profit. Some pastors in these Catholic, white enclaves strongly defended the parish against any attempt by African Americans to move into their boundaries. They often claimed that African Americans would be better off in their own parishes, just as other Catholic immigrants had been in the past. These pastors urged their people to hold onto the houses they had saved for and bought in the late 1940s and 1950s and to remain a part of the ethnic neighborhood so dominated by the parish and its activities. Liberal Catholics, often in conjunction with Catholic interracial groups or similar associations, worked for the integration of neighborhoods. The struggle caused great tensions among Catholics. The integrationists had the moral high ground and also, somewhat belatedly, the support of archbishops in many large northern cities such as Chicago. But Catholic white flight to the suburbs could not be stopped.[66]

Catholics were never in the forefront of the struggle for racial justice in the United States. A few bishops took courageous stands, and Catholic interracial councils and other groups tried to educate other Catholics and work for justice, but they fought an uphill battle. In the 1950s and early 1960s some laity worked for integrated housing in some northern cities, but were ultimately unsuccessful.

Community Organizations

The problems of urban America occasioned a significant new approach in the social mission of the Church, which became even more prominent in the post–Vatican II era—the support of community organizations. Saul D. Alinsky, an agnostic Jew, organized the Back of the Yards neighborhood in Chicago in the late 1930s and started the Industrial Areas Foundation in 1940 to promote community organizations and to train community organizers.[67] Alinsky organized poor neighborhoods so that people who were powerless could improve their lot by organizing and gaining political power that commanded the respect of local authorities. These peoples' organizations, a true example of grassroots democracy, were composed of representatives from groups and associations in the neighborhood such as clubs and churches, but with indigenous leadership. Opposition to community organization came from different sources. Some Christians feared that the conflictual approaches used by these organizations were in opposition to Christian charity. Others feared that Alinsky's earlier organizations tended to preserve the white neighborhood against encroachment by African Americans. But Alinsky later organized even within the black community.

In the early 1940s, Alinsky became friendly with Msgr. John O'Grady, the secretary of the National Conference of Catholic Charities; O'Grady advocated for Church support of Alinsky's community organization projects.[68] In the 1940s and 1950s Alinsky's primary support came from the Archdiocese of Chicago, especially through the efforts of John Egan, who was put in charge of urban ministry in 1958.[69] Alinsky developed a personal friendship with distinguished Catholic philosopher Jacques Maritain. His blurb of Alinsky's *Reveille for Radicals* calls Alinsky "one of the few really great men of our century."[70] As time went on Alinsky's organizations became strongly ecumenical, but there is no doubt that the institutional Catholic Church was the strongest supporter of his work in the 1940s and 1950s.

Support for community organizations provided an entirely new approach to the social mission of the Church. Other approaches focused on what Catholics could do to help bring about social justice by their activity. Supporting community organizations provides a structure that allows the poor and the powerless to help themselves. Catholic support for community organizing came to the fore in the 1960s and afterward.

The Jocist Movement and the Christian Family Movement (CFM)

Lay involvement in many areas of social mission, especially during the 1930s and thereafter, sprung from an emphasis on Catholic action in its narrower and broader senses, together with the theology of the mystical body of Christ and the importance of participation in the liturgy. These movements affected comparatively few Catholics and were often unknown to the ordinary Catholic in the pew. One important social action movement—the Catholic Family Movement (CFM)—incorporated the ideas of so-called specialized Catholic action groups founded in Europe by Father, later Cardinal, Joseph Cardijn. Cardijn started the Young Christian Workers (YCW) and the Young Christian Students (YCS) based on his principle of the like-to-like approach of the apostolate to change a milieu. Members belonged to cells of about ten or twelve who followed the method of see, judge, act—observe the situation, judge it on the basis of the Gospel, and act to restore all things in Christ. This Jocist Movement (from the French name for young Catholic workers) spread throughout Europe in the 1930s among elite Catholics.[71]

The Jocist Movement in the United States ultimately found its greatest strength in the Chicago area thanks to priests like Louis Putz of Notre Dame and Reynold Hillenbrand of Chicago and the support of the Archdiocese of Chicago. Louis Putz, who had experience with Jocist groups in Europe before World War II, brought the YCS to Notre Dame in the 1940s and 1950s and also strongly supported the YCW and the CFM.[72] Msgr. Reynold Hillenbrand was truly the father of Catholic action in Chicago and probably in the United States in the pre–Vatican II era. His advocacy of the Jocist approach, together with his role as rector of the Chicago seminary, made him a dominant figure. He served as the priest head of both YCW and CFM. In both organizations, however, the role of the priest was secondary; leadership and active participation in the meetings came from the laity themselves.[73] The YCW influenced a few committed Catholics but reached its zenith in the 1950s.[74] The CFM became the largest Catholic action movement in the United States and had at one time a membership of nearly fifty thousand couples, but its influence far surpassed these numbers.[75]

The CFM developed from a number of groups, especially at Notre Dame and in the Chicago area. A Chicago couple, Pat and Patty Crowley, became the leaders of the movement and devoted themselves to its development—even on an international level.[76]

As Jeffrey Burns points out in his history of the CFM, this was a new type of movement in a time of change for the Catholic Church. The CFM was primarily a suburban middle-class movement in a Church that had been urban and working class. CFM was primarily a lay movement in a clerically dominated Church; its members were young couples who had moved to the suburbs. Despite the fact that most of its male members were college-educated professionals and most of the women were housewives, there was a basic gender equality. Unlike other Catholic movements dealing with marriage such as the Cana Conference, which sought to strengthen Catholic marriages and family, CFM emphasized the need for the family and the group to influence and transform the milieu around them, which would also strengthen their families. CFM was based on the theology of the mystical body, the importance of celebrating and living out the liturgy, and the Cardijn method—which were strongly associated with other forms of Catholic action. Like Jocist groups it was primarily geared toward action, not education. Group meetings were prepared by one couple and the chaplain, and occurred every two weeks. The meetings included discussion of a scriptural passage, a liturgical topic, and a larger social inquiry—all following the "see, judge, act" approach.

The CFM became a national movement in 1949; its coordinating committee published *For Happier Families* to introduce couples to the movement. Annual national meetings began in 1950. The movement grew rapidly and membership reached thirty-two thousand couples in 1957. CFM held its third and subsequent conventions at Notre Dame during the summer. The conventions featured well-known theological speakers and exciting participative liturgies, and had a different theme each year. *ACT*, its monthly newsletter or bulletin, went to all the couples. In the late 1950s the movement went international, expanding to more than forty countries. The expectation was that CFM would continue to grow and expand in the aftermath of Vatican II, but by the late 1960s the largest and most influential lay movement of social action in the U.S. Catholic Church was already in decline.

CONCLUSION

What can and should one learn from the historical overview of the social mission of the Church in the United States before Vatican II? History exists not just to tell us about the past but also that we might learn what is helpful for the present and the future.

In general the understanding of the Church and its different relationships to broader U.S. society strongly affected its social mission. From the viewpoint of ecclesiology, the Church often meant the hierarchy and the bishops who played an important role in the social mission of the Church, especially through the instrumentality of the NCWC. Sometimes the bishops were able to mobilize the whole Church behind their activity, as was the case for the struggle against indecent movies and the Legion of Decency. This social involvement was successful at least for a time precisely because all the people of God were involved. Other movements came primarily from lay creativity and participation—as exemplified by the Catholic Worker Movement, Friendship House, and the Catholic Peace Movement. The CFM was primarily a lay movement, even though clergy served as chaplains.

The changing historical situation of the Catholic Church in the United States greatly influenced its social mission. In the colonial period the Catholic Church was a small minority of landowners rather than the poor. It is not surprising that these Catholics primarily conformed to the social, political, and economic situation in which they found themselves. The tremendous influx of immigrants in the nineteenth century overwhelmed the Church in its efforts to provide for its own—spiritually and also materially. There was no time to think about broader societal issues with the exception of trying to counter the anti-Catholic and anti-immigrant movements by proclaiming to be as patriotic as other Americans.

As the Catholic Church grew and Americanized somewhat, it could and did express growing concern over the conditions of the society surrounding it. Before World War II the Catholic Church was monolithic and self-contained. The majority of the Catholic population lived in northern cities where the Catholic parish was the center of their religious life and of their social and cultural life. Catholics looked to their priests and bishops for leadership and generally followed them.

Things began to change after World War II. Catholics further mainstreamed into American society, and became part of the economic middle class. They moved to the suburbs where the ethnic, cultural, and religious neighborhoods largely did not exist. They went to college in record numbers thanks to the G.I. Bill and their elevated economic status. As a result, the monolithic and self-contained Catholic Church changed. The parish no longer dominated all aspects of Catholic lives. In this context Catholics no longer looked to their priests or bishops to provide leadership. Likewise, Catholics associated with non-Catholics, making it even harder to form Catholic-only groups who were concerned about a particular cause or issue.

Three aspects of the social mission before Vatican II stand out. First, it is always easier to be concerned for the rights of the poor when the poor are one's own. Care for poor Catholic children was supported by all Catholics. Concern for the rights and needs of workers was a major issue in the Catholic Church precisely because most of its members were blue-collar workers. But Catholic commitment to racial justice was not as prevalent or strong.

Second, the involvement of the whole Church, from the bishops to all the laity, was best exemplified by the Legion of Decency. But this approach lost its effectiveness in the late 1950s precisely because the hearts of the Catholic laity were no longer wholly in it. By this time members of the Catholic laity were not ready to follow unreservedly the prudential judgment of the bishops. Now and in the future it will be exceedingly difficult to find agreement among Catholics on matters involving prudential judgments.

Third, the late 1930s through the 1950s were a golden period of Catholic action. The CFM at first seemed to indicate that Catholic action groups would continue to thrive in the suburbs and with a well-educated Catholic laity in the Vatican II era. Without doubt the changed social, economic, and cultural circumstances of U.S. Catholics played a significant role in CFM's decline in the late 1960s. The cohesive Catholic culture no longer existed. At the same time there were significant elements within the Church, especially Vatican II (1962–65) and *Humanae vitae* (1968), that had a dramatic effect on the self-understanding of Catholics in this country and worldwide. The recognition of the Church as the pilgrim people of God, all of whom are called to holiness, while at the same time recognizing the importance of ecumenical relations, could not help but have a profound effect on the understanding and structuring of the social mission of the Church. The next chapter will develop a contemporary understanding of the Church as a basis for understanding its social mission and how it should be structured.

NOTES

1. For my analysis of Ryan's social ethic, see Charles E. Curran, *American Catholic Social Ethics: Twentieth Century Approaches* (Notre Dame, Ind.: University of Notre Dame Press, 1982), 26–91.

2. John A. Ryan, *Declining Liberty and Other Papers* (New York: Macmillan, 1927), 180–81.

3. John A. Ryan, *The Church and Socialism and Other Essays* (Washington, D.C.: University Press, 1919), 152–55.

4. Ryan, *Declining Liberty*, 181–84.

5. Ryan, *Church and Socialism*, 157–62; John A. Ryan, *Seven Troubled Years, 1930–36: A Collection of Papers on the Depression and on the Problems of Recovery and Reform* (Ann Arbor, Mich.: Edwards Brothers, 1937), 33–39.

6. John A. Ryan, "The Church and the Working Man," *Catholic World* 89 (September 1909): 776–78.

7. John Courtney Murray, "Contemporary Orientation of Catholic Thought on Church and State in the Light of History," *Theological Studies* 10 (1949): 215–27.

8. John Courtney Murray, "Toward a Theology for the Layman I," *Theological Studies* 5 (1944): 64–68.

9. John Courtney Murray, "The Roman Catholic Church," *Catholic Mind* 46 (1948): 580–88.

10. Murray, "Toward a Theology for the Layman I," 71–75.

11. John Courtney Murray, "Intercredal Cooperation," *Theological Studies* 4 (1943): 260–61.

12. For an in-depth study of these documents and their influence, see Kenneth R. Himes, ed., *Modern Catholic Social Teaching: Commentaries and Interpretations* (Washington, D.C.: Georgetown University Press, 2004).

13. Raphael A. Huber, ed., *Our Bishops Speak, 1919–1951* (Milwaukee, Wisc.: Bruce, 1952).

14. Administrative Board of the NCWC, "Church and Social Order," in *Our Bishops Speak*, ed. Huber, 324–43.

15. Douglas J. Slawson, *The Foundation and First Decade of the National Catholic Welfare Council* (Washington, D.C.: Catholic University of America Press, 1992), 70–95.

16. Mark A. Miller, "The Contribution of Reverend Raymond A. McGowan to American Catholic Social Thought and Action, 1930–1933" (MA thesis, Catholic University of America, 1979).

17. George G. Higgins with William Bole, *Organized Labor and the Church: Reflections of a "Labor Priest"* (New York: Paulist, 1993).

18. H. W. Flannery, "Social Movements," *New Catholic Encyclopedia*, 13:331–32.

19. Slawson, *Foundation and First Decade*, 94.

20. Patricia Ann Lamoreux, "Justice for Wage Earners," *Horizons* 28 (2001): 222–25.

21. Dorothy M. Brown and Elizabeth McKeown, *The Poor Belong to Us: Catholic Charities and American Welfare* (Cambridge, Mass.: Harvard University Press, 1997), 71–72.

22. John F. Cronin, *Catholic Social Action* (Milwaukee, Wisc.: Bruce, 1948), 75–88.

23. Mary Harrita Fox, *Peter E. Dietz: Labor Priest* (Notre Dame, Ind.: University of Notre Dame Press, 1953).

24. Higgins, *Organized Labor and the Church*, 30–62.

25. For different views of the ACTU, see Neil Betten, *Catholic Activism and the Industrial Worker* (Gainesville: University Press of Florida, 1976), 124–45, and Douglas P. Seton, *Catholics and Radicals: The Association of Catholic Trade Unionists and the American Labor Movement from the Depression to the Cold War* (Lewisburg, Pa.: Bucknell University Press, 1981).

26. Philip Gleason, *Keeping the Faith: American Catholicism Past and Present* (Notre Dame, Ind.: University of Notre Dame Press, 1987), 67–70.

27. Bernard W. Dempsey, "Ability to Pay," *Review of Social Economy* 63 (2005): 336–46; Thomas F. Devine, "The Origins of the Catholic Economic Association," *Review of Social Economy* 2 (1944): 102–3.

28. My primary source for what follows is Frank Walsh, *Sin and Censorship: The Catholic Church and the Motion Picture Industry* (New Haven, Conn.: Yale University Press, 1996); see also James M. Skinner, *The Cross and the Cinema: The Legion of Decency and the National Catholic Office for Motion Pictures* (Westport, Conn.: Praeger, 1993), 81–107.

29. John Courtney Murray, "The Bad Arguments Intelligent Men Make," *America* 96 (November 3, 1956): 120–23; Harold C. Gardiner, *The Catholic Viewpoint on Censorship* (Garden City, N.Y.: Hanover, 1958).

30. Gardiner, *The Catholic Viewpoint on Censorship*, 108–30; Una M. Cadegan, "Guardians of Democracy or Cultural Storm Troupers? American Catholics and the Control of the Popular Media," *Catholic Historical Review* 87 (2001): 252–82.

31. In this section I follow closely the important study by Patricia McNeal, *Harder than War: Catholic Peacemaking in Twentieth Century America* (New Brunswick, N.J.: Rutgers University Press, 1992).

32. McNeal, *Harder than War*, 5–20, 73–74, 83–85, 97–98, 155–56; see also Harry W. Flannery, "CAIP Fights for International Peace," *U.S. Catholic* (September 1963): 20–25; H. W. Flannery, "Catholic Association for International Peace," *New Catholic Encyclopedia*, 3:264.

33. William D. Miller, *A Harsh and Dreadful Love: Dorothy Day and the Catholic Worker Movement* (Garden City, N.Y.: Image, 1974), 79. See also Mel Piehl, *Breaking Bread: The Catholic Worker and the Origin of Catholic Radicalism in America* (Tuscaloosa: University of Alabama Press, 2006), 63–64. This book was first published by Temple University Press in 1982. See also my interpretation in Curran, *American Catholic Social Ethics*, 131–32.

34. Piehl, *Breaking Bread*, 63–64.

35. Piehl, *Breaking Bread*, 109.

36. Dorothy Day, "Aims and Purposes," *Catholic Worker*, February 1940, 7; www.catho licworker.org/dorothyday/.

37. Piehl, *Breaking Bread*, 109–14.

38. Piehl, *Breaking Bread*, 104–5.

39. Miller, *A Harsh and Dreadful Love*, 24–25.

40. Curran, *American Catholic Social Ethics*, 164–65.

41. Miller, *A Harsh and Dreadful Love*, 253–54.

42. Piehl, *Breaking Bread*, 128, 157–59, 175–76. Piehl devotes one chapter (145–180) to "The Catholic Worker and Catholic Liberalism."

43. In this section I depend heavily on Miller, *A Harsh and Dreadful Love*, 157–85, and Piehl, *Breaking Bread*, 189–240; see also Eileen Egan, "Dorothy Day: Pilgrim of Peace," in *A Revolution of the Heart: Essays on the Catholic Worker*, ed. Patrick G. Coy (Philadelphia: Temple University Press, 1988), 69–133; also "Part 10: Catholic Worker Pacifism 1933–1945," in *Dorothy Day and the Catholic Worker Movement: Centenary Essays*, ed. William J. Thorn, Phillip Runkel, and Susan Mountin (Milwaukee, Wisc.: Marquette University Press, 2001), 445–81.

44. For the story of Catholic conscientious objectors in World War II, see Gordon C. Zahn, *Another Part of the War: The Camp Simon Story* (Amherst: University of Massachusetts Press, 1979).

45. McNeal, *Harder than War*, 75–103.

46. McNeal, *Harder than War*, 105–30. See also Thomas Merton, *On Peace*, with an introduction by Gordon C. Zahn (New York: McCall, 1971).

47. McNeal, *Harder than War*, 94–100.

48. Geoffery Gneuhs, "Radical Orthodoxy: Dorothy Day's Challenge to Liberal America," in *Dorothy Day and the Catholic Worker Movement*, 219–20.

49. Piehl, *Breaking Bread*, 92–93.

50. U.S. Catholic Bishops, "The Pastoral Letter on War and Peace: The Challenge of Peace: God's Promise and Our Response," *Origins* 13 (1983): 12, 13.

51. Charles R. Morris, *American Catholic: The Saints and Sinners Who Built America's Most Powerful Church* (New York: Random House, 1997), 229. Subsequent paragraphs depend heavily on Morris, *American Catholic*, 228–54.

52. Will Herberg, "The Social Philosophy of Karl Barth," in Karl Barth, *Community, State, and Church: Three Essays*, with an introduction by Will Herberg (Garden City, N.Y.: Anchor, 1960), 58.

53. John Timothy Donovan, "Crusader in the Cold War: A Biography of Fr. John F. Cronin, 1908–1994" (PhD diss., Marquette University, 2000), 33–146.

54. Donald F. Crosby, *God, Church, and Flag: Senator Joseph R. McCarthy and the Catholic Church* (Chapel Hill: University of North Carolina Press, 1978).

55. P. E. Hogan, "Negroes in the U.S., IV (Apostolate To)," *New Catholic Encyclopedia*, 10:314.

56. Cyprian Davis; *The History of Black Catholics in the United States* (New York: Crossroad, 1990), 234.

57. Marilyn Wenzke Nickels, *Black Catholic Protests and the Federated Colored Catholics, 1912–1933* (New York: Garland, 1988).

58. David W. Southern, *John LaFarge and the Limits of Catholic Interracialism, 1911–1963* (Baton Rouge: Louisiana State University Press, 1996), 186–213.

59. John LaFarge, *Interracial Justice: A Study of the Catholic Doctrine of Race Relations* (New York: America, 1937); see also John LaFarge, *The Catholic Viewpoint on Race Relations* (Garden City, N.Y.: Hanover House, 1956).

60. Southern, *John LaFarge*, 220–37.

61. D. M. Cantwell, "Friendship House," *New Catholic Encyclopedia*, 6:206–7.

62. Hogan, "Negroes in the United States," 313–14.

63. U.S. Catholic Bishops, "Discrimination and the Catholic Conscience," in *Pastoral Letters of the American Hierarchy*, ed. Hugh J. Nolan (Huntington, Ind.: Our Sunday Visitor, 1971), 506–10.

64. Donovan, "Crusader in the Cold War," 133–46.

65. John T. McGreevy, *Parish Boundaries: The Catholic Encounter with Race in the Twentieth Century Urban North* (Chicago: University of Chicago Press, 1996), 56–63; see also Steven M. Avella, *This Confident Church: Catholic Leadership and Life in Chicago, 1940–1965* (Notre Dame, Ind.: University of Notre Dame Press, 1992), 283–88.

66. McGreevy, *Parish Boundaries*, 79–110. For Chicago, see Avella, *This Confident Church*, 289–322.

67. For the best study of Alinsky and his work, see Sanford D. Horwitt, *Let Them Call Me Rebel: Saul Alinsky—His Life and Legacy* (New York: Alfred A. Knopf, 1989); from a more Catholic perspective, see P. David Finks, *The Radical Vision of Saul Alinsky* (New York: Paulist, 1984).

68. Finks, *The Radical Vision*, 72–89.

69. In addition to Horwitt and Finks, see Avella, *This Confident Church*, 221–47. For a biography of John Egan, see Margery Frisbie, *An Alley in Chicago: The Ministry of a City Priest* (Kansas City, Mo.: Sheed & Ward, 1991).

70. Saul D. Alinsky, *Reveille for Radicals* (New York: Vintage, 1969).

71. Michael De La Bedoyère, *The Cardijn Story: A Story of the Life of Msgr. Joseph Cardijn and the Young Christian Workers' Movement Which He Founded* (New York: Longmans Green, 1958).

72. Walton R. Collins, "A Lifetime of Action," originally published in *Notre Dame Magazine* (Autumn 1998); www.nd.edu/~ndmag/putzf98.html.

73. Steven M. Avella, "Chicago's Sons: George G. Higgins and Reynold Hillenbrand," *U.S. Catholic Historian* 19 (Fall 2001): 25–32; Steven M. Avella, "Reynold Hillenbrand and Chicago Catholicism," *U.S. Catholic Historian* 9 (Fall 1990): 353–70; Avella, *This Confident Church*, 151–86.

74. Mary Irene Zotti, *A Time of Awakening: The Young Christian Worker Story in the United States* (Chicago: Loyola University Press, 1991).

75. On CFM I closely follow Jeffrey M. Burns, *Disturbing the Peace: A History of the Christian Family Movement* (Notre Dame, Ind.: University of Notre Dame Press, 1999).

76. In addition to Burns, *Disturbing the Peace*, see John Kotre, *Simple Gifts: The Lives of Pat and Patty Crowley* (Kansas City, Mo.: Andrews and McMeel, 1979). On their role in the papal birth control commission, see Robert McClory, *Turning Point* (New York: Crossroad, 1995).

3

The Understanding of the
Church after Vatican II

The previous two chapters show how the U.S. Catholic Church structured its social mission before Vatican II. Theological understanding of the Church and different Catholic cultural and social situations in this country greatly influenced how the Church carried out its social mission. This chapter develops a contemporary understanding of the Church— especially in light of Vatican II. Ecclesiology, or the theology of the Church, provides an important structural foundation for the social mission of the Church.

THE CHURCH IN VATICAN II

The changes brought about by Vatican II were quite significant. Pre–Vatican II treatises on the Church reflected an attempt to defend those aspects of the Church that had been denied or seriously downplayed by Protestant reformers. Thus, these treatises emphasized the organizational and institutional Church with its papal, hierarchical, and clerical leadership. Vatican II treats the Church as primarily a mystery and a sacrament, not an institution or organization.[1] The first chapter of the Council's Dogmatic Constitution on the Church (*Lumen gentium*) discusses the Church as mystery. The Church has the nature of a sacrament and is a sign and an instrument of communion with God—a people brought into unity from the unity of the triune God. The first chapter proposes various images of the Church—a sheepfold, a cultivated field, the building of God, Jerusalem, our Mother, the spouse of the Lord—rather than an institutional definition. The Church is best described as the people of God who strive to acknowledge God and serve God and human beings in holiness. The whole people of God share in the threefold office of Jesus—the priestly, the kingly, and the prophetic. Only in chapter 3 does the constitution discuss hierarchical structure and the institutional Church. Vatican II recognizes that the Church is a communion of local churches that are true churches in their own right and not just administrative subdivisions of the Church of Rome. Pre–Vatican II theology tends to identify the Church with the kingdom of God. Vatican II, however, takes an eschatological approach, according to which the Church is endowed with a sanctity that is real but imperfect; it is a sign of the kingdom and will reach its perfection only in the glory of heaven. The Church is a pilgrim Church, and all Christians are called to holiness, the fullness of the Christian life, and the perfection of love. Formerly there was a division between those called to perfection, who left the world for the religious life and followed the evangelical counsels, and the ordinary Christian, who lived in the world and obeyed the Ten Commandments.[2]

CATHOLICITY OF THE CHURCH

Without doubt Vatican II changed the understanding of the Catholic Church from the former manualistic approach to ecclesiology that emphasized institutional aspects denied by the Protestant reformers. But there also has been significant continuity in the understanding of the Catholic Church throughout the centuries. Protestant theologian and sociologist Ernst Troeltsch (1865–1923) discusses in *The Social Teaching of the Christian Churches* three different approaches to the structure of Christian religious institutions—church, sect, and mystical types.[3] Max Weber's distinction between church and sect has been accepted, used, and developed by subsequent sociologists.[4] The sect type is best exemplified by the Anabaptist Movement (sometimes called the left wing of the Protestant Reformation).[5] Anabaptist groups saw themselves as a small minority of committed voluntary believers who followed the Gospel imperative totally and saw themselves in opposition to the world around them. The Gospel calls for one to turn the other cheek, take no oaths, and practice nonviolence; if one does not detach from the rest of the world one ultimately has to compromise these Christian tenets. Sectarians believe themselves to be called as faithful witnesses to the Gospel message, not called to transform society. Attempts to work with others in transforming the world inevitably involve compromises and watering down the radical Gospel message. In the United States today the Amish typify such an approach.

Troeltsch treated the term sect as a nonevaluative, descriptive concept. Note that sociologically the concept of sect does not have the pejorative connotations often found in contemporary uses of the word. For Troeltsch the sect is distinguished from the church type exemplified by the Catholic Church.[6] The church type is a large group of believers—including saints and sinners—that exists within the world and works to influence existing cultural, political, and economic structures. The church type moderates the radical ethic of Jesus. One significant difference is that sects are often identified with pacifism, whereas church types recognize the occasional need to use force to preserve and promote justice. The church has a hierarchical organization and structure. Different approaches to baptism demonstrate clear differences between church and sect. The church practices infant baptism. Infants are brought to the church by their parents and in a certain sense are born into the church as the family of God. The sect approach practices adult baptism because only an adult can make the radical commitment to the Gospel demanded by the sect.

Troeltsch's approach is sociological and descriptive but it points to aspects that are normative for the Catholic Church. In my judgment the most significant characteristic of the Catholic Church is its (lowercased) catholicity. The Catholic Church is universal and inclusive. Four important aspects of this inclusivity are inclusivity of membership, of concerns, of its basic moral and theological approaches, and of its aspects of morality with differing levels of certitude.

Inclusive in Membership

The church catholic is universal in its calling all human beings to the Church. In the church catholic there are people of all races, sexes, and classes. In the church catholic there is neither Jew nor Greek, neither free nor slave, neither male nor female nor any other distinction that might exist among human beings.

The inclusive or all-embracing aspect of the Church recognizes great diversity among its members. The Church is not just a community of the spiritually elite and perfect—all are called to perfection and holiness, but also its membership includes sinners. The Catholic tradition distinguishes between two types of sin—venial and mortal. I do not always agree with the ways in which these have been understood, but the basic reality of sinful members of the Church illustrates its spiritual diversity. Mortal (from the Latin word for death) sin involves spiritual death and separates one from God. Venial (from the Latin word for "pardon") sin refers to sin that does not break one's relationship with God and may be more readily forgiven. No one in this world is perfect; all fall short and are guilty of venial sin. But even those in mortal sin still belong to the Church. Boundaries may distinguish among Church membership, but there is expansiveness to it.

The Catholic Church includes people who differ on many political, social, cultural, and economic issues. In the United States Church there are Democrats and Republicans. Some Catholics are pacifists and some recognize the need for force in order to preserve and promote justice. Some Catholics oppose the death penalty; some support it. Catholics take differing positions on the question of immigration. Catholics have to varying degrees supported or opposed particular wars. Catholics cannot agree on health care delivery in our country. There is no doubt that Catholics hold a variety of many different and even opposing positions on many issues facing our society.

The Catholic Church also recognizes the need for both diversity and unity regarding theology, faith, and practice. There are different levels and categories of Church teaching. The most important distinction exists between what is a core matter of faith and what is removed from the core. Basic doctrines illustrate the core aspects of faith—belief in a loving God, the mother and father of all, who created all things, who has redeemed us from sin and death itself in Christ Jesus, and who through the gift of the Holy Spirit has animated the Church as the pilgrim people of God. Faith in the Catholic Church includes recognizing the importance of the sacraments and the existence of the Petrine and hierarchical office in the Church.

Most Catholics today are familiar with the distinction between infallible and noninfallible Church teaching. Even pre–Vatican II manuals of theology included different "theological notes" to indicate how central certain positions are to Catholic faith.[7] One textbook includes ten different theological notes of various positions ranging from something that is a matter of faith to what is more probable or merely probable.[8] Pope Leo X's 1520 bull *Exsurge domine* condemned forty-one propositions in the writings of Martin Luther as heretical, being in opposition to Catholic truth, false, scandalous, seductive of simple minds, or offensive to pious ears.[9] Obviously what is offensive to pious ears does not involve core doctrines of the Church.

The Catholic Church will always experience tension between unity and diversity. There is no doubt that in the period immediately before Vatican II Church emphasis was on unity. But there always has been a legitimate diversity among Catholics, not only on issues involving society, culture, politics, and economics, but even in matters of theological theory and practice. There has been and always will be difficulty maintaining unity of faith and legitimate diversity. This recognition has great implications for the understanding and structuring of the social mission of the Church.

Inclusive in Its Concern for All Reality

The church catholic acknowledges the role and importance of all created reality. This is a characteristic of the Church that clearly distinguishes it from the sect type. The Church does not withdraw from the world; it is deeply concerned about all its aspects. The opening words of Vatican II's Pastoral Constitution on the Church in the Modern World make this point very clearly: "The joys and hopes, the grief and anguish of the people of our time, especially of those who are poor or afflicted, are the joys and hopes, the grief and anguish of the followers of Christ as well. Nothing that is genuinely human fails to find an echo in their hearts."[10]

In many ways the church-state relationship is paradigmatic of Catholic acceptance of all other created and human realities. This is also the primary area of difference between the church type and the sect type. This relationship between church and state also shows what historically has caused problems in the Church's relation to all other human realities. In the post-Constantinian era the Church recognized the state as a separate reality with its own functions and purposes but insisted that the state must serve the Church. The danger in the Catholic approach was the temptation to see the relationship of the Church to all human realities in light of a hierarchical ordering in which the temporal serves the spiritual.[11] The church catholic tends to recognize the basic goodness of all that is human but also wants to see that Christian virtues and approaches have some effect on these earthly and temporal realities.

Vatican II seeks to resolve this tension between temporal and spiritual by insisting that earthly realities can and should be affected by the participation of believers, but are not directly subordinate to the Church. Vatican II's Declaration on Religious Liberty set out the proper relationship between church and state, recognizing both the limited and independent role of the state and avoiding the total separation between them that would reduce the Church simply to a private reality that has no influence whatsoever on public and societal life. The state, or human political society, exists to protect, defend, and promote the public order of society. As such the state is limited and should not directly serve any religious end. But the Church, whose members are both Catholics and citizens, can and should try to work for justice in state and society.[12]

The U.S. understanding of the separation of church and state does not relegate the Church entirely to the private realm. The church catholic, through the activities of its members, can and should try to work for justice and peace without the state being subservient in any way to the Church. The pastoral letters that U.S. Catholic bishops wrote in the 1980s on peace and the economy illustrate the acceptance of a limited idea of the state and an attempt to gain influence through the actions of Christian citizens working with all people of goodwill.[13] Subsequent chapters will discuss some of the complexities in the church-state relationship.

Vatican II's Pastoral Constitution on the Church in the Modern World stresses the rightful autonomy of earthly affairs, the important word being "rightful": "If by the autonomy of earthly affairs is meant the gradual discovery, utilization, and ordering of the laws and values of matter and society, then the demand for autonomy is perfectly in order: it is at once the claim of humankind today and the desire of the Creator." But there is also a false meaning to this autonomy, as if to say earthly realities do not depend upon God and human beings can do with them whatever they please without regard to the fact of their God-given purpose.[14]

The church catholic is concerned with everything that is truly human. The Catholic Church, for example, has always encouraged and supported the arts. The search for and enjoyment of beauty is an important part of humanity and its cultivation, which the church catholic seeks to develop. The Church uses painting, music, and architecture to enhance its own worship, but it respects the basic criteria of good art regardless of whether a work takes religion as its subject matter.

The Catholic Church was the first patron and supporter of universities in the Western world.[15] The Church has consistently supported human reason not only in the disciplines of theology and canon law, but in improving knowledge of all that there is in this world. The church catholic wants to help human beings come to understand all that God has made. In addition, the development of the mind is itself an important aspect of human development. The pursuit of knowledge and the pursuit of art are ends in themselves.

This inclusivity and catholicity with regard to all earthly realities—including sex, ethnicity, nationality, and social class—also affects the lives of Church members, who share aspects of human life with all God's people. Church people live in families, neighborhoods, and nations. In addition to belonging to all of what the Catholic tradition has called natural societies, or groups, Church people also belong to many different voluntary associations such as professional organizations or clubs.

Universality and inclusivity present a significant challenge to the Church in terms of its social mission. People possess not only their Catholic identity but also many other identities and commitments that affect their assessment of how to live and act. Positions associated with one's gender, ethnicity, race, social class, and professional organizations might at times run counter to the social teaching of the Church.

Why is the church catholic committed to the type of catholicity that embraces all human reality? Its ultimate foundation is the belief in creation. All that exists has been created by a good God. Consequently, Catholic Christians have to be concerned and involved with all aspects of existence. In addition, redemption affects all that God has created. We are called to work on behalf of the new heaven and the new earth whose fullness will only come as God's gift at the end of time.

The catholicity that sees Christian realities as affecting all aspects of the human grounds the characteristic Catholic acceptance of mediation. Mediation refers to the fact that the divine comes to us in and through the human and the natural. The created, the natural, and the human are not evil. They are not only good, but they contain within themselves a manifestation of the Creator. Just as in Jesus the divine became incarnate in the human, so too in the Church the divine becomes present in and through the human. The Church is not an invisible society in which the individual Christian is immediately related to God and saved. The Church is a visible human community—the people of God—with visible human officers. God works in and through the human. The visible church community is the means by which God comes to us and we go to God.

The sacramental system so central to Catholic belief and practice illustrates the reality of mediation based on creation, redemption, and the eschatological future. In the primary sacrament, the Eucharist, the Church celebrates the gift of God's love to the covenant people and the people's grateful response and commitment to give thanks to God and live out the covenant call to discipleship. The Eucharist is basically a celebratory meal recalling the many meals Jesus celebrated with his disciplines, including what we call the Last Supper. The celebratory meal is the primary way in which human families and friends gather together to celebrate their love and friendship for one another. On holidays or special occasions such as birthdays, weddings, and even funerals people share food and drink, tell stories, laugh, cry, and sustain and nurture one another. So the liturgy takes over the fundamental sharing inherent in a meal and makes the meal the primary way in which Christians celebrate God's love and their commitment to love God and neighbor. Jesus's love is present to us in and through the meal. The Eucharistic meal also anticipates the eternal banquet, when God's people will live forever in God's house.

The other sacraments also illustrate the basic reality of mediation. God's salvific presence is mediated in and through natural realities. Baptism is conferred by the pouring of water. Water is life sustaining, refreshing, and cleansing to humans. The sacrament of baptism uses water to signify the life-sustaining, refreshing, and cleansing love of God. Oil used in the sacraments makes present the reality of God's anointing and healing gifts.

Inclusivity in Its Basic Approach to Theology

The Catholic approach to theology is characterized by "both-and" approaches rather than "either-or" approaches. Karl Barth, the great mid-twentieth-century Reformed theologian, once remarked that his greatest problem with Catholic theology was its "and."[16] Barth thus points to differences between the typical Catholic and some classical Protestant approaches. The Catholic approach insists on scripture and tradition; some Protestants stress scripture alone. The Catholic approach insists on grace and works; some Protestants stress grace alone. The Catholic approach insists on faith and reason; some Protestants stress faith alone. The Catholic approach insists on Jesus and the church; some Protestants stress Jesus alone.

In constructing social teaching that serves as the basis of its social mission, the Catholic Church insists on both faith (scripture and tradition) and (human) reason. In today's ecumenical climate many contemporary Protestants accept a similar approach, such as the Wesleyan Quadrilateral and its four sources of scripture, tradition, reason, and experience.[17]

The Catholic acceptance of human reason has often been understood in terms of natural law. The natural law well illustrates the principle of mediation. How do we know what God wants us to do? Do we go immediately to God and ask what we should do? No. God gave us reason. Human reason reflecting on the human nature that God made can determine how God wants human beings to act. Natural law has traditionally been understood as the participation of eternal law in the rational creature. Eternal law is God's plan for the world and human behavior. By the reason God gave us, we human beings can know this divine plan and ordering.[18]

Before Vatican II the realm of the natural was often seen as distinct and even separate from the supernatural. The supernatural involved grace, faith, and the divinizing mission of the Church. The natural involved the temporal and earthly, and emphasized reason. The distinction between the divinizing mission of the Church and the humanizing mission discussed in the previous chapter exemplifies the separation of the supernatural from the natural. Vatican II, as illustrated in the Pastoral Constitution on the Church in the Modern World, overturned this dualism. Faith, grace, and Jesus Christ must influence what takes place in the temporal and worldly realms, and are mediated in and through the human. The social mission of the Church and the transformation of the world are thus constitutive dimensions of the preaching of the Gospel and the overall mission of the Church.

Inclusivity in Recognizing Different Levels of Morality with Different Degrees of Certitude

The Catholic theological tradition recognizes different aspects or levels of morality, from the general to the specific and from the more certain to the less certain. For instance, in my judgment the basic and most general aspect of personal morality is the fundamental orientation of the person.[19] This has been described in terms of the commitment to discipleship, the love of God and neighbor, or in more technical terms as the fundamental option. Lack of certitude and different possible understandings arise when one tries to discuss in practice what constitutes love of neighbor—for example in situations such as a sick drug addict asking for money.

In addition to the general orientation of the person there are virtues that characterize the life of the Christian person. The Catholic tradition recognizes, for example, the three theological virtues of faith, hope, and love; and the cardinal virtues of prudence, justice, fortitude, and temperance. All agree that the Christian person should be just, but lack of certitude and differing opinions arise in determining what is just in a particular situation. The fundamental orientation and the virtues characterize the person on the subjective pole of morality.

Societal values are central in addressing the objective pole of reality. The U.S. bishops' pastoral letter on the economy mentions love, solidarity, justice, participation, and human rights. These values are general, and all would agree on the need for them, but in particular cases there will often be conflicts among them.[20]

On the objective pole of morality there is an important place for moral principles to guide action. Some are very general principles and about these there is no dispute—good is to be chosen and evil is to be avoided. Who would disagree? But what is good and what is evil? There are other more specific principles, such as the professional obligation of confidentiality. But the Catholic tradition has recognized that in certain circumstances the obligation of professional confidentiality gives way to other significant moral principles or values. For example, our society maintains that physicians must report all gunshot wounds to the police.[21] The more specific and complex the circumstances, the greater the possibility for exceptions to a particular principle. Prudential judgments are the final decision that one makes in a particular situation, bringing together the subjective and objective poles of morality. In situations where certitude of virtues or principles is lacking, a judgment cannot be said to be made with absolute certitude. For example, if one adheres to the just war theory, one cannot claim certitude about the justification of a particular war—whether it be World War II or the war in Afghanistan.

Thomas Aquinas proposed a nuanced approach to the question of the certitude involved in moral matters.[22] A significant difference exists between speculative reason and practical reason that deals with moral judgments. Speculative judgments concern those things that are necessary and cannot possibly be anything else. The measures of the interior angles of all triangles add up to 180 degrees. But someone might be deceived because a particular figure does not conform to his idea of a triangle and not realize that its combined angle measures equal 180 degrees. Specific conclusions reached through speculative reason are always true, but they might not be known by every human being because of insufficient intelligence.

Practical reason, however, deals with contingent reality. Aquinas admits that the first principles of natural law are always and everywhere true, and states as his example that good is to be done and evil is to be avoided. As an example of a secondary principle of natural law, Aquinas states that deposits should always be returned. A deposit is something entrusted to another under the condition that the owner can have it back whenever she asks for it. Circumstances could arise, however, in which the deposit should not be returned to the owner. Think, for example, of a man who is raving drunk and is threatening to kill an enemy and wants his sword. In this case the deposited sword should not be returned. Aquinas recognizes that the more specific and concrete the circumstances, the lesser the certitude and the greater the possibility of exceptions to a moral principle.

There is a fascinating history regarding this lack of certitude. In their important pastoral letters in the 1980s on peace and the economy, U.S. bishops made known their particular prudential judgments, such as no first use of even the smallest of nuclear weapons. In the early 1980s bishops' conferences in Europe also contemplated pastoral letters on peace, deterrence, and war. Cardinal Joseph Ratzinger, as head of the Congregation for the Doctrine of the Faith, arranged for an informal consultation with Vatican officials and the bishops' conferences drafting letters on the subject. The Vatican did not want bishops' conferences making authoritative statements that might contradict one another. Memoranda from the meeting pointed out the need to distinguish clearly between moral principles and their application to particular realities. This distinction avoids attaching an unwarranted level of authority to prudential contingent judgments and safeguards what has been called the legitimate freedom of the believer. In this case Cardinal Ratzinger himself recognized the freedom of the believer in the Church.[23]

The final version of the U.S. pastoral letter on peace distinguishes between universal moral principles, quotations from universal Church teaching, and prudential judgments based on these principles. These latter are not binding in conscience on Catholics, but Catholics should seriously consider them. The economic pastoral makes a similar point. The U.S. bishops, like Aquinas, agree that as a situation becomes more specific the level of certitude decreases and the possibility of legitimate diversity exists.[24] But the bishops did not go as far as Aquinas, who recognized that even secondary and specific principles themselves—not simply their application—cannot claim absolute certitude.

The Church as catholic, inclusive, and big has roots in all of theology. Even the manualistic pre–Vatican II theology recognized the universal salvific will of God. Historically this position existed in tension with the recognition that outside the Church there is no salvation. But the universal salvific will is more fundamental, as evidenced by the recognition of the fact that all who are in God's grace belong to the Church by desire. Explicitly conscious membership in the Church was not required. In 1953 in the United States, Leonard Feeney was silenced because of his narrow interpretation of the necessity of the Church for salvation. Recent discussion has centered on the role of non-Christian religions as mediators of salvation.[25]

Catholic theology stresses the mercy of God and acknowledges the sinful reality present in Christians and all people. The Catholic Church recognizes penance as one of its seven sacraments. Catholic anthropology realizes that we are all pilgrim people who constantly fall short and are in need of God's mercy and forgiveness. Every Christian person knows the eschatological tension between the imperfections and sinfulness of the present and anticipation of the fullness of the future. Every Eucharistic liturgy begins with a confession of sins.

Catholic moral theology recognizes that members of the Church often lack certitude about what they are called to do, and thus the pluralism of moral judgments and actions within the Church. From the seventeenth until the twentieth century Catholic moral theology paid great attention to what was called the probabilism controversy, which centered on a legalistic understanding of how to act when there is no moral certitude. But this long and acrimonious controversy highlighted the difficulty of making judgments or acting with provisional knowledge. More often than not, Christians do not have moral certitude, owing to the great complexity involved in specific human judgments; thus the role of prudence in moral decision making comes to the fore.[26]

Sociological Evidence

Contemporary sociological studies of Catholics in the United States, albeit descriptive and in no way normative themselves, point to a normative view of the Church as catholic and inclusive. A team of sociologists undertook four surveys of U.S. Catholics—in 1987, 1993, 1999, and 2005—in which they often asked Catholics the same basic questions.[27] Over a period of nearly twenty years, they amassed a significant amount of data. The study recognizes that some Catholics are more committed to the Church than others. But the percentage of highly committed U.S. Catholics declined from 27 percent in 1987 to 21 percent in 2005. The percentage of moderately committed Catholics grew from 57 percent to 64 percent. The percentage of less-committed Catholics remained at 15 percent over the period studied. The decline in the most highly committed Catholics is due to the decline in the older age group (born before 1940) and the growing number of young Catholics.[28]

The (again, purely descriptive) study shows that Catholics as a whole generally agree on matters considered central to faith, but their opinions diverge on more peripheral matters. Over three-quarters of the Catholics interviewed said that helping the poor, belief in Jesus's resurrection, the sacraments, and Mary as the mother of God were most important to them and their faith. The authors of the study conclude that these four teachings are deeply rooted in the Catholic tradition and can be said to be accepted as basic or core elements of Catholic faith.[29]

In the 2005 study less than one-fourth of the Catholics interviewed looked to Church leaders as the only authoritative teaching source on sexual issues such as contraception, divorce and remarriage, homosexual behavior, and nonmarital sexuality. Of those interviewed, 42 percent to 61 percent looked only to individuals themselves for moral wisdom on these questions. Both the individual conscience and Church teaching authority served as guides for 27 percent to 35 percent. The four teachings least often said to be very important to respondents in the 2005 study were teachings that oppose abortion (44 percent), teachings that oppose the death penalty (35 percent), and the need for a celibate male clergy (29 percent).[30] Sociological surveys by their very nature can never be normative or prescriptive, but they indicate in their own way that the Catholic Church is a big church, inclusive of saints and sinners and of the more and less committed, in which there is both unity on core issues and diversity on more peripheral issues.

DISSENT FROM NONINFALLIBLE HIERARCHICAL TEACHING

Since Vatican II a new illustration of the catholicity of the Church as a big church emerged in the form of dissent from noninfallible hierarchical teachings. This came to the fore in reaction to Pope Paul VI's 1968 encyclical *Humanae vitae,* which condemned artificial contraception for spouses. Catholic theologians in various parts of the world maintained that in theory and practice one could disagree with this teaching and still be a good Roman Catholic. It is safe to say that the majority of Catholic theologians have recognized the legitimacy of dissent on this issue but a vocal minority strongly opposes such dissent. Many regional and national conferences of bishops strongly supported the encyclical, some conferences seemed to hedge, and a third smaller group explicitly or implicitly accepted the legitimacy of dissent.[31] In 1974 Andrew M. Greeley and his associates at the National Opinion Research Center found that 83 percent of U.S. Catholics approved of artificial contraception for spouses.[32]

Proponents of such dissent appeal to three aspects of Catholic theology connected with the characteristic of catholicity. First, the accepted distinction between infallible and noninfallible teaching recognizes that noninfallible teachings might be wrong. Second, on specific complex moral issues it is difficult to claim a certitude that excludes the possibility of error. Third, the Catholic "both-and" approach also applies to the teaching role of the Church. All the baptized, and not only the hierarchical magisterium, contribute to the teachings of the Church. Today theological dissent exists on many different issues such as committed homosexual relationships, the beginning of individual human life, divorce, and other issues of sexuality.[33]

The papal teaching office has strongly condemned public theological dissent but recognizes the possibility of private theological dissent. The hierarchical magisterium has been reluctant to recognize the legitimacy of dissent.[34] However, many Catholics disagree in practice with a number of noninfallible teachings.

CONCLUSION

At this stage it is important to recall the most significant conclusions about the Church and its social mission that stem from the characteristic of catholicity. The Catholic Church is universal or inclusive with regard to its membership, its concerns, its basic moral and theological approaches, and its different aspects of morality with differing levels of certitude. Catholicity, however, involves a possible pitfall.

The greatest danger facing the church catholic is that the light of the world will dim and the salt of the earth will lose its savor. History shows how often individual Catholics and the church as a whole have too readily conformed to the larger world. Only in the nineteenth century did the Catholic Church finally condemn slavery.[35] And throughout the centuries, the Church and its people have too often been identified with the powerful, the rich, and the influential.

The sect type has a much clearer and simpler approach since it stands in opposition to what is happening in the world and is by definition always countercultural. But the church catholic with its "both-and" approaches has a more complex and tension-filled relationship to the world. At times the Church must strongly confront and challenge what is taking place in the culture, such as the individualism and materialism that so often characterize the contemporary U.S. ethos. At other times the Church has learned from the U.S. experience and gained a greater appreciation of freedom, human rights, and the equal role of women.

The church catholic and its individual members must be constantly aware of the danger of too readily conforming to the existing ethos. In and out of season the Church must bring to mind the call to holiness for itself and all its members, and the need for continual conversion on the part of individuals and the Church itself. We must become more conscious of our continuing sinfulness and the need to grow and develop in our relationships with God, neighbor, and the world itself.

The Church can never forget its commitment to a preferential option for the poor. At all levels—the individual, the family, the local, national, and universal Church—there must be a continual examination of conscience to guarantee that the baptized and their community are faithful to this commitment. Deeds are more important than words.

The Church must also encourage and support the prophetic role in the Church. Most of us would prefer not to be disturbed by prophets, but without prophets the church catholic can readily lose its savor; the prophetic office remains a very high priority as regards carrying out the social mission of the Church.

NOTES

1. For the most comprehensive volume on the theology of the Church, see Richard P. McBrien, *The Church: The Evolution of Catholicism* (New York: HarperCollins, 2008), 91–214.

2. "Dogmatic Constitution on the Church," in *Vatican Council II: Basic Sixteen Documents*, ed. Austin Flannery (Northport, N.Y.: Costello, 1996), 1–96.

3. Ernst Troeltsch, *The Social Teaching of the Christian Church*, 2 vols. (New York: Harper Torchbooks, 1960).

4. William H. Swatos, ed., *Twentieth Century Religious Movements in Neo-Weberian Perspective* (Lewiston, N.Y.: Edwin Mellen, 1992).

5. Troeltsch, *Social Teaching*, 2:691–706.

6. Troeltsch, *Social Teaching*, 1:201–445.

7. Harold E. Ernst, "The Theological Notes and the Interpretation of Doctrine," *Theological Studies* 63 (2002): 813–25.

8. Sixtus Cartechini, *De valore notarum theologicarum et de criteriis ad eas dignoscendas* (Rome: Gregorian University Press, 1951).

9. Jimmy Akin, "Identifying Infallible Statements," www.catholic.com/thisrock/2001/0109bt.asp.

10. Pastoral Constitution on the Church in the Modern World, n. 1, in *Vatican Council II*, ed. Flannery, 163. Church documents usually number paragraphs. The abbreviation n. refers to a single paragraph, and nn. to multiple paragraphs.

11. McBrien, *Church*, 253–54.

12. Declaration on Religious Liberty, in *Vatican Council II*, 551–68; Leslie Griffin, "Commentary on *Dignitatis humanae*," in *Modern Catholic Social Teaching: Commentaries and Interpretations*, ed. Kenneth R. Himes (Washington, D.C.: Georgetown University Press, 2005), 244–65.

13. U.S. Catholic Bishops, "Challenge of Peace: God's Promise and Our Response" and "Economic Justice for All," in *Catholic Social Thought: The Documentary Heritage*, ed. David J. O'Brien and Thomas A. Shannon (Maryknoll, N.Y.: Orbis, 1992), 492–680.

14. Pastoral Constitution on the Church in the Modern World, n. 36, in *Vatican Council II*, 201–2.

15. Charles Homer Haskins, *The Rise of Universities* (Ithaca, N.Y.: Cornell University Press, 1972).

16. For a Catholic critique of Barth and on differences between Barth and the Catholic theologian Hans Urs von Balthasar, see Christopher Steck, *The Ethical Thought of Hans Urs von Balthasar* (New York: Crossroad, 2001), 58–122.

17. Albert Cook Outler, "The Wesleyan Quadrilateral in John Wesley," in *Doctrine and Theology in the United Methodist Church*, ed. Thomas Langford (Nashville, Tenn.: Abingdon, 1991), 75–88.

18. Thomas Aquinas, *Summa theologiae*, 4 vols. (Rome: Marietti, 1952), Ia IIae, q. 93–94.

19. For my understanding of these different levels, see Charles E. Curran, *The Catholic Moral Tradition Today: A Synthesis* (Washington, D.C.: Georgetown University Press, 1999).

20. U.S. Bishops, "Economic Justice," nn. 63–84, in *Catholic Social Thought*, ed. O'Brien and Shannon, 594–99.

21. James F. Keenan, "Confidentiality, Disclosure, and Fiduciary Responsibility," *Theological Studies* 54 (1993): 142–59.

22. Aquinas, *Ia IIae*, q. 94, a. 4.

23. "Rome Consultation on Peace and Disarmament: A Vatican Synthesis," *Origins* 12 (1983): 691–95.

24. "Challenge of Peace," nn. 9–10, in *Catholic Social Thought*, ed. O'Brien and Shannon, 494; "Economic Justice for All," n. 20, in *Catholic Social Thought*, ed. O'Brien and Shannon, 576.

25. Josephine Lombardi, *The Universal Salvific Will of God in Official Documents of the Roman Catholic Church* (Lewiston, N.Y.: Edwin Mellen, 2007).

26. Julia Fleming, *Defending Probabilism: The Moral Theology of Juan Caramuel* (Washington, D.C.: Georgetown University Press, 2006), 141–51.

27. William V. D'Antonio, James D. Davidson, Dean R. Hoge, and Mary L. Gautier, *American Catholics Today: New Realities of Their Faith and Their Church* (Lanham, Md.: Rowman and Littlefield, 2007).

28. D'Antonio et al., *American Catholics Today*, 40.

29. D'Antonio et al., *American Catholics Today*, 93.

30. D'Antonio et al., *American Catholics Today*, 92–97.

31. Joseph A. Selling, "The Reaction to *Humanae vitae*: A Study in Special and Fundamental Theology" (STD diss., Catholic University of Louvain, 1977); William H. Shannon, *The Lively Debate: Responses to* Humanae Vitae (New York: Sheed and Ward, 1970).

32. Andrew M. Greeley, William C. McCready, and Kathleen McCourt, *Catholic Schools in a Declining Church* (Kansas City, Mo.: Sheed and Ward, 1976), 35.

33. For the spectrum of theological positions on the question of dissent, see Charles E. Curran and Richard A. McCormick, eds., *Readings in Moral Theology No. 6: Dissent in the Church* (New York: Paulist, 1988).

34. Congregation for the Doctrine of the Faith, "Instruction on the Ecclesial Vocation of the Theologian," *Origins* 20 (1990): 117–26.

35. John T. Noonan, Jr., *A Church That Can and Cannot Change: The Development of Catholic Moral Teaching* (Notre Dame, Ind.: University of Notre Dame Press, 2005), 3–123.

4

Vatican II and a New Understanding of the Social Mission

In the pre–Vatican II period the social mission of the Church was twofold—divinization and humanization. Divinization was the work of sanctifying God's people, whereas humanization was the mission of working for the betterment of the world. This distinction, and even separation, between the spiritual and temporal served as the basis for the different roles of clergy and laity. Divinization was the work of hierarchy and clergy; humanization was the work of laity—and obviously the work of divinization was more important than that of humanization.

The One Mission of the Church

Vatican II and subsequent developments changed this understanding of the twofold mission of the Church. In the words of the 1971 International Synod of Bishops document *Justitia in mundo*: "Action on behalf of justice and participation in the transformation of the world fully appear to us as a constitutive dimension of the preaching of the Gospel, or, in other words, of the Church's mission for the redemption of the human race and its liberation from every oppressive situation."[1]

Three developments in Vatican II contributed to this newer understanding of the one mission of the Church, which was to include the transformation of the world. First, the Dogmatic Constitution on the Church emphasizes the Church as the sign of the kingdom or reign of God. Jesus inaugurated the Church by preaching the good news of the coming of the kingdom of God. The kingdom shines out in the word and work of Jesus and in his very presence. Jesus, through the gift of the spirit, gave the community of his disciples

57

the mission of proclaiming the kingdom of God, with a realization that the fullness of the kingdom will come only at the end of time.[2]

Chapter 6 of the Constitution describes the different symbols that scripture uses for the revelation of the kingdom and the nature of the Church. The Church is a sign or sacrament of the kingdom. Just as Christ was sent to bring good news to the poor and to heal the brokenhearted, the Church encompasses with its love all those who are afflicted by human infirmity; it recognizes in the poor and suffering the likeness of its own founder, and so does all in its power to relieve their need.[3]

A second Vatican II development is the change in moral theology from an approach based almost entirely on natural law. Moral theology dealt with the temporal life of Catholics. Natural law recognizes that human reason reflecting on human nature can determine how God wants us to act in the world. Scripture, at best, was a proof-text to confirm the results of natural law. Grace and Christ played no significant role in this moral theology.[4] The Decree on the Training of Priests (*Optatam totius*) of the Second Vatican Council called for the renewal of moral theology. Theological subjects were to be renewed by a more lively contact with the mystery of Christ and the history of salvation. The document points out moral theology for special consideration: "Its scientific presentation, drawing more fully on the teaching of holy Scripture, should highlight the lofty vocation of the Christian faithful and their obligation to bring forth fruit and charity for the life of the world."[5]

The Pastoral Constitution on the Church in the Modern World pointed out that one of the gravest errors of our time is the dichotomy between the faith people profess and their daily lives.[6] In its first three chapters—dealing with the human person, human community, and human action—the Pastoral Constitution employs a methodology that tries to overcome this dichotomy. The first chapter, for example, begins with an understanding of the human person based on creation in the image of God, but then recognizes the reality of sinfulness and the resulting dramatic struggle between good and evil in human life. The chapter closes with a consideration of Christ the new man. Only in light of the mystery of the Word made flesh does the mystery of humanity become clear. Christ, the New Adam, is the revelation of the mystery of the Father and his love, fully revealing humanity to itself and bringing to light humanity's very high calling.[7]

A third Vatican II development that grounded the one mission of the Church in the transformation of the world comes from the understanding of the Church-world relationship. In the early days of Vatican II, Cardinal Leo Suenens of Belgium proposed the need for the council not only to address the

Church in its internal life but also the Church *ad extra*—its relationship to the world. The leadership and members of the Council quickly recognized the importance of Suenens's proposal. Thus came into existence what was first called Schema 13 and ultimately the Pastoral Constitution on the Church in the Modern World, *Gaudium et spes*. The Dogmatic Constitution on the Church, *Lumen gentium*, considered the Church's internal life; *Gaudium et spes* considers the Church in relation to the world.[8]

Gaudium et spes goes beyond the two-mission understanding that had been the basis for the role of the laity in the pre–Vatican II Church. *Gaudium et spes* maintains that the Church enters into dialogue with the world, throwing the light of the Gospel on human problems and—with the prompting of the Holy Spirit—supplying humanity with the saving resources of its founder. The key to this discussion is the human person in her or his totality, body and soul, heart and conscience, mind and will.[9] *Gaudium et spes* develops this mission of transformation in accordance with the concept of catholicity. The Church respects the legitimate autonomy of earthly realities and at times learns from these realities. But together with all people of goodwill the Church attempts to transform the world.[10]

In his 1975 apostolic exhortation *Evangelii nuntiandi*, Pope Paul VI makes this point very succinctly: "[E]vangelizing means bringing the Good News into all the strata of humanity, and through its influence transforming humanity from within and making it new." Evangelization is a question not only of spreading the Gospel, but also using the power of the Gospel to affect—or even upset—humankind's judgment, values, points of interest, lines of thought, sources of inspiration, and models of life.[11]

Political and liberation theologians have gone beyond hierarchical church documents in their understanding of the Church-world relationship. Such documents see the Church and the world as two previously constituted entities that then enter into dialogue and relationship with one another. But political and liberation theologians do not understand faith as an independently constituted reality illuminating the political or economic sphere. The prior question is how the commitment to struggle for the poor and against injustice affects faith itself. Commitment to this struggle is the horizon that shapes our understanding of faith itself and of the Church. Joseph Komonchak has phrased the question in this way: What, in light of human existence as a political problem, is the meaning of the Word of God and of the Church?[12]

The Church's mission to struggle for justice in the world, which has been accepted in post–Vatican II Catholic theology in various ways, has roots in scripture itself. John R. Donahue points out that biblical justice—which involves a concern for the poor, the weak, and the vulnerable—is embedded in the narratives that describe the self-identity of God's people and has become incorporated into law. Biblical justice has always had a prophetic dimension that opposes oppressive structures of injustice. Both Old and New Testaments unfailingly stress that God hears the cries of the poor and is on their side. Liberation theologians insist that the Exodus experience manifests that the freeing and liberation of God's people involve a freedom from slavery and bondage in political and economic orders. Prophetic literature strongly criticizes cultic worship that does not also call for justice and concern for the needy.[13]

The New Testament likewise points to the one mission of the Church. Jesus came to preach good news to the poor in Luke 4, and the gospel on the whole shows a special concern for the poor.[14] The famous parable of the Last Judgment in Matthew 25 asks when people came to the assistance of Jesus—who was hungry, thirsty, naked, and in prison. When?—when you did it to the least of these my sisters and brothers. Indeed, his execution makes Jesus himself one with all victims of injustice.

Hierarchical teaching and Catholic theologians generally agree that the social mission of the Church is tied to that of preaching the Gospel, but there has been some dispute about how exactly the social mission is related to the proclamation of the good news of salvation in Christ Jesus. As mentioned earlier, according to *Justitia in mundo*, working for the transformation of the world is a constitutive dimension of the preaching of the Gospel and the mission of the Church.

The principal author of its introduction, in which this phrase occurs, was Vincent Cosmao, a Dominican priest working in France and a member of the drafting committee. To Cosmao, this means that the preaching of the Gospel occurs by means of action on behalf of justice. The 1974 Synod revisited the term constitutive. Bishop Ramon Torella, then vice president of the Vatican's Pontifical Justice and Peace Commission, understood constitutive to mean that action on behalf of justice is an integral, but not an essential, part of preaching the Gospel. Others disagreed. Gregorian University theologian Juan Alfaro insisted that integral was an insufficient descriptor, because a thing can exist in the absence of certain integral parts: although the hand is an integral part of the human body a human can live without it. For Alfaro, action on behalf of justice is an essential dimension of Gospel proclamation, but not a unique one.[15]

Evangelii nuntiandi—Paul VI's apostolic exhortation based on the synodal deliberations—distinguishes between primary and secondary elements of the complex process of evangelization. The primary element is the proclamation of the good news of salvation; the secondary elements, without which evangelization would be incomplete, are the personal and social aspects of human life and the call for liberation in these areas.[16]

In his first encyclical, *Deus caritas est*, Pope Benedict XVI emphasizes charity as the spirit that moves us to love one another as Christ first loved us, and thus distinguishes charity from (the less fundamental) justice.[17] In his 2009 encyclical *Caritas in veritate* Benedict sees justice as inseparable from charity and intrinsic to it. Justice calls us to give another what is due, but charity transcends justice because it involves giving what is ours to another.[18]

In interpreting Benedict, Charles M. Murphy concludes that the ambiguous role of justice in the proclamation of the Gospel and the mission of the Church stems from different understandings of justice. If justice is understood to be a natural virtue, as is held in classic philosophy, then justice (giving to the other what is due) must be considered integral but inessential to preaching the Gospel. If, however, justice is understood in the biblical sense—as God's liberating action, which demands a human response—then it must be recognized as the essence of the Gospel message itself.[19]

Role of Laity

Vatican II's insistence on the one mission of the church, which includes working for the transformation of the world, undercuts the pre–Vatican II understanding of the laity as having a mission of humanization in the temporal order as distinguished from divinization in the spiritual order.

The Decree on the Apostolate of Lay People (*Apostolicam actuositatem*) makes this point and develops its consequences. Its second paragraph explicitly states, "Lay people too, sharing in the priestly, prophetical, and kingly office of Christ, play their part in the mission of the whole people of God in the Church and in the world. In the concrete, their apostolate is exercised when they work to evangelize people and make them holy; it is exercised, too, when they endeavor to have the Gospel spirit permeate and improve the temporal order."[20] Lay people thus exercise an apostolate of evangelization and sanctification, but the ministry of Word and sacrament of clergy are the principal means of bringing it about.[21]

Apostolicam actuositatem describes the fivefold makeup of the lay apostolate.[22] First, in Church communities, the laity have an active role in the life and activity of the Church—especially at the parish level. Second, the family is the primary vital cell of society. Christian parents inculcate faith and commitment in their children by word and example and should collaborate with others to protect the good and promote the importance of the family and human society. The document refers to the family as a domestic Church—a concept that has subsequently been developed in Church documents and by individual theologians.[23] Third, young people exert a major influence on modern society. Their social importance demands a corresponding apostolate activity that is supported by their own ardor and exuberance. Fourth, the lay apostolate includes the social and work environment in which people live. In this regard *Apostolicam actuositatem* embraces the pre–Vatican II emphasis on the apostolate of like to like. Fifth, there is a broad apostolate for lay people at the national and international levels. One sign of the times is the growing sense of solidarity among all peoples. Presenting these five aspects of the lay apostolate without ranking their importance stands in some tension with other pronouncements in the documents, such as the distinctive task of lay people being the renewal of the temporal order.[24]

Role of Laity in the Church

Since Vatican II, involvement in the Church community has received much more emphasis than other areas of the mission of the laity—including the transformation of the temporal order—and in practice the increased role of the laity has been most striking. Lay people now have a very conspicuous role in the liturgy, especially as Eucharistic ministers and as readers of the Word. Pastoral staffs now include many lay people working in religious education, catechesis, visiting the sick and homebound, bereavement, marriage preparation, and also justice and peace ministries. Pastoral councils are widespread; they may have only an advisory role, but do allow lay people some say in what goes on in their parishes. Also, there has been recent emphasis on providing theological education for laity. Today those involved in the Catholic theological enterprise of higher education are predominantly lay people.

In addition, much theoretical writing treats the need to increase the role of the laity in the life of the church. Child molestation scandals, and especially their coverups by U.S. bishops, have occasioned a significant body of literature about greater lay participation in the Church. The organization Voice of the Faithful was formed to respond to the handling of the pedophilia issue.[25] The National Leadership Roundtable on Church Management uses the expertise of the laity to help with Church management and finances.[26] Paul Lakeland's books make a strong case for a much greater role for the laity. The books build on the Vatican II understanding of the role and the theology of the laity developed in the post–Vatican II era to make practical recommendations.[27]

This emphasis on the laity has not gone unchallenged. In December 1977, forty-seven prominent clergy, religious, and especially lay Catholics issued the Chicago Declaration of Christian Concern. (Recall that Chicago had been in the forefront of the development of Catholic action in the 1950s and 1960s, using Canon Cardijn's "see, judge, act" approach with its emphasis on like to like.) The statement claims that a welcome and significant movement within the Church—the involvement of lay people in many Church ministries—has led to a dereliction of the unique ministry of lay women and men. Lay ministry is now seen as involvement in Church-related ministries such as religious education, pastoral care for the sick and elderly, or readers at the liturgy—work traditionally assigned to priests and religious. Unfortunately, this has led to a devaluation of the unique ministry of lay men and women to transform the temporal order.[28]

Clergy and Religious in the Transformation of the World

In the post–Vatican II Church the former bifurcation of the role of clergy and religious in the spiritual realm and the role of laity in the temporal realm was challenged not only by the laity's role in the internal life of the Church but also by the recognition that the transformation of the world is intimately connected with the Gospel and the Church's mission of redemption. Clergy and religious cannot be concerned only with the spiritual.

Events in the United States also greatly influenced the involvement of clerics and religious working directly for social transformation. Civil rights and the Vietnam War were the most pressing social issues in the United States in the 1960s and early 1970s, and occasioned dissention and division within the country. But clergy and religious groups played significant roles on both fronts. Many white churches and white clergy supported the mission of the Reverend Martin Luther King Jr., especially in the 1963 march on Selma. Clergy from all denominations played a significant role in the struggle against the Vietnam War. The best-known interfaith group was the Clergy and Laity Concerned about Vietnam—headed by Rabbi Abraham Heschel; the Reverend Richard John Neuhaus, then a Lutheran pastor; and Daniel Berrigan, a Jesuit priest.[29]

Catholic religious and clergy involvement in the peace movement was more pronounced than in the civil rights movement, which had begun even before the completion of Vatican II. Perhaps the best example of white Catholic clergy involvement in the civil rights movement was the work of Milwaukee priest James Groppi. In the mid- and late 1960s Groppi organized protests and marches against segregation in schools and in housing in Milwaukee, and also picketed judges who belonged to the Fraternal Order of Eagles (which refused to admit nonwhites to membership). He led over one thousand welfare mothers into the Wisconsin State Assembly for a sit-in to protest cuts in the welfare budget. Groppi's activities in Milwaukee were publicized even outside the city. His superiors did not always support his actions, and he gradually became disenchanted and left the active ministry.[30]

EXAMPLE OF THE CATHOLIC RESISTANCE

The late 1960s and early 1970s saw the emergence of a loosely knit group known as the Catholic Resistance, or the American Catholic Left. The group numbered about two hundred members and included laity, although clergy and women religious were disproportionately represented. The acknowledged leaders in the group were the Berrigan brothers: Daniel, a Jesuit priest; and Philip, a Josephite priest. The fact that Catholic priests and nuns were involved brought more public attention to their nonviolent—but felonious—direct actions in protest of the war in Vietnam.[31]

The Berrigan brothers had been involved in earlier protests supporting the civil rights movement—Philip more so than Daniel. Philip joined the Josephite religious order precisely because he wanted to work with blacks. Dorothy Day, the Catholic Worker Movement, and Thomas Merton's writings on peace also had an important influence on their development. In the mid-1960s Philip Berrigan was stationed in Baltimore and formed a small group that practiced civil disobedience. In October 1967 Philip and three others poured blood on Selective Service files at the Customs House in Baltimore. Daniel became one of the founders of the Clergy and Laity Concerned about Vietnam and participated in demonstrations and civil disobedience.[32]

The Catonsville Action on May 17, 1968, was a galvanizing event. Nine people led by Daniel and Philip Berrigan seized draft records from Selective Service Local Board 33, in Catonsville, Maryland, and burned them with napalm. Television stations, having been alerted beforehand, filmed the entire episode. When the police arrived, they waited to arrest the perpetrators until Daniel Berrigan had finished leading the Lord's Prayer.

The Catonsville Action went beyond previous efforts in destroying government property—the draft files. Some proponents of nonviolent resistance found this unacceptable, but the perpetrators insisted that nonviolence referred primarily to life—not to property that was used for immoral purposes. The Berrigan brothers' trial, conviction, and sentencing brought great publicity for their cause and positions.

The Berrigan brothers then took civil disobedience one step further: they did not willingly surrender themselves to serve their jail sentences. Philip Berrigan was arrested in the rectory of St. Gregory the Great Church in New York on April 21. Daniel Berrigan, who was working in the Cornell United Religious Work, appeared before ten thousand people at the university, but managed to escape capture. He then went underground, wrote extensively about his positions, and occasionally surfaced at public events before he was finally arrested in August at William Stringfellow's Block Island home. Throughout the country, other draft board raids took place under the aegis of the Catholic Resistance.

In early 1971 the Justice Department announced an indictment of the East Coast Conspiracy to Save Lives for plotting to blow up the heating systems of government buildings in Washington and to kidnap presidential advisor Henry Kissinger. Philip Berrigan was among those indicted. Their three-month trial began in January 1972 in Pennsylvania. The government's case was based on the testimony of an informer and letters to Philip Berrigan smuggled into prison by Sister Elizabeth McAlister, who was to become his wife. The trial culminated in a hung jury—10–2 in favor of acquittal. Many saw this trial as a political move to embarrass and weaken the Catholic peace movement, but the Catholic Resistance was already fading away. The waning era of protest, the closing of the war, and internal divisions all contributed to the demise of the Catholic Resistance.

RELIGIOUS ORDERS OF WOMEN AND MEN

The Catholic Resistance received considerable media exposure, but it was only a small part of the larger involvement of religious women and men in social ministry. No group in the Catholic Church took more seriously the Vatican II emphasis on the Church serving the world and working for the kingdom of God in the world than religious orders of women and men, who truly put into practice the recognition that action toward justice is a constitutive dimension of the Gospel and the mission of the Church.

The role of Catholic women religious in the United States changed dramatically as a result of Vatican II. They had for the most part been "active" rather than "contemplative" in the cloistered sense, and their apostolate defined the way in which they lived their religious lives. In large part this apostolate involved serving in institutions of the Church such as schools, hospitals, and orphanages. In addition to historical factors mentioned earlier in this chapter, the developing women's movement also changed the understanding of ministry for women religious in this country.[33]

After Vatican II women religious saw the call to discipleship as a challenge to participate in Jesus's mission of building the reign of God. The commitment to mission and ministry calls for continual conversion because the reality of personal and social sin still permeates individuals and the world. Conversion involves a question of consciousness. The movement of God's Spirit in our times involves a growing consciousness of the ecclesial, social, economic, and political structures that perpetuate the oppression and dehumanization of people—and demands that religious women and their congregations create lifestyles and structures that witness to the values of the Gospel.[34]

The priority of justice in the mission of U.S. religious women after Vatican II is exemplified by the work of the Leadership Conference of Women Religious (LCWR), the commitment of individual congregations, and certain organizations formed by women religious.

The national association of religious women was first organized in 1956 with the name of the Conference of Major Superiors of Women (CMSW). Despite Vatican objections, in 1971 the group voted to change its name to the Leadership Conference of Women Religious. By this time, many nuns were leaving congregations because they found religious life to be too confining, but others continued the work of reforming the life and mission of religious sisters.[35] The LCWR made social justice a priority, and the theme of its 1971 assembly was "The Church Is for the World." The more conservative *Consortium Perfectae Caritatis* broke off from the LCWR because its members believed the directions taken by the LCWR were sacrificing spiritual concerns for political goals.[36]

The LCWR website emphasizes its continuing commitment to social justice: "Working for a more just and peaceful world is an integral component of LCWR's vision and goals." Many member congregations are actively engaged in promoting social, economic, and earth justice. As an umbrella group, LCWR provides opportunities for addressing concerns with a corporate voice by taking action on resolutions approved by the national assembly.[37]

It is impossible in this space—or perhaps in any space—to adequately describe the approaches of the various religious congregations of women making the mission for social justice a priority.[38] The Adrian Dominican Sisters must suffice as an illustration. The general chapters of the Adrian Dominican Sisters mention four elements necessary to be a sign of God's salvation in the world: the allocation of resources in critical areas of need for people least able to support themselves; the initiation of social change to alleviate injustice and the attainment of rights basic to dignified human life; the involvement of each member in an educative process in social justice as an essential element of her Gospel commitment; the Gospel imperative that inspires and directs our congregation and its education, stewardship, and ministries.[39]

NETWORK, a national Catholic social justice lobby, exemplifies Catholic religious women's working to change unjust structures.[40] NETWORK began with a meeting of forty-seven sisters in Washington in December 1971. The purpose of the meeting was to create a network of sisters working with social policy issues. These sisters had been influenced by the changes occurring in religious life in the United States after Vatican II and by the changing times. The movement grew dramatically from this small beginning. Its website describes NETWORK as a progressive voice within the Catholic community that has sought to influence Congress toward peace and justice for more than thirty years. Through lobbying and legislative advocacy they aim to close the gap between the rich and the poor and to dismantle policies based on racism, greed, and violence. NETWORK's membership of more than one hundred thousand actively communicates with elected representatives to promote a national agenda.

NETWORK has been supported by LCWR (which has passed three resolutions in its favor) and many individual religious congregations. Its founders, leaders, staff, and members come from a variety of religious communities, but today religious women are not the only ones involved. NETWORK recognizes that systemic change is slow in coming and perseverance is an important virtue. They see themselves as speaking out of the Catholic social justice tradition, but also are influenced by the feminist movement: they supported the Equal Rights Amendment when the U.S. bishops did not; and decided that all employees should receive equal pay, in place of the differential pay scales that exist in U.S. businesses—and even in most other justice and peace organizations. NETWORK is a recognized Catholic organization and is listed in the Official Catholic Directory (OCD), but at times it has been at odds with the positions of U.S. bishops.

Another group of women religious working for structural change was the National Assembly of Women Religious (NAWR), founded in 1970. The group later agreed to open its membership to lay women and changed its name to the National Assembly of Religious Women (NARW). The driving force behind this group was a Dominican sister, Marjorie Tuitte, who had been trained in Saul Alinsky's community organizing approach. Tuitte insisted on the creative use of power to pursue and empower a truly human agenda. NARW/NAWR fought against racism, classism, militarism, clericalism, and later against heterosexism and destruction of the environment, and also explicitly opposed official Church policy in areas such as the ordination of women and abortion laws. At its peak in the 1970s NAWR's membership included one hundred sisters' councils across the country and some five thousand individual members. The organization distributed resource packets and pamphlets to its members, as well as a newsletter called *Probe*. However the organization folded in 1995 due to financial constraints and other factors.[41]

Religious orders and congregations of men made similar commitments to work for social justice. The Society of Jesus (Jesuits) founded in the sixteenth century is an exemplar. The thirty-second General Congregation of the Jesuit Order met between December 1974 and March 1975—notably, after the 1971 International Synod that emphasized action on behalf of justice as a constitutive dimension of the Gospel and of the Church's mission. Decree 4 of this Congregation maintained that the promotion of justice is an absolute requirement of the Jesuit mission today, both individually and corporately.[42] The Jesuits have taken this mandate very seriously. In the United States the Jesuit Conference Office of Social and International Ministries (JSIM) seeks to fulfill its mission in collaboration with twenty-eight Jesuit colleges and universities, more than sixty high schools and middle schools, eighty parishes, and twenty-eight retreat houses, in addition to individual social ministry efforts. This office engages in legislative and corporate advocacy—focusing on domestic issues such as poverty; housing; minimum wage; international issues such as immigration, war, and violence; and HIV/AIDS. The JSIM also seeks to raise awareness and facilitate dialogue on social justice issues throughout the Ignatian family, and among Jesuits doing social research and analysis themselves and with various social ministries. This office works closely with other Jesuit apostolates such as the Ignatian Volunteer Corps, the Ignatian Solidarity Network, and the Jesuit Refugee Service.[43] The U.S. Jesuits maintain the social ministry database "Iggy," which provides a comprehensive listing of Jesuit- and Ignatian-inspired social ministries in the United States—including direct service ministries; university social research institutes; and social outreach programs at Jesuit parishes, schools, and provinces.[44]

The Jesuits constitute one of the largest and most influential religious communities of men in the U.S. Catholic Church. Their commitment to social justice, however, is not unique, and has been shared by almost all other male religious orders and communities. For our purposes it is sufficient to use the

Jesuits to illustrate the commitment to social justice among male religious groups.

This commitment to social justice among female and male religious communities marks a significant change in carrying out the social mission of the Church after Vatican II. Religious took on different forms of social justice ministry and also became heavily involved in advocacy and working to change social policies and unjust structures. Individual religious and clergy also adopted their own approaches to social justice involvement. Those that received the most publicity usually involved some type of civil disobedience, as illustrated by the actions of the Catholic Resistance. Note that religious involvement in advocacy corresponds with the same emphasis in Catholic institutions such as Catholic Charities and Catholic health care.

However, some objected to the prominent role of religious and clergy in social justice and advocating for social change because it diminished the rightful role of the laity in the temporal order. Many explicit objections came from people who had been associated with lay Catholic action in Chicago. The aforementioned Chicago Declaration of Concern noted that in the preceding decade many priests have acted as if the primary responsibility to work for justice and peace rested with ordained ministers, thus bypassing the laity and their role. These religious and priests sought to impose their own agendas on the laity. Today we may now have a clericalism from the left: social transformation is the work of the laity in their various roles. Many have the impression that one can change society only as an outsider and not in the day-to-day activity of Christian people in their families, neighborhoods, voluntary assemblies, workplaces, and political groups. In this light the Declaration notes with regret the demise of many lay organizations and movements that had once thrived. Movements for justice and peace are now built into Church bureaucracy, but there is no evidence that bureaucratization has led to a greater involvement of the laity. In fact, we have lost a generation of lay leaders.[45]

Andrew M. Greeley, the well-known Chicago priest, sociologist, and later novelist, strongly disagreed with the Berrigans' new approach and the peace movement's methods of protest and confrontation. Unlike previous generations of social activists, these new Catholic social activists are crusaders who are not interested in forming unions or organizing communities. This new approach has not produced any real results.[46] In a 1971 essay Msgr. George G. Higgins discussed "old breed" and "new breed" approaches to Catholic social action. Higgins, a Chicago priest and early disciple of Msgr. Reynold Hillenbrand in Chicago in the 1930s, worked for the Social Action Department of the U.S. Bishops for thirty-six years. His primary area of expertise was labor, but he was the best-known proponent of Catholic social action in the United States as a result of his work for the U.S. bishops. Higgins was a believer in social action as primarily the work of the laity, and identified with the old breed. He characterized the new breed as too churchy; too interested in seeing problems in terms of pushing the church hierarchy to take particular positions rather than recognizing the primacy of the laity in the secular realm; too enthralled with marches and demonstrations rather than recognizing the need for long-term education and structural reform; and too moralizing and quick to make prophetic denunciations without recognizing professional expertise and the complexity of moral issues such as the Vietnam War. He admired many of the qualities of the new breed, but believed their approach could only go so far and would not ultimately solve social problems. Nevertheless, in the same article he cautions the reader that the new breed–old breed distinction is something of a rhetorical device.[47]

A CATHOLIC "BOTH-AND" SOLUTION

In my judgment the central issue in this discussion is the role of bishops, clergy, and religious in changing public policy and political, economic, and social structures; this issue has received considerable attention in both the public media and the Church. Working for structural change is a significant aspect of the social mission of the Church—but it is only a part of that mission and also involves substantial input from lay people. Lay people have the indispensable and unique role in trying to transform all the aspects of the temporal realm in their daily lives. Such a solution is in keeping with the characteristic Catholic "both-and" approach.

Importance of Structural Change

The Vatican II approach and subsequent developments—by emphasizing the struggle for justice and a preferential option for the poor—recognized the need for a change of social, political, and economic structures. Injustice in our world is above all a structural reality. An important goal is to change public policy and legislation.

Nontheological factors such as the post–World War II ethos also emphasize the need for structural change through changes in public policy.[48] An emphasis on democracy and democratic institutions called for change in many different political structures. In 1948 the United Nations issued the Universal Declaration of Human Rights, thus making human rights a central social, political, and economic concern. One major change worldwide was the end of colonialism and the establishment of indigenous local governments throughout Asia and Africa. Existing political systems were no longer seen as divinely established and unchangeable. Only after the war did people become more conscious of the evil of the Holocaust. As time went on the world became more aware of the huge disparities between the developed and the developing world. At the same time the threat of nuclear war and Cold War injustices perpetrated by both East and West became more apparent.

In the 1960s the United States saw a tremendous growth in the awareness of injustices and attempts to right them. The campaigns of Martin Luther King and others sought to eliminate racial injustices. More and more people became convinced of the injustice of the U.S. support of the government of South Vietnam, and responded with public protests and demonstrations. In the decades that followed people in the United States became aware of other injustices, including domestic economic disparities and the ecological problems that had been created by human hubris. From a theoretical perspective, there is no doubt that structural change is a very effective way to correct injustice, which explains the Church's present-day emphasis on change in public policy on a number of issues.

In the 1960s and early 1970s the initial call for structural change took the form of public protests and demonstrations, and it was very helpful to have priests and religious in religious garb leading these demonstrations. This was a comparatively new and novel role for Catholic nuns and priests, and newspaper pictorials and televised images of religious and clergy helped to give a greater prominence to a cause. As time went on, nuns and priests were no longer the attention getters they had been.

In fairness, many of the religious and priests recognized that demonstrations alone were not enough, and that change would not be easy. Demonstrations at best were a first step to mobilize public opinion to bring about structural change. Some naïvely thought that demonstrations would effect rapid change, but history points to long-term commitments to struggles over a period of years.

It was only natural for Catholic activists to want Church leaders to support the cause of social justice and denounce injustice. In light of the role of the Church as bearing witness to the kingdom and promoting transformation, the bishops themselves are now working for more just institutions. The documents of the universal papal and hierarchical magisterium that treat Catholic social teaching since the late nineteenth century have strongly emphasized the need to create just structures in all aspects of our social life. The best efforts of the United States bishops in this regard were their 1980s letters on peace and the economy.[49]

But as leaders of the Church bishops have to be careful about how they work for change in public policy and legislation. Since the last quarter of the twentieth century there have been "culture wars" between two competing ideas of what U.S. public policy should be.[50] Chapter 7 discusses the way in which bishops should propose their positions on public policy in light of the need to respect legitimate diversity in the Church and the freedom of the believer.

Thus, all members of the Church—laity, clerics, religious, and bishops—play a role in working for structural change. The laity vote and work to change public opinion in various milieux. Also it is the laity who hold the executive, judicial, and legislative offices that immediately and directly bear on public policy. The laity have the primary role, even though their role seldom receives primary emphasis. The attention in the post–Vatican II Church rightfully given to the role of clerics, religious, and bishops should not detract from the primary role of the laity in effecting structural change.

The Unique Role of the Laity

Public policy is important for social change, but it is by no means the whole of social, cultural, and economic life. Catholic social teaching has insisted on the principle of subsidiarity, and its understanding of the limited role of government and the need for mediating institutions in public society.[51] The fundamental Catholic view of society looks something like this: At the very foundation of society stands the human person with God-given dignity, rights, and responsibilities. The person precedes the state and can never be subordinated to it. However, the person is not just an individual; but in the Catholic tradition the human person is social by nature. The next level is that of family, the basic unit of society that develops human beings. As a natural society the family comes before the state and cannot be absorbed by it. At the next level are institutions and structures such as neighborhoods or extended families. We live in and through these realities.

Then come voluntary or independent structures and institutions that are necessary to any society. Think, for example, of the significant public role played by the press and the media. Cultural institutions of all kinds exist to develop the higher aspects of human existence. Educational groups of great variety foster people at every level. Religious groups, synagogues, mosques, and churches bring people together for religious and other purposes. Business and economic corporations also should work for the common good. Professional societies and labor unions work for the good of their members and also for the public good. Groups that people join of their own free will are called voluntary groups; we need such groups for human fulfillment but also for the greater public good. In the Catholic understanding, only after these other aspects of society come local, state, and national government.

The Catholic understanding thus coheres with the democratic notion of a limited constitutional government. In a well-organized society all persons, organizations, structures, institutions, associations, and corporations have a role to play in addition to the subsidiary role of government. The public or societal order embraces many realities—social, cultural, educational, associational, and work oriented—beyond the political realm.

The term subsidiarity derives from the Latin word *subsidium*, which means "help." According to this theory of subsidiarity, the upper levels are not to annihilate or absorb the lower, more basic levels, but to enable the lower levels to do what they can and to intervene only when the lower levels are incapable of doing what has to be done. Thus, voluntary associations help individuals and families function as best they can and should only do what individuals and families cannot accomplish on their own or with the help of others. Likewise, government should intervene to help voluntary associations and do only what the voluntary groups cannot do on their own. Government itself should start at the grassroots level, and the state and federal governments in turn should take upon themselves only what is beyond the capabilities of local government.

The principle of subsidiarity reminds us of the different areas in which the baptized Christian is called to live out the social mission that is part and parcel of the baptismal commitment. These activities do not receive much public attention but they are very important if the total Church is to transform society. The social mission of the Church involves much more than just the political order.

As might be expected, the Vatican II Decree on the Apostolate of Lay People stresses this point. The most important fields of lay action include church, communities, the family, youth, the social milieu, and national and international affairs. Without much elaboration the document refers to the family, in accord with Catholic tradition, as the first and vital cell of society; it also insists that the infusion of Christian spirit into the mentality, customs, laws, and structures of the community in which one lives and works is so much the duty and responsibility of the laity that it cannot be performed by others.[52]

In *Family Ethics: Practices for Christians*, Julie Hanlon Rubio insists on the social role of the family. She recognizes and to an extent agrees with those who claim that the body of Catholic social teaching has little developed the social role of the family, but shows how the Family Life Bureau of the bishops' conference and many Catholic authors in the pre–Vatican II period treated the family as the basic unit of society. She calls special attention to the writings of Pope John Paul II that detail the role of the family in society. John Paul II frequently refers to the family as the domestic Church that has an important social mission attached to it.[53]

The importance of transforming the mediating institutions of society or the milieus in which people live and work in the United States is well developed in the book *Habits of the Heart*.[54] This book by Robert Bellah and four coauthors was first published in 1985, but is now widely recognized as a classic. Its basic thesis is that the primary language spoken by people in the United States is the language of individualism. The authors do not say that everyone acts in a totally individualistic way, but that even those who are committed to others have a difficulty finding a language to express what they are trying to do. Individualism takes two forms. Utilitiarian individualism sees every other person or thing simply as means to one's own ends. A reaction to utilitarian individualism, expressive individualism insists on the right of the person at any time or place to express her unique core of individuality and feeling without any concern for others. *Habits of the Heart* contrasts this language of individualism with the language of biblical religion and civic republicanism, which still is spoken in the United States but as a very secondary language. The book then shows how this individualism affects private life in terms of finding oneself, love and marriage, reaching out, and individualism itself. Although the book describes these four aspects or areas as part of private life, these aspects also have an important social dimension. Individualism also strongly affects four aspects of public life—getting involved, citizenship, religion, and the national society.

Habits of the Heart indicates how the language and attitude of individualism affects many of the mediating institutions and milieux in which we live. The Christian and biblical traditions take a communitarian approach, which avoids the two extremes of individualism and collectivism. Christian and biblical communitarianism does not deny the importance of the fulfillment and happiness of the person, but hold that the person arrives at such fulfillment and happiness only in the context of community.

In accord with a Catholic understanding, I do not see a total opposition between Christianity and culture that renders the Church always countercultural. The Catholic Church in the Vatican has perhaps the most significant library and museum in the Western world. How can such an institution claim to be totally countercultural? The Christianity-culture relationship is complex. Human culture at times reveals the goodness of creation and of grace which exists beyond the explicitly Christian, but at other times it exhibits the imperfection and especially the effects of sin that characterize all human reality. At times the Church can learn from culture; the U.S. Catholic Church has learned the values of democracy, freedom, human participation in institutions of society, and the rights of women. At other times the Church should criticize culture for its failings and shortcomings. In my judgment, the major problem in contemporary U.S. culture today is the danger of individualism. In this context, the Catholic is called both in his or her own actions and especially in concert with like-minded people to inject a more communitarian approach into public life in the United States. The most significant way in which Catholics can transform existing culture and mediating institutions is by changing this predominate individualism into a more communitarian reality.

CONCLUSION

The post–Vatican II role of the laity in transforming the temporal order in the United States differs from pre–Vatican II Catholic action in three important ways. First there is only one mission of the Church working for justice and the transformation of the world seen as a constitutive dimension of the one mission of evangelization and redemption. The sharp distinction between the supernatural and the natural existing in the pre–Vatican II approach that grounded the role of the laity has been replaced with a recognition that faith, grace, and Jesus must affect reality.

Second, earlier Catholic action rested on a very triumphalistic understanding of the Church, supported both by a pre–Vatican II ecclesiology and the role that the Church played in the lives of Catholics in this country. A good illustration of this triumphalism is the song of student Catholic Action, often called "An Army of Youth." The first stanza illustrates the triumphalistic, and even militaristic and nationalistic, character of such an approach:

> An army of youth flying the standards of Truth,
> We're fighting for Christ the Lord.
> Heads lifted high, Catholic Action our cry,
> And the Cross our only sword.
> On Earth's battlefield

Never a vantage we'll yield
As dauntlessly on we swing.
Comrades true, dare and do
Neath the Queen's white and blue,
For our flag, for our faith
For Christ the King.[55]

Third, the role of the laity in transforming the world usually involves working with many people who are not Catholic. Earlier Catholic action insisted on the organized activity of Catholics as such, and the laity worked together precisely as Catholics. Such an approach presupposed a very homogeneous Catholic culture distinct from the surrounding culture and society. In the early-twentieth-century United States, people still referred to the "Catholic Ghetto." Catholics were very conscious of their identity, and this affected much of what they did in their lives. Before Vatican II there was little emphasis on ecumenical cooperation; Catholics were even forbidden to share in Protestant worship services. An old adage held that Catholics were born in a Catholic hospital, baptized in a Catholic Church, educated in Catholic schools, lived in Catholic neighborhoods, and were buried in Catholic cemeteries. As noted earlier, throughout the twentieth century Catholics assimilated into U.S. society. This process became much more pronounced after World War II, when Catholics moved into the suburbs and formed many new relationships with non-Catholics.

In addition, Vatican II saw a new emphasis on ecumenical relationships, which called for Catholics to work together with other Christians and people of other religions or of no religion. Catholicism had insisted on organized action to effect social change. Since Vatican II, organized activity has had to include people other than Catholics in order to be effective. Thus, sociological and theological grounds call for Catholics to cease working only by themselves for social change.

There will continue to be some comparatively small activity of Catholics working separately, but the primary way to transform the temporal order will be by working with others in a pluralistic society. The next chapter will discuss how specifically Catholic institutions and movements in the pre–Vatican II Church have evolved in the face of changing theological and sociological circumstances.

However, the laity can use two significant aspects of the Catholic action approach developed by Canon Cardijn. The first is the transformation of the

milieu in which people find themselves. Different milieux should be understood in light of the principle of subsidiarity, which recognizes many different
aspects of the social reality in addition to the role of government. Second, "see,
judge, and act" is still applicable today. One must first see what is going on,
judge how best to change or transform what is happening, and then act in
accord with that judgment.

This chapter treats the changing focus of the social mission of the Church
due to theological factors stemming from Vatican II as well as changing social
situations. The older distinction and even dichotomy between the role of the
clergy and religious in the spiritual realm and the laity in the temporal realm no
longer holds. The whole Church—all the baptized—work for transformation as
part of preaching the Gospel and the redemptive mission of the Church. This
approach recognizes the need for all Catholics to work to change public policy.
Lay people now also have a role in the spiritual life of the Church, but continue
to be called to transform all the milieux in which they live and work—now in
conjunction with others who are not Catholic.

NOTES

1. Synod of Bishops, 1971, *Justitia in mundo*, in *Catholic Social Thought: The Documentary Heritage*, ed. David J. O'Brien and Thomas A. Shannon (Maryknoll, N.Y.: Orbis, 1992), 289.

2. Dogmatic Constitution on the Church, n. 5, in *Vatican Council II: The Basic Sixteen Documents*, ed. Austin Flannery (Northport, N.Y.: Costello, 1996), 3–4.

3. Dogmatic Constitution on the Church, no. 8, in *Vatican Council II*, 10.

4. For my evaluation of the manuals, see Charles E. Curran, *Catholic Moral Theology in the United States: A History* (Washington, D.C.: Georgetown University Press, 2008), 2–11.

5. Decree on the Training of Priests, n. 16, in *Vatican Council II*, 376.

6. Pastoral Constitution on the Church in the Modern World, n. 43, in *Vatican Council II*, 211.

7. Pastoral Constitution on the Church in the Modern World, nn. 12–22, in *Vatican Council II*, 174–87.

8. Charles Moeller, "History of the Constitution," in *Commentary on the Documents of Vatican II*, vol. 5: *Pastoral Constitution on the Church in the Modern World*, ed. Herbert Vorgrimler (New York: Herder and Herder, 1969), 11ff.

9. Pastoral Constitution on the Church in the Modern World, n. 3, in *Vatican Council II*, 164.

10. Pastoral Constitution on the Church in the Modern World, nn. 40–45, in *Vatican Council II*, 207–17.

11. Pope Paul VI, *Evangelii nuntiandi*, nn. 18–19, in *Catholic Social Thought*, 309–10.

12. Joseph A. Komonchak, "Clergy, Laity, and the Church's Mission in the World," *Jurist* 41 (1981): 439–44; see also Francis Schüssler Fiorenza, "Church: Social Mission of," in

New Dictionary of Catholic Social Thought, ed. Judith A. Dywer (Collegeville, Minn.: Liturgical, 1994), 151–71.

13. John R. Donahue, "The Bible and Catholic Social Teaching: Will the Engagement Lead to Marriage?" in *Modern Catholic Social Teaching: Commentaries and Interpretations*, ed. Kenneth R. Himes (Washington, D.C.: Georgetown University Press, 2005), 9–40.

14. Donahue, "The Bible and Catholic Social Teaching," 24–31.

15. Charles M. Murphy, "Action for Justice as Constitutive of the Preaching of the Gospel: What Did the 1971 Synod Mean?" *Theological Studies* 44 (1983): 300–305.

16. *Evangelii nuntiandi*, nn. 25–29, in *Catholic Social Thought*, 312–13.

17. Pope Benedict XVI, *Deus caritas est*, Origins 35 (2006): 541–57.

18. Pope Benedict XVI, *Caritas in vertiate*, n. 6, in *Origins* 39 (2009): 128–29.

19. Charles M. Murphy, "Charity not Justice as Constitutive of the Church's Mission," *Theological Studies* 68 (2007): 284.

20. Decree on the Apostolate of Lay People, n. 2, in *Vatican Council II*, 405–6.

21. Decree on the Apostolate of Lay People, n. 6, in *Vatican Council II*, 411.

22. Decree on the Apostolate of Lay People, nn. 9–14, in *Vatican Council II*, 416–23.

23. Florence Caffrey Bourg, *Where Two or Three Are Gathered: Christian Families as Domestic Church* (Notre Dame, Ind.: University of Notre Dame Press, 2004); Joseph C. Atkinson, "Family as Domestic Church: Developmental Trajectory, Legitmacy, and Problems of Appropriation," *Theological Studies* 66 (2005): 592–604.

24. Decree on the Apostolate of Lay People, n. 7, in *Vatican Council II*, 413.

25. Voice of the Faithful, www.votf.org.

26. National Leadership Roundtable on Church Management, www.nlrcm.org.

27. Paul Lakeland, *Liberation of the Laity: In Search of an Accountable Church* (New York: Continuum, 2003); Lakeland, *Catholicism at the Crossroads: How the Laity Can Save the Church* (New York: Continuum, 2007).

28. "The Chicago Declaration of Christian Concern," in *Challenge to the Laity*, ed. Russell Barta (Huntington, Ind.: Our Sunday Visitor, 1980), 21.

29. Mitchell K. Hall, *Because of Their Faith: CALCAV and Religious Opposition to the Vietnam War* (New York: Columbia University Press, 1990).

30. Patrick Jones, "'Not a Color but an Attitude': Fr. James Groppi and Black Power Politics in Milwaukee," in *Groundwork: Local Black Freedom Movements in America*, ed. Jeanne Theoharis and Komozi Woodard (New York: New York University Press 2005), 259–81.

31. Charles A. Meconis, *With Clumsy Grace: The American Catholic Left 1961–1975* (New York: Seabury, 1979).

32. In this section on the Berrigans, I follow, especially, Patricia McNeal, *Harder than War: Catholic Peacemaking in Twentieth Century America* (New Brunswick, N.J.: Rutgers University Press, 1992), 173–210; see also William VanEtten Casey and Philip Nobile, eds., *The Berrigans* (New York: Avon, 1971).

33. Anneliese Sinott, "Mission and Ministry," in *Journey in Faith and Fidelity: Women Shaping Religious Life for a Renewed Church*, ed. Nadine Foley (New York: Continuum, 1999), 101.

34. Sinott, "Mission and Ministry," 107–9.

35. On the changing lifestyles of religious women, see Lora Ann Quinones and Mary Daniel Turner, *The Transformation of American Catholic Sisters* (Philadelphia: Temple University Press, 1992).

36. Kenneth A. Briggs, *Double Crossed: Uncovering the Catholic Church's Betrayal of American Nuns* (New York: Doubleday, 2006), 142.

37. See "LCWR and Social Justice," lcwr.org/lcwrsocialjustice/socialjusticeoverview.htm.

38. For an overview, see Briggs, *Double Crossed*, 133–51.

39. Sinnott, "Mission and Ministry," 110.

40. Carol Coston, "Women Religious Engage the Political Process," in *Journey in Faith and Fidelity*, ed. Foley, 198–217; available online at www.networklobby.org.

41. Anne E. Patrick, "A Ministry of Justice: The 25 Year Pilgrimage of the National Assembly of Religious Women," in *What's Left? Liberal American Catholics*, ed. Mary Jo Weaver (Bloomington: Indiana University Press, 1999), 176–87; see also Briggs, *Double Crossed*, 143–44.

42. *Documents of the 32nd General Congregation* (Washington, D.C.: The Jesuit Conference, 1975), Decree 4.

43. See "Social Justice," www.jesuit.org/index.php/main/jesuits-worldwide/social-justice/.

44. See "Social Ministries Database," iggy.jesuit.org/.

45. "Chicago Declaration of Concern," in *Challenge to the Laity*, 22–23.

46. Andrew M. Greeley, "Catholic Social Activism, Real or Rad-Chick," *National Catholic Reporter*, February 7, 1975; Andrew M. Greeley, "L'Affaire Berrigan," *The New York Times*, February 19, 1971.

47. George G. Higgins, "Historical Resume of the Teaching, Policy, and Action of the Church in 'Social Mission,'" in *Metropolis: Christian Presence and Responsibility*, ed. Philip D. Morris (Notre Dame, Ind.: Fides, 1970), 144–72.

48. Marvin L. Krier Mich, *The Challenge and Spirituality of Catholic Social Teaching* (Louisville, Ky.: Just Faith, 2005), 5–6.

49. For my analysis of these documents, see Charles E. Curran, *Catholic Social Teaching 1891–Present: A Historical, Theological, and Ethical Analysis* (Washington, D.C.: Georgetown University Press, 2002).

50. James Davison Hunter, *Culture Wars: The Struggle to Control the Family, Art, Education, Law, and Politics in America* (New York: Basic, 1992).

51. For my understanding of the principle of subsidiarity in Catholic social teaching, see Curran, *Catholic Social Teaching*, 141–44.

52. Decree on the Apostolate of Lay People, nn. 7–13, in *Vatican Council II*, 412–22.

53. Julie Hanlon Rubio, *Family Ethics: Practices for Christians* (Washington, D.C.: Georgetown University Press, 2010), 37–65.

54. Robert N. Bellah, Richard Madsen, William M. Sullivan, and Ann Swidler, *Habits of the Heart: Individualism and Commitment in American Life* (Berkeley: University of California Press, 1985).

55. Daniel Lord, "For Christ the King," www.giamusic.com/sacred_music/tabletalk/63.cfm.

5

Post–Vatican II Development of Three Earlier Instances of the Social Mission

The preceding chapters treat the changed understanding of the Church and the social mission of the Church together with the assimilation of Catholics into the U.S. cultural mainstream. This chapter considers three earlier initiatives of the social mission in light of the developments discussed in the previous chapters. Catholic health care facilities and Catholic Charities continue to exist with the same basic purpose of caring for the sick and the needy, but they have changed dramatically. Changes in how our society funds and cares for the sick and needy have also greatly affected these two institutions. The Catholic Worker Movement remains today the most enduring illustration of a voluntary group of committed people, but it, too, has undergone significant development.

Catholic health care institutions and Catholic Charities share many common questions and proposed solutions regarding protection and promotion of Catholic identity today. Both types of institutions are far more pluralistic than they were in the first half of the twentieth century: they serve both Catholics and non-Catholics; their staffs and even their leaders include Catholics as well as non-Catholics; most significantly, their funding does not come primarily from the Catholic Church—government money plays a major role, especially for Catholic Charities.

What, then, is the Catholic identity of such institutions today? These new developments are not incompatible with Catholic identity. Recall the discussion in chapter 2 of Catholic identity being also catholic (with a lowercase c). The Catholic Church recognizes that Catholics can and should work together with all people of goodwill for the public good. If Catholic identity were exclusive it would have much more clearly defined boundaries, but this would make the Church into a discrete sect, and would no longer be catholic.

In theory, the Catholic identity of institutions and the social mission are not unique but are distinctive.[1] For example, care for the poor distinguishes Catholic identity and the Catholic social mission, but many other religious and non-religious people share this concern. Precisely because Catholic identity is also catholic (again, with a lowercase c) and is distinctive in its embracing of certain concepts, values, and realities that are shared by others, the Catholic social mission and even the institutions involved in such a mission are open to participation by people who are not themselves Catholics.

Ronald P. Hamel, an ethicist with the Catholic Health Association, refers to Catholic identity as the character of the institution.[2] One must first define Catholic identity, then develop and put into practice the means to manifest this identity in all aspects of institutions. Catholic identity cannot be limited to a single element of an institution, such as the service of chaplains in hospitals.

A basic problem comes from tension between the importance of the bottom line, or institutional profit; and the mission of the Catholic institution to show, for example, special concern for the poor and needy. The entry of many for-profit institutions into the health care field, and to a much lesser degree into Catholic Charities, has exacerbated this problem. The problem is greater for health care institutions than for Catholic Charities because they are huge businesses with large landholdings, buildings, and very extensive and expensive equipment. How does one negotiate the tension between Catholic identity and the bottom line?[3]

CATHOLIC HEALTH CARE INSTITUTIONS

Theological changes brought about by Vatican II have not influenced the basic mission of Catholic hospitals and health care institutions. Care for the sick, even in institutional settings, has a long history in the Roman Catholic tradition. But Vatican II, changes in Catholic life and culture, and also significant changes in health care delivery in the United States have had a profound effect on Catholic health care facilities.

Scientific and technological breakthroughs have made accessible very expensive equipment necessary to the modern hospital. The country as a whole is very conscious of the rising cost of health care, and health care institutions have attempted to reduce their costs. Insurance companies and government regulations have also been interested in cutting health care expenses both inside and outside health care institutions. The move from fee for service to managed care has made the hospital world more competitive. In many areas individual hospitals have closed because they are no longer viable in the twenty-first century. Health care facilities now compete for patients and market shares. In this economic climate larger hospital systems have emerged in order to cut down on expenses and provide better services. For-profit health care facilities and national corporations have now entered the realm of health care facilities. The danger today is that health care facilities are primarily a business and not a service to those who are sick or in need.

As discussed in chapter 1, Catholic hospitals and health care facilities were created with the sponsorship and work of congregations of women religious; a much smaller number were sponsored by congregations of lay brothers. The CEO of the hospital was usually a religious sister, and many religious women served as nurses and administrators. Their distinctive garb made the Catholic presence all the more visible. Most Catholics automatically gravitated to the Catholic hospital, which was an integral part of the Catholic subculture. Today this is no longer the case.[4]

How have Catholic health care facilities coped with changes both in broader health care delivery and in the internal life of the Church? First, the sponsoring Catholic religious congregations incorporated their health care institutions as separate legal corporations. to serve a twofold purpose—to enhance their ability to receive public funding, and to protect the religious congregation from legal and financial liabilities stemming from the activities of the hospital.[5] Much more dramatic were the demise of the freestanding individual Catholic hospital and the emergence of Catholic health care systems encompassing several different hospitals. For example, in 1998 Catholic Health East brought together smaller, already existing health care facilities that had been sponsored by individual congregations, and strives to ensure their continued Catholic identity and operational strength. The system covers eleven East Coast states from Maine to Florida and includes thirty-three acute care hospitals, four long-term acute care hospitals, thirty-six long term–care facilities, twelve assisted living facilities, five continuing care retirement communities, eight rehabilitation facilities, and twenty-five home health/hospice agencies.[6]

Headquartered in St. Louis, Missouri, Ascension Health—the nation's largest Catholic and largest nonprofit health care system—serves patients in twenty states and the District of Columbia through a network of hospitals and related facilities providing acute care services; long-term care; community health services; and psychiatric, rehabilitation, and residential care. The system is sponsored by the religious communities of the Daughters of Charity, the Congregation of St. Joseph, and the Sisters of St. Joseph of Carondelet.[7] Catholic health care facilities have undergone dramatic changes but still provide significant health care delivery in the United States. As of 2006, there were sixty

Catholic hospital systems and more than six hundred hospitals—or about 12.5 percent of all non–federally funded community hospitals—in addition to innumerable other health care facilities.[8]

Catholic Identity of Health Care Institutions

Recent developments have brought to the fore the question of the Catholic identity of Catholic health care institutions. Kevin O'Rourke, who has spent forty years as a Catholic theologian and ethicist involved in health care—often in association with the Catholic Health Association—has proposed twelve constituent elements of Catholic identity. O'Rourke is the first to recognize that many of these characteristics are vague and general, but perhaps this is the nature of mission statements. The twelve constitutive elements include these: carrying on the ministry of Christ; expressing Gospel values; respecting human dignity; supporting the sanctity of life; fostering a holistic vision of health care; ensuring high-quality health care; demonstrating a preferential option for the poor; forming a community dedicated to social justice; fostering the common good; observing Catholic ethical and religious directives; being a not-for-profit institution; and being approved by the Church hierarchy.[9]

O'Rourke insists, "The quality of care will not be sacrificed for any other factor which is important for Catholic identity." The Catholic health care facility must be a good facility, and thus needs efficient and high-caliber medical and nursing staffs, as well as up-to-date medical approaches and managerial skills.[10] Ron Hamel insists that Catholic institutions must maintain the highest professional standards, provide top-quality services, adapt to the changing expressions of their secular counterparts, correspond to all legal and operational requirements for such facilities, and remain financially solvent. Church institutions are part of the world and not exempt from its requirements.[11]

Some non-Catholic Christians insist that Christian and even Catholic health care should differ from other forms of health care. In a symposium on Catholic health care two non-Catholic contributors insisted that Catholic health care facilities should in some sense challenge the health care delivered in non-Catholic settings. Their basic thrust is that Catholic health care today focuses too much on bodily healing and ignores the spiritual and transcendent aspects of healing. Tristram Englehardt, for one, observes that the Catholic hospital emphasizes the immanent aspect of Catholic health care but downplays the transcendent. The Christian facility, some argue, should primarily be concerned with excellence in spiritual care and only secondarily with excellence in medical care.[12]

William E. Stempsey, the editor of this symposium, points out that the Catholic contributors all basically agree with the approach proposed by O'Rourke: that the Catholic health care facility must be a good health care facility. Catholic spirituality for the most part seeks to find God in all things, and for Catholics the healing process does not bring one to Christ; Christ is already part of physical healing. Even in the New Testament, the healings of Jesus demonstrate the importance of the temporal.[13]

The understanding that a Catholic institution needs to be a good health care facility is based on Catholic theology, with its characteristic note of mediation: the divine is mediated in and through the human. God's healing takes place in and through all that is involved in the human healing process. An older scholastic axiom maintained that God works through secondary causes. Note here the Catholic emphasis on "both-and": a health care institution should be both high quality and Catholic. Certainly the Catholic approach may criticize health care delivery and institutions today, but such criticism should be based on what it means to provide good health care, and all may enter into discussion with Catholic institutions.[14]

Means to Promote Catholic Identity

One practical problem concerns promoting and ensuring the complex Catholic identity of these health care facilities. Three players are involved—bishops, the Catholic Health Association, and, especially, those entrusted with making the Catholic mission present throughout its institutions.

Individual Catholic health care institutions are connected to the bishop of the diocese in which they are located. The bishop has Church-related obligations to the hospital, especially with regard to maintaining the Catholic identity of the institution. In 2001 the Catholic bishops of the United States as a whole issued the fourth edition of "Ethical and Religious Directives for Catholic Health Care Services."[15] Although approved by the national body of bishops, these Directives must be implemented by each individual bishop.

The Directives have an interesting history. The original Directives were developed in 1949 by a group of United States and Canadian theologians and health care professionals. In 1956 a revised second edition, with heavy input from Jesuit moral theologian Gerald Kelly, was published by the Catholic Hospital Association of the United States and Canada. This edition became official policy only where individual diocesan bishops promulgated it. The 1971 edition has served as the official policy of United States bishops as a whole, but still must be adopted by individual diocesan bishops. Note that the writing and preparation of these Directives has been taken over by the bishops themselves but they continue to consult a fair amount in the process.[16]

There has been another significant change to these Directives. Early versions dealt with the ethical dilemmas that arise in a Catholic hospital, but the 2001 Directives are much broader in scope. The Directives now comprise six comparatively short parts—the social responsibility of Catholic health care services, pastoral and spiritual responsibilities, the professional-patient relationship, issues concerning the beginning of life, issues in care for the dying, and forming new partnerships with non-Catholic health care organizations and providers. These Directives thus account for new Catholic health care contexts and, above all, have moved away from the exclusive casuistic approach of the earlier Directives, which dealt only with controversial issues and cases occasioned by Catholic moral teaching.

The Catholic Health Association is a voluntary membership, professional organization of more than two thousand health care sponsors, systems, facilities, health plans, and related organizations. The CHA thus serves its members in their ministry and works closely with the United States bishops, but it is not an official Church organization. The CHA publishes *Health Progress*, a bimonthly professional journal; *Catholic Health World*, a semimonthly newsletter; and *Health Care Ethics USA*, a quarterly newsletter published jointly by the CHA and the Center for Health Care Ethics at Saint Louis University.[17]

The CHA thus sees itself as a spokesperson for Catholic health care in the United States. Catholic health care is a ministry continuing the loving and healing ministry of Jesus. Catholic health care plays the roles of provider, employer, advocate, and citizen in working with and serving people of diverse faiths and background: "Our ministry is rooted in our belief that every person is a treasure, every life a sacred gift, every human being a unity of body, mind, and spirit." Each facility in Catholic health care has its own mission statement based on its historical charism and contemporary situation, but the CHA proposes six general commitments: providing compassionate and high-quality care, promoting health and well-being for all, paying special attention to the poor and vulnerable, acting to end poverty and injustice, using resources responsibly, and acting in harmony with the Catholic Church.[18]

One recent CHA development that obviously stems from the initiatives of Vatican II involves advocacy for better health care for all—especially the poor and the vulnerable. CHA, through its Washington office, advocates for health care reform in collaboration with other Catholic health care facilities—and, often, with non-Catholic groups. Its agenda is twofold—to strengthen the viability of Catholic health care ministry and to encourage the current health care system to be more compassionate and just. Above all, the CHA advocates for a health care system that provides accessible and affordable health care for all; it views health care as a right and the number of uninsured in the United States today (47 million) to be a national disgrace.[19]

The primary responsibility for promoting Catholic identity rests with the Catholic health care system and especially the individual health care institution. Three strategies have emerged to carry out this function—sponsorship, offices of mission effectiveness, and training for lay leadership.

Sponsorship is a nontechnical term for the way in which religious congregations (especially those made up of women) in decline have tried to ensure the continuing Catholic identity of their institutions. Health care institutions are now incorporated separately from the religious community, but in many cases religious community leaders have retained powers over the corporation, which gives them some control and influence over the Catholic identity of these institutions. "Reserved powers" is a term in not-for-profit institutions that refers to powers not given to the governing board but maintained and exercised by so-called corporate members. In Catholic hospitals these reserved powers generally include appointing boards of trustees; amending corporate statutes and bylaws; setting corporate philosophy and mission; deciding to merge, sell, or dissolve the corporation; approving budgets; and appointing chief executive officers—all with an eye toward ensuring the Catholic identity of the institution.[20]

As a general rule Catholic health care facilities now have a mission leader or supervisor of mission effectiveness. The purpose of this office is to integrate values and mission into the daily operations of health care facilities. People holding this position see themselves as catalysts, tone and direction setters, facilitators, resource persons, and educators. This office is usually at the vice presidential level and reports directly to the CEO.[21]

Leadership development of the laity is a third essential way to promote Catholic identity. The Catholic Health Association and broader Catholic health systems educate the leaders of the individual institutions themselves. Within each institution the mission leader or mission effectiveness person provides for the development of lay leaders and all staff in that particular institution.[22] Their challenge is to make sure that the Catholic identity permeates the entire institution and all its decisions and activities—not an easy assignment. Catholic health care institutions must be well run and efficient. A well-known adage in Catholic health care is "No margin, no mission." This phrase sums up the basic tension between the bottom line and the Catholic mission. But the Catholic recognition of catholicity (with a lowercase c) and "both-and" approaches maintain that one can have a health care facility that is both efficiently run and Catholic. The margin may make the mission possible, but the mission makes the margin necessary.[23] In practice this means that the primary responsibility for the Catholic mission lies with the CEO herself, and all leadership decisions within the institution should be made with the Catholic mission in mind.[24]

Mission integration aims to influence the culture and ethos of the entire institution—from leadership to the physicians, nurses, social workers, and entire support staff. One such device is to start every institutional meeting with a prayer or reflection that highlights values pertinent to what is being done. Such reflections or prayers are not to be led by "the religious person" but by all involved in the meeting.[25]

The challenge to develop and maintain the Catholic identity of health care institutions is daunting in light of diversity within institutions and the demands of efficiency. The forces of depersonalization, secularization, and the bottom-line mentality have to be overcome. Richard A. McCormick was somewhat negative in his evaluation of the Catholic identity of health care institutions.[26] But ethnographer Simon J. Craddock Lee, himself not a Catholic, maintains on the basis of his research in a Catholic health care system that retaining Catholic identity and implementing its mission is possible. Craddock's study involves a health care system that includes some non-Catholic institutions, but he maintains that the Catholic identity is apparent.[27]

There are two other factors that complicate the Catholic identity of health care institutions. The first involves mergers or some form of cooperation with for-profit institutions. Do such things water down Catholic identity? The second concerns actions forbidden by the bishops' Directives. Directive no. 70 explicitly states that Catholic health care facilities are not to perform or immediately cooperate in abortion or direct sterilization. There has been a somewhat lengthy discussion of the possibility of cooperating in providing sterilization in Catholic hospitals. In the post–Vatican II Church many Catholic theologians have dissented from the official condemnation of direct sterilization, and many Catholic spouses have been sterilized. Thus some would argue that Catholic health care facilities should perform sterilizations under certain circumstances. Other Catholics, however, support the condemnation of direct sterilization and Catholic hospitals' refusal to perform them.[28] Some reproductive rights groups have tried to block secular hospitals from merging with Catholic institutions because of their position on sterilization.[29] In practice arrangements have often been made for some way to provide these services.[30]

Catholic health care institutions and Catholic Charities share a structural problem that also detracts from Catholic identity: they are not primarily funded by the Church. Catholics as a whole do not feel any ownership of these institutions and therefore do not identify much with them. The next section discusses this in greater detail.

Catholic health care institutions have a very strong presence in society today and will endure. However, smaller institutions may close. All will continue to wrestle with the question of their Catholic identity.

CATHOLIC CHARITIES

Before Vatican II a significant development in Catholic Charities occurred with the introduction of the government provision of services plan. In 1959 the federal government began to purchase services from nonprofit agencies serving the general public. Catholic Charities had always had a close working relationship with governments of all kinds, but the new approach resulted in a large infusion of funding that permitted a significant increase in the number of services provided. This, together with the war on poverty and the creation of Medicare and Medicaid programs, expanded the involvement of Catholic Charities agencies in issues such as drug abuse, housing, and care for the mentally ill and developmentally disabled.[31]

In 1967 the National Conference of Catholic Charities (which later changed its name to Catholic Charities USA) initiated a renewal process in light of Vatican II, which resulted in the 1972 publication of *Toward a Renewed Catholic Charities Movement* and its acceptance by the membership. This document, produced by Catholic Charities leaders, has been called the "Cadre Report." It called for Catholic Charities to be involved in three areas: the provision of direct services to all people and use of government money to provide some of these services, advocacy for the poor, and convening people to work on social issues. Subsequent statements have built on the Cadre Report.[32]

In the 1990s a three-year evaluation process called Vision 2000 outlined four strategic directions: continued direct services to all people, not just Catholics; efforts to change sinful structures of society that create poverty and undermine wholesome family life; helping people to deal with problems themselves; and strengthening Catholic Charities' relationships with the rest of the Church and promoting Catholic social teaching.[33] One sees in it a recognition that the provision of direct services is not enough—charities must also work toward structural change and individual empowerment. In 2010 Catholic Charities USA, the umbrella organization, celebrated its centennial.

Individual Catholic Charities organizations are legally incorporated in each diocese and are themselves umbrella organizations involving many different agencies and ministries. The Catholic Charities of the Archdiocese of New York website, for example, describes the five activities it carries out through different agencies—protecting and nurturing children, sheltering the homeless, strengthening families and resolving family crises, supporting the physically and emotionally challenged, and welcoming immigrants and refugees.[34] Charities USA, an umbrella group headquartered near Washington, D.C., emphasizes advocacy work and empowerment, but some dioceses also become involved in social change and empowering the poor and needy.

The Catholic Charities USA website suggests, if not in so many words, that Catholic Charities can be both Catholic and catholic. Catholic Charities in the United States involves over 1,700 agencies and institutions, over 62,000 staff, and 240,000 volunteers. Despite this incredible variety of people—of many faiths and none—Catholic Charities is truly Catholic. As the website indicates, Catholic Charities is rooted in scripture; it is an integral part of the Catholic Church; it promotes the sanctity of human life and the dignity of persons; it is authorized by the diocesan bishop to exercise ministry; it respects the religious beliefs of those it serves; it recognizes physical, mental, and spiritual needs; it enjoys a special relationship to the Catholic diocese and parishes; it works in active partnership with religiously sponsored charities; it supports an active public-private relationship, and it advocates for those in need.[35] Catholic Charities is more heavily dependent on the local bishop than are Catholic health care institutions.

The national organization's 2007 Code of Ethics consists of four parts— scriptural and theological considerations; principles of Catholic social teaching; ethical standards; and the fundamental values of truth, justice, love, and freedom. Most non-Catholics readily agree with these values and the need to develop them in charitable works.[36]

Catholic Charities is aware of the need at all levels to ensure that workers and volunteers recognize and work to promote its Catholic identity and ethos. Catholic Charities does not have the sponsorship and mission-effectiveness coordinator positions that Catholic hospitals have. However, Catholic Charities leaders see the need to train leaders with a Catholic vision, and to share that vision with staff and volunteers in mission and spirituality workshops. Many dioceses also provide retreats for Catholic Charities personnel. Some agencies hold liturgical or paraliturgical services to celebrate the appointments of boards and officers.[37]

Catholic Charities, however, faces a greater problem of identity than does Catholic health care. Throughout the first half of the twentieth century, Catholic Charities meant Catholics taking care of Catholics. Funding was heavily Catholic and the staff and volunteer personnel were predominantly Catholic. Catholic Charities thus grew from the heart of the Church.

Catholic Charities has expanded greatly since the 1960s, thanks especially to government funding, but most Catholics no longer recognize it as coming from the heart of the Church. Catholic Charities is now the largest private human service provider in the United States. Almost two-thirds of its budget comes from government funding, and many employees and clients are non-Catholics. Catholic Charities may do much more good today than it did in the past, but most Catholics no longer feel any ownership of its works.

Catholic Charities leadership is well aware of this, and seeks to involve Catholic Charities more deeply into the life of the local Catholic Church. Leaders have called for a parish-based Catholic Charities that makes their work very visible at the local level. The need to recruit more Catholic volunteers to carry on the work of Catholic Charities has been emphasized. In many dioceses as well as nationwide, Catholic Charities has supported and participated in Catholic social education.[38]

Problems also arise from the opposition between Catholic teaching and practice and government regulations. One such case concerns state laws requiring that employee medical plans cover contraception, although most make exceptions for religions or churches. However, courts in California and New York hold that Catholic Charities must cover contraception in their medical insurance programs. Catholic Charities argued before the courts for their religious freedom as a church organization. Opponents maintained that Catholic Charities is a service organization and not a church. Ultimately it was decided that if a service organization accepts government money, it must also abide by laws made for the common good. In 2007 the Supreme Court declined to hear an appeal of the New York State Court decision.[39]

A second issue concerns adoption by same-sex couples. In Boston, Catholic Charities would have lost its funding if they did not abide by the state law permitting same-sex couples to adopt children. After lengthy discussion Boston Catholic Charities announced on May 10, 2006, that they would cease adoption work rather than facilitate what they believed to be morally wrong.[40] In both cases many Catholics found themselves disagreeing with the Church's moral position—especially that regarding contraception. These two cases thus illustrate the conflicts that may arise when a Catholic agency relies heavily on government funding.

Like health care institutions, Catholic Charities has a strong and visible role in providing for the poor and needy of the United States, and will surely continue to function. In the immediate future these institutions will continue to defend and act in accord with official Catholic teachings. The problem with this is that many Catholics disagree with official positions. Both institutions face the ongoing challenge to make Catholic identity permeate all aspects of their institutional life. Catholic Charities stands a better chance of achieving an improved relationship with the Church because of its connection to local bishops, the fact that in many dioceses annual collections are taken in support of Catholic Charities, and recent attempts at parish-based Catholic Charities operations.

THE CATHOLIC WORKER

Vatican II and its impact on the Catholic Church in the United States meant that many pre–Vatican II social action movements ceased to exist. The Catholic opposition to immoral films began to die out even before Vatican II. The Catholic Family Movement continues to exist, but with greatly diminished numbers and strength. The very concept of Catholic Action no longer made sense after Vatican II, when action on behalf of justice and the transformation of the world were seen as the constitutive dimension of the preaching of the Gospel and the mission of the Church. But one very significant lay movement has survived and even prospered—the Catholic Worker Movement.

The contemporary Catholic Worker Movement website lists over 185 Catholic Worker communities worldwide, most in the United States.[41] Many of the Worker communities also continue to put out some type of publication, but the New York community still publishes the paper that was first edited by Dorothy Day. The Catholic Worker website describes its purpose in the May 2008 *Catholic Worker* article "Aims and Means of the Catholic Worker Movement," first published in 1992. It opposes the capitalistic system that creates unequal distribution of wealth and fosters a consumerist society of disposable goods that results from unbridled technology. Centralized and bureaucratic politics makes accountability ineffective, and an effective political forum for redressing grievances next to impossible. Class, race, sex, and wealth often define personal worth and value in our society. The arms race illustrates the direction and spirit of our age. In contrast, the Catholic Worker advocates personalism, a decentralized society, a green revolution, nonviolence, works of mercy, voluntary poverty, and the significance of manual labor. The statement ends with a recognition that the Worker is prepared to accept failure with these aims, but success as the world understands it is not the final criterion for judgment. What is most significant is the love of Jesus Christ and living His truth.[42]

Changes after Vatican II

Tensions in the post–Vatican II Catholic Worker Movement mirror the tensions found in the broader Catholic Church today. Dorothy Day totally accepted Catholic Church teachings on faith and morals. In Dorothy Day's time people who divorced and remarried no longer felt comfortable at the Worker. She herself in the 1960s actually expelled some younger people because of their attitudes toward drugs and sex.[43] A post–Vatican II Church has seen the rise of dissent from Church teaching, especially in the areas of morality and sexuality. In her 1993 *Voices from the Catholic Worker*, Rosalie Riegle Troester reports, "The issue of homosexuality is the most disturbing conflict within the Catholic Worker according to many of the 208 people I interviewed."[44]

The issue of homosexuality was especially pressing at the New York Catholic Worker. In 1983 sexuality was discussed at a national meeting of Catholic Workers. The New York Catholic Worker community sponsored a roundtable discussion on the Church's attitude towards gays followed by a series of articles. The editorial board of the *Catholic Worker* then published a statement of editorial policy: no article may deviate from what is understood to be the *Catholic Worker* view, and no one who publicly disagrees with any Church teaching—no matter whether as an individual, in conscience, sensitively, or nonviolently—may be an editor of the *Catholic Worker*. As a result, two gay editors were removed and two others resigned. However, the turmoil in the New York Catholic Worker did not have significant effect on other Worker communities. One observer pointed out that at most of the Catholic Worker communities he visited, support for gay and lesbian rights was widespread and virtually taken for granted.[45] One can readily conclude from this that the *Catholic Worker* in New York was much more attuned to Dorothy Day's positions on Church teaching.

Homosexuality occasioned the most conflict in the Catholic Worker movement in the late twentieth century, but other divisions and disputes within the broader Church were also present in the Catholic Worker. Pat Coy, who himself edited a book on the Catholic Worker Movement, claimed, "These areas—especially the gay and lesbian issues, the abortion issues in particular, the women's issues—have torn communities apart. And people have left bitterly."[46] Troester's book has separate sections on abortion as well as feminism and the Worker and the Church.[47] The Catholic Worker website and many community websites do not mention these disputes.

The Catholic Worker has also faced two additional post–Vatican II realities. The first is the disillusionment that many Catholics have with the Church, and the second is the fact that social action today is often on an ecumenical or even broader basis. These realities have occasioned other divisions within the Catholic Worker.

Troester's book has a section on "The Worker and the Church" in the literary form of a roundtable discussion. The editor points out there are many in the movement who are not Catholic and many more like her who live uneasily with the Church.[48] Dan McKanan recognizes great diversity in the movement as regards its relationship to the Catholic Church. At a workshop on "Forging Community and Spiritual Diversity" at the 2006 National Gathering of Catholic Workers, fifty participants were asked to describe their spiritual identities. Perhaps eight of the fifty identified themselves as unambiguously Catholic; a roughly equal number said such things as "photosynthesis is my God" or "Jerry Garcia was my first prophet." A larger number described themselves as committed to the Sermon on the Mount.[49] McKanan also mentions a growing number of communities that describe themselves as being "in the Catholic Worker tradition" rather than simply saying they are Catholic Workers.[50]

Ann O'Connor and Peter King claim that non-Catholics now dominate the movement and are assisted by the silence of the more faithful Catholics. O'Connor and King, of the Unity Kitchen Community in Syracuse, have been the strongest voices protesting ecclesial diversity in the Catholic Worker Movement. In their view, if a community is a faithful Catholic community as the Church defines "Catholic," then it should say so. If it is not Catholic in union with the Church, it should not call itself a Catholic Worker community.[51]

Another significant development and area of dispute in the Catholic Worker Movement does not involve Catholic identity. Dorothy Day made it very clear that the Catholic Worker would not apply to the government for tax-exempt status or for financial help. Personalism calls for the individual Christian to take responsibility for other persons. Anarchism recognizes that the government ultimately treats the person in need as an object. Also, Christians are called to feed the hungry at personal expense—not because they can obtain a tax deduction by giving money to charity. Contemporary Catholic Workers still insist on the importance of both personalism and anarchism, but debate ensued when numerous Catholic Worker communities incorporated, obtained tax-exempt status, and received federal financial or food assistance.[52] However, even in

Dorothy Day's time the three most enduring houses of hospitality outside New York City established nonprofit boards. Dorothy Day gave less support to these communities than to other communities, but she never forced them out of the movement.[53]

There is the related question of how the present ecclesial diversity and other developments within the Catholic Worker Movement relate to the ideas and approach of Dorothy Day. Ann O'Connor and Peter King see great discontinuity and insist on the need to reestablish the Catholic identity of the movement. Historian James Fisher maintains that the present movement has definitely departed from the approach of Dorothy Day.[54]

Others hold that the present developments, although they depart from Dorothy Day's understanding of the Church, are still in some accord with her approach. Brian Terrell points out that Dorothy Day lived in a state of permanent dissatisfaction with the Church; if we come to the Church with a spirit of docility and subservience, then we have not loved the Church as much as Dorothy did.[55] Fred Boehrer, who has written a doctoral dissertation on anarchism, the Worker, and Roman Catholic authority,[56] claims that the anarchism proposed by Dorothy Day has been reinterpreted by many contemporary Catholic workers to justify dissent from the teaching of the Church and even leaving the Church.[57] McKanan's book as a whole emphasizes continuity between the present movement and the approach of its founders. He concedes that Dorothy Day might have been disturbed by the decision of some Catholic Workers to leave the institutional Church. Such a move, however, is consonant with the Worker's longstanding teaching to appeal to the Sermon on the Mount rather than to the entire body of Catholic teaching in articulating its identity.[58]

Durability and Future of the Movement

What explains the longevity of the Catholic Worker movement? The Catholic Worker stands out as the longest lasting lay social action movement in the United States Church. Two characteristics help to explain its longevity. First, the movement is based on the Sermon on the Mount. The radical call of the Gospel, which emphasizes corporal works of mercy, is a perennial attraction for some followers of Jesus. The Catholic Worker is not based on a single issue or a particular understanding of the social mission of the Church. There have been and always will be Christians who are called to a literal following of the Sermon on the Mount. I doubt that the attractiveness and the call of the Sermon on the Mount are going to change much over time.

But there is a second important explanation for the movement's continued existence over a seventy-five-year period that has witnessed great changes in the U.S. Catholic Church. Dorothy Day did not believe in structure or organization; personalism, anarchism, and decentralization are logically opposed to structural organization beyond the local level. Even Dorothy Day did not establish rules for the different Catholic Worker communities to follow. She developed the basic ideas of the movement, but various editors of the paper contributed their own nuances and approaches. Dorothy often traveled to meet the other houses and to encourage them in their work. The movement was open to developments and adaptations precisely because there was no rigid organizational structure. This explains why some developments have occurred that seem to be in discontinuity with approaches taken by Dorothy Day herself. However, the Catholic Worker today is much more diffuse because it no longer has its founders' commitment to the institutional Catholic Church.

The evolving pluralistic identity of the Catholic Worker vis-à-vis the Catholic Church raises one last significant question: Will the Catholic Worker continue to grow and develop as it has in previous generations? The very lack of organizational structure makes it much easier for the movement to change and prosper, but that Catholic identity today is so diffuse that it might not be able to hold the movement together. Until her death in 1980 Dorothy Day was the heart and soul of the movement. Many of today's Catholic Workers have not had any personal contact with her and know her only from history. How will these pluralistic communities continue in the same movement? However, the diversity in the Catholic Worker movement mirrors the life of the Catholic Church in the United States today. There is no doubt that today the primary identity of the movement derives from its commitment to the Sermon on the Mount and corporal works of mercy. Such a commitment might be strong enough to bind people who have differing approaches to the institutional Catholic Church.

Dan McKanan indicates a very practical way in which the Worker today can still maintain its own identity despite various house differences regarding the institutional Church. In the early days of the movement the charismatic leadership of Dorothy Day and her friendship with other Catholic Worker communities constituted the glue of the movement. But by her death in 1980 the movement had evolved into a genuine community of communities. No longer did the individual Worker community depend only on Dorothy Day and the New York Worker; the different communities supported and encouraged one another. Today there are regional and national get-togethers, and Workers often visit other houses and share their stories and experiences. The Worker today is truly an organism and not an organization, and it can continue to grow and prosper.[59] Only time will reveal the future of the Catholic Worker Movement.

Notes

1. Charles E. Curran, *Ongoing Revision: Studies in Moral Theology* (Notre Dame, Ind.: Fides, 1975), 1–36.

2. Ronald P. Hamel, "Caring for Catholic Institutions," *New Theology Review* 14, no. 2 (2001): 31.

3. For an in-depth discussion of these issues, see Charles J. Fahey and Mary Ann Lewis, eds., *The Future of Catholic Institutional Ministries: A Continuing Conversation* (New York: Third Age Center, Fordham University, 1992); for my earlier discussion on these issues, see Charles E. Curran, "The Catholic Identity of Catholic Institutions," *Theological Studies* 58 (1997): 90–108.

4. For a symposium on the Catholic identity of Catholic health care institutions, see *Christian Bioethics* 7 (April 2001): 1–172.

5. John Beal, "Catholic Hospitals: How Catholic Will They Be?" in *Catholic Identity*, ed. James H. Provost and Knut Wolf (Maryknoll, N.Y.: Orbis, 1994), 83–84.

6. Catholic Health Care East, www.che.org.

7. Ascension Health, www.ascensionhealth.org.

8. Benedict M. Ashley, Jean K. deBlois, and Kevin D. O'Rourke, *Health Care Ethics: A Catholic Theological Analysis*, 5th ed. (Washington, D.C.: Georgetown University Press, 2006), 230.

9. Kevin O'Rourke, "Catholic Hospitals and Catholic Identity," *Christian Bioethics* 7, no. 1 (2001): 20–23.

10. O'Rourke, "Catholic Hospitals and Catholic Identity," 21.

11. Hamel, "Caring for Catholic Institutions," 29.

12. H. Tristram Englehardt, "The DeChristianization of Christian Health Care Institutions, or, How the Pursuit of Social Justice and Excellence Can Obscure the Pursuit of Holiness," *Christian Bioethics* 7, no. 1 (2001): 151–61; Corinna Delkeskamp-Hayes, "Christian Credentials for Roman Catholic Health Care: Medicine versus the Healing Mission of the Church," *Christian Bioethics* 7, no. 1 (2001): 117–50.

13. William E. Stempsey, "Institutional Identity and Roman Catholic Hospitals," *Christian Bioethics* 7, no. 1 (2001): 6–7.

14. See, for example, Clarke Cochran, "Another Identity-Crisis: Catholic Hospitals Face Hard Choices," *Commonweal*, February 25, 2000, 12–16.

15. United States Conference of Catholic Bishops, "Ethical and Religious Directives for Catholic Health Care Services," www.usccb.org/bishops/directives.shtml.

16. Lisa Sowle Cahill, *Theological Bioethics: Participation, Justice, and Change* (Washington, D.C.: Georgetown University Press, 2005), 104–5.

17. Cahill, *Theological Bioethics*, 83–85; see also Catholic Health Association, www.chausa.org.

18. Catholic Health Association, "Ministry," www.chausa.org/pub/mainnav/ourcom mitments/mission.

19. Catholic Health Association, "Advocacy," www.chausa.org/pub/mainnav/advocacy/ default.htm.

20. Canon Law Committee of the Catholic Health Association of the United States and Peter Campbell, *The Search for Identity: Canonical Sponsorship of Catholic Health Care* (St. Louis, Mo.: Catholic Health Association, 1993).

21. Teresa Stanley, "Mission in a Time of Transition," *Health Progress* 74, no. 2 (March 1994): 28–32; Eileen Wrobleski, "Measuring Mission Integration," *Health Progress* 84, no. 1 (January–February 2003): 43–45.

22. Curran, "The Catholic Identity of Catholic Institutions," 96–97.

23. Simon J. Craddock Lee, "Ethics of Articulation: Constituting Identity in a Catholic Hospital System," in *Listening to the Silences: Re-thinking Ethics in Healthcare*, ed. C. Sorrell Dinkins and J. M. Sorrell (Madison: University of Wisconsin Press, 2006), 98–110.

24. John O. Mudd, "From C.E.O. to Mission Leader," *America*, July 18–25, 2005, 14–17.

25. Lee, "Ethics of Articulation," in *Listening to the Silences*, ed. Dinkins and Sorrell, 110.

26. Richard A. McCormick, "The Catholic Hospital: Mission Impossible?" *Origins* 24 (1995): 648–53.

27. Lee, "Ethics of Articulation," 69–129. Lee's long chapter is based on his doctoral dissertation, "*Caritas et communitas*: An Ethnographic Account of the Ethics and Social Values of Catholic Health Care in Contemporary California" (PhD diss.: University of California, San Francisco, with University of California–Berkeley, 2003).

28. On support for dissenting positions and a review of some of the controversies, see Richard A. McCormick, "Sterilization: the Dilemma of Catholic Hospitals," in *History and Conscience: Studies in Honor of Father Sean O'Riordan, CSSR*, ed. Raphael Gallagher and Brendan McConvery (Dublin: Gill and Macmillan, 1989), 105–33; on strong opposition to direct sterilization, see Eugene Diamond, "Sterilization in Catholic Hospitals," *Linacre Quarterly* 55 (1988): 57–66.

29. Francis A. Butler, "Will Charity Laws Close Catholic Hospitals?" *America*, October 29, 2001, 12–15.

30. Ashley, deBlois, and O'Rourke, *Health Care Ethics*, 78–80.

31. Jack Balinsky, "Introduction: The Evolution of Catholic Charities in the United States," www.dor.org/Charities/AHistorybyJackBalinsky.htm; also Curran, "The Catholic Identity of Catholic Institutions," 101.

32. For the document itself and two essays by Edward J. Ryle and Thomas J. Harvey assessing its influence twenty years later, see *Cadre Study: Toward a Renewed Catholic Charities Movement* (Arlington, Va.: Catholic Charities USA, 1992).

33. Dennis M. Doyle, *The Church Emerging from Vatican II: A Popular Approach to Contemporary Catholicism* (Mystic, Conn.: Twenty-Third Publications, 1992), 335–36.

34. Catholic Charities of New York, "What We Do," www.catholiccharitiesny.org/what-we-do.

35. "Ten Ways Catholic Charities Is Catholic," www.catholiccharitiesusa.org/netcom munity/page.aspx?pid = 296.

36. "Code of Ethics," www.catholiccharitiesusa.org/netcommunity/document .doc?id = 657.

37. Curran, "The Catholic Identity of Catholic Institutions," 102.

38. Curran, "The Catholic Identity of Catholic Institutions," 101.

39. "Supreme Court Turns Down Cases of Religious Separation," *New York Times*, October 2, 2007, nytimes.com/2007/10/02/washington/02scotus.html; "Uncharitable Interpretation," *Commonweal*, March 26, 2004, 5–6.

40. "Boston's Catholic Charities to Stop Adoption Service over Same-Sex Law," www.catholic.org/national/national_story.php?id=19017.

41. The Catholic Worker Movement, www.catholicworker.org.

42. "The Aims and Means of the Catholic Worker," *The Catholic Worker*, May 2008, www.catholicworker.org/aimsandmeanstext.CFM?Number=5.

43. William D. Miller, *All Is Grace: The Spirituality of Dorothy Day* (Garden City, N.Y.: Doubleday, 1987), 156–77.

44. Rosalie Riegle Troester, ed., *Voices from the Catholic Worker* (Philadelphia: Temple University Press, 1993), 525.

45. Dan McKanan, *The Catholic Worker after Dorothy: Practicing the Works of Mercy in a New Generation* (Collegeville, Minn.: Liturgical, 2008), 194–98.

46. Troester, *Voices from the Catholic Worker*, 551.

47. Troester, *Voices from the Catholic Worker*, 545–60.

48. Troester, *Voices from the Catholic Worker*, 518–24.

49. McKanan, *The Catholic Worker after Dorothy*, 181–82.

50. McKanan, *The Catholic Worker after Dorothy*, 79.

51. Ann O'Connor and Peter King, "What's Catholic about the Catholic Worker Movement? Then and Now," in *Dorothy Day and the Catholic Worker Movement: Centenary Essays*, ed. William J. Thorn, Phillip M. Runkel, and Susan Mountin (Milwaukee, Wisc.: Marquette University Press, 2001), 128–43.

52. Fred Boehrer, "Diversity, Pluralism, and Ambiguity: Anarchism in the Catholic Worker Movement," in *Dorothy Day and the Catholic Worker*, 102–3, 122.

53. McKanan, *The Catholic Worker after Dorothy*, 26.

54. James T. Fischer, *The Catholic Counterculture in America 1933–1962* (Chapel Hill: University of North Carolina Press, 1989), 253.

55. Brian Terrell, "Dorothy Day, Rebel Catholic: Living in a State of Permanent Dissatisfaction with the Church," in *Dorothy Day and the Catholic Worker*, 144–49.

56. Frederick George Boehrer III, "Christian Anarchism in the Catholic Worker Movement: Roman Catholic Authority and Identity in the United States" (PhD diss.: Syracuse University, 2001).

57. Boehrer, "Diversity, Pluralsim, and Ambiguity," in *Dorothy Day and the Catholic Worker Movement*, 123.

58. McKanan, *The Catholic Worker after Dorothy*, 190.

59. McKanan, *The Catholic Worker after Dorothy*, 27–28.

6

Three Significant Issues in the Post–Vatican II Church

Catholic social action sometimes takes the form of organized and concerted efforts targeting particular issues. This chapter discusses three such issues in the post–Vatican II Church that occasioned this type of action. Abortion became the most significant issue for the Church following the *Roe v. Wade* Supreme Court decision in 1973, and has remained so ever since. Peace and war have been perennial moral issues for Christians. Some social action responds to a particular historical cause or event, such as the Church support of César Chávez and the United Farm Workers in the 1970s. In these three cases both bishops and lay people were involved, but the lay people often acted independently of the bishops' leadership.

ABORTION

There can be no doubt that Catholics have played a major role in the opposition to abortion in this country. Vatican II reiterated traditional Catholic teaching that proscribed direct abortion. To the present day, however, Catholic teaching recognizes a theoretical doubt about when truly individual human life begins. In practice, however, one must give human life every benefit of the doubt. Just as the hunter cannot shoot if what she sees is either a deer or a human being, so one cannot directly abort a fetus—note the word *direct*. The Catholic tradition has recognized the existence of conflictual situations, but only in the late nineteenth and early twentieth centuries did the hierarchical magisterium clearly distinguish what was direct abortion and what was indirect abortion. A direct abortion is an act that by the nature of the act or the intention of the agent aims at aborting the fetus either as a means or as an end.

Thus, it is a wrongful direct abortion to abort the fetus to save the life of the mother. The two best-known examples of indirect abortion are the removal of a cancerous pregnant uterus and the removal of an infected fallopian tube that contains a fertilized ovum or fetus.[1] Indirect abortion may be permissible with a proportionate reason.

Abortion was not much discussed until the 1960s. In 1962 the American Law Institute (ALI) approved a model law procedure permitting abortion for the physical or mental health of the mother, for fetal abnormality, and for rape or incest. In 1967 the American Medical Association voted to change its longstanding opposition to abortion and basically agreed with the exceptions listed in the ALI's proposal. Later that year a few states passed legislation similar to the ALI proposal.[2]

In the 1960s the issue of abortion was confined to the states and did not involve the country as a whole. But *Roe v. Wade* changed that by establishing the right to an abortion in the first two trimesters with no restrictions except in the second trimester to protect the mother's health. In the third trimester some consideration is given to the fetus, but abortion is legal to protect and promote the health of the mother. The U.S. bishops were the earliest significant body in the United States to oppose the Supreme Court decision.

The basis for the position of the bishops and all others who oppose abortion is their understanding that from the moment of conception the conceptus is to be treated as a human being. The fetus is the weakest of all human persons and needs the protection of society to guarantee its right to life. From the very beginning the bishops insisted that abortion is not an issue of sectarian morality but one that concerns the basis of a truly civilized society. Notice here the emphasis on catholicity with a lowercase c. Abortion concerns the moral order of society and public virtue. The bishops appeal to biological and scientific reason to support their position, which is consistent with the values put forward in the Declaration of Independence and the United States Constitution. Opposition to abortion is not just a matter of Catholic teaching, although at times the bishops did make appeals based on scripture, particularly "Choose life that you and your descendents may live" (Deuteronomy 30:19). This biblical injunction has been a part of U.S. public consciousness since John Winthrop and the Plymouth colony; thus, the bishops insist, opposition to legal abortion is firmly rooted in U.S. values and traditions.[3]

The Secretariat of Pro-Life Activities of the U.S. Conference of Catholic Bishops teaches respect for all human life from conception to natural death, and works for its protection. Specifically, the Secretariat develops educational material on pro-life issues; conducts educational programs in the Church—

especially the Respect Life Program, which begins on the first Sunday of October in every Catholic diocese and parish in the United States; conducts educational campaigns in the public square; publishes *Life Issues Forum*, a biweekly column for Catholic newspapers; publishes *Life Insight Newsletter*; enables programs to meet the needs of pregnant women and other vulnerable persons; provides dioceses with pro-life liturgical suggestions each month; coordinates and advises on relevant public policy; and assists diocesan implementation of pro-life programs.[4]

There can be no doubt that since the early 1970s to the present the U.S. Catholic bishops have played a major role in the pro-life movement in this country. The final chapter discusses in great detail the approach that the bishops have taken to abortion legislation in this country and how abortion relates to other pro-life issues.

Catholic laity have been obviously influenced by the words and actions of U.S. bishops. Many Catholic laity have also worked on their own pro-life initiatives. Even before bishops as a group responded to *Roe v. Wade*, the first abortion opponents were disproportionately Catholic, largely self-recruited, and independently financed. They often used Catholic parishes for recruitment and meeting places but also complained of lack of support from the clergy.[5]

Antiabortion and Pro-Life Approaches

Catholic laity have been a strong, even leading, force in the pro-life movement since *Roe v. Wade*, and have continued to be so even after evangelical and fundamentalist Protestant churches joined the movement in the late 1970s. Many have failed to recognize that the pro-life movement, even for Catholics, is not monolithic. Michael W. Cuneo identifies two clearly different approaches within the pro-life movement. The pragmatic and reformist approach has the ultimate goal of an abortion-free society, but in the interim, within the limits of civility and legality, they strive to protect fetal life as much as possible. Their methods include cultivating popular support for the pro-life position, educating the general public, lobbying for more restrictive abortion legislation, and offering concrete assistance to pregnant women. They try to convince as many people as possible of their position, and thus tend not to emphasize religious language and arguments and avoid confrontational tactics.[6]

The second approach is more radical, militant, and confrontational. In the judgment of its followers, the reformist approach does not seem to be achieving its purpose: The time for direct action has arrived and one must take the pro-life movement to the streets—blockading clinics, engaging in civil disobedi-ence, and sometimes even being arrested. This approach is religious in empha-sis. Even before evangelical and fundamentalist Protestants joined the anti-abortion movement some Catholics took this direction. These militant Catho-lic anti-abortionists were deeply conservative both culturally and religiously, and quite disturbed by many post–Vatican II developments. They feared that the Catholic Church was losing its basic moorings and its transcendent mean-ing. Fighting abortion by protesting, marching, and praying at abortion clinics became a sacred crusade and a manifestation of their countercultural spirituality.[7]

Cuneo outlines these two different approaches in sociological terms, but they correspond to the general theological underpinnings of two different approaches to the social mission of the Church. The first is an approach that strives to be effective in transforming the attitudes and structures in society. By definition, such an approach uses both theoretical and practical means that try to convince all others of the rightness of their position. Such an approach is very much in keeping with catholicity. Furthermore, if one wants to change society, one must work together with what the recent popes have called all people of goodwill; Catholics using primarily Catholic religious reason and working only as Catholics will not work effectively. But there is a downside to such an approach: By necessity this approach requires compromises and set-tling for something short of one's own ideals and goals.

The second approach is the witness approach, whose proponents are greatly troubled by the effectiveness approach. Christians are not called to be effective; they are called by baptism to bear witness to the Gospel message of Jesus. The Gospel has a radical ring to it, and by being pragmatic one loses the salt of the Gospel message. In my judgment the Church Catholic, with its emphasis on a big Church, needs to have room for both approaches, but in individual cases there have been problems with the ways in which both these approaches have operated.

The National Right to Life Committee (NRLC) exemplifies a pragmatic reformist approach to ending legalized abortion. The NRLC is the largest right-to-life organization in the United States. According to its website it has affiliates in all fifty states and the District of Columbia, and over three thousand local chapters. Its primary concern has been abortion, but it also works with related issues of euthanasia and infanticide.[8]

NRLC owes its existence to the institutional support of the Roman Catholic Church. In 1967 James McHugh, then the director of the Family Life Bureau of the United States Bishops' Conference (and later a bishop), created this national network of pro-life leaders. His purpose was to connect diverse groups that had sprung up in the middle and late 1960s to oppose abortion. The group's first actual meeting took place in Chicago in 1970; at the June 1973 meeting in Detroit the NRLC renewed its commitment to do everything possible to protect fetal life after *Roe v. Wade*, but also severed its formal connection with the Catholic Church. Some worried that Catholic bishops had too much control over the organization; others recognized that the group would be more effective if it were independent of the Catholic Church. It was important for the United States to see that abortion was not just a Catholic issue. The NRLC elected Marjorie Mecklenburg—a Protestant—its first president, and four other Protestant women as members of its first board of directors. However, the NRLC remained inextricably Catholic; upwards of 75 percent of its grassroots advocates had a Catholic background.[9]

One potentially divisive issue was artificial contraception. Almost all non-Catholics and even many Catholics did not want the organization to oppose artificial contraception, as this would hurt its efforts to limit and ultimately eliminate legal abortion in the United States. However, conservative Catholics strongly urged the organization to oppose artificial contraception for spouses. The NRLC papered over its internal division by declaring that it was scrupulously neutral on the question of contraception.[10]

NRLC seeks to change public opinion on abortion; its ultimate goal is a constitutional amendment to nullify *Roe v. Wade*. In the meantime it lobbies at both national and state levels for laws that prohibit the use of public funds for abortion services and that require waiting periods or parental consent. They believe it counterproductive to appeal to religious perspectives; scientific facts alone—as illustrated, for example, in photographs of the fetus—should convince Americans to support legal protection for the unborn. They frequently analogize their efforts to the abolitionist movement, which involved a commitment to defend an entire class of humanity that was not extended basic human rights. As such the NRLC recognizes the need for strategic flexibility based on some political expedience.[11]

Objections to a reformist approach involving education and legislative change began to surface within NRLC. Some conservative Catholics claim that the contraception mentality has led to the increased public acceptance of abortion. The conventional wisdom maintains that the availability of contraception lessens the acceptance and number of abortions, but in their view the contraceptive mentality of separating intercourse from procreation inevitably leads to easy acceptance of abortion. Based on this understanding Judie and Paul Brown founded the American Life League (ALL) in 1979. Judie Brown had worked as an NRLC administrator for some years, but grew dissatisfied with its approach. ALL basically accepts the positive relationship between the contraceptive mentality and abortion and urges a strong religious approach to countering abortion. ALL opposes any coalition that requires even an apparent compromise of the principle that all abortion is murder. This group has received financial and other support from conservative right-wing groups. ALL also adopts a militaristic strategy in its opposition to abortion clinics, and looks upon other right-to-life groups as heretical because of their willingness to compromise and not demand the prohibition of all abortion.[12]

ALL also answers the call by some within the NRLC to take a more activist and radical approach in opposition to abortion. These militaristic purists of the pro-life movement (most of whom are Catholic) committed themselves in the late 1980s to what Michael Cuneo calls "veritable careers of civil disobedience"—blocking access to abortion clinics, vandalizing the property of such clinics, and engaging in sit-ins at the clinics. In 1980 Joseph M. Scheidler founded the Pro-Life Action League, which aimed at stopping abortion via public protest and confronting abortionists.[13] NRLC leadership strongly opposed the use of civil disobedience as a tactic, as it would hinder the NRLC's ability to convince other Americans of the truth about abortion. For example, at the May 1986 NRLC national meeting in Denver, the president, Catholic John Wilke, urged all those in attendance to abstain from acts of civil disobedience.[14]

The most militant antiabortion group is Operation Rescue, founded in 1987 by Randall Terry, then a Binghamton, New York, Pentecostal minister. At the time Terry was inspired by Joseph M. Scheidler's book.[15] Terry has frequently been arrested, and by 1988 approximately 10,000 of its members had been arrested for blocking abortion clinics throughout the country. Court fines drove Operation Rescue into bankruptcy.[16] In 2005 Terry converted to Roman Catholicism and was arrested again for protesting President Obama's 2009 graduation address at the University of Notre Dame.[17] Operation Rescue today describes itself as one of the leading pro-life Christian activist organizations, working on the cutting edge of the opposition to abortion by taking direct action in accord with biblical mandates.[18]

Other Approaches

These differing approaches in the pro-life movement share a commitment to the understanding that the fetus from the moment of conception is a human person, and outrage at the fact that about 50 million abortions have been performed in the United States since 1973.[19] They differ on tactics but agree that abortion is *the* primary social issue in the United States. James R. Kelly describes these two positions as "antiabortion" and "right to life." There exists, however, a third position, which Kelly calls the "pro-life" or "consistent ethic" approach, which sees abortion as one of many life issues, all of which must be addressed by our society.[20] The antiabortion and right to life proponents reject the consistent ethic approach because it detracts from the primacy of abortion.

The consistent ethic approach takes its name from the theory developed by Cardinal Joseph Bernardin in the 1980s to link together all life issues. His approach attempted to show that the Catholic understanding in general and the U.S. bishops' approach in particular did not involve single-issue politics. Many Catholics had been upset that the Catholic position on social justice in this country was reduced only to abortion, neglecting other issues such as poverty, war, discrimination, and capital punishment.[21] Chapter 8 shows how—unfortunately—U.S. bishops themselves have moved away from this consistent ethic of life approach.

The pro-life or consistent ethic movement itself is not monolithic, but in Kelly's understanding three characteristics distinguish its approach:

1. Abortion is one important issue, but other issues such as economic poverty, human inequality, war, capital punishment, and all forms of discrimination are also significant life issues.
2. The issues are linked not only in theory but also in practice. Statistics show that poor women have more abortions than other women. By overcoming poverty one will be able to decrease the number of abortions.
3. Many who take this approach also consider the feasibility of what can be done to prevent abortion. In the U.S. situation today it is not realistic to think that *Roe v. Wade* will soon be overturned, but it is possible to limit the number of abortions.

Bernardin would not have agreed with this understanding of the consistent ethic approach.

James R. Kelly has been called the "foremost social historian" of the pro-life movement, and I have followed Kelly quite closely throughout this section.[22] However, Kelly was not only a social historian; he also developed his own approach to the pro-life movement, which in recent years seems to have been adopted by others who do not necessarily recognize that it originated with Kelly.[23] Kelly's basic thesis is the possibility of limiting the number of abortions by dealing especially with the poverty of women, which is a major factor in their decision to have an abortion: 14 percent of all women fall below the poverty line, whereas one-third of all women who have abortions fall below the poverty line.

One of the factors contributing to the sharp division between pro-choice and pro-life positions is the Republican Party's embracing the pro-life position and the Democratic Party's embracing the pro-choice position. Even in the late 1980s, however, there were signs that these identifications were eroding somewhat. Social conservatives in the Republican Party strongly opposed abortion, but fiscal conservatives were beginning to have some problems with the pro-life position. The social conservatives insisted on the basic equality and intrinsic worth of every human life and the claim that these human lives can make on the community. Fiscal conservatives opposed arguments based on equality and claims on the community. Kelly pointed to a study indicating that the cost of medical intensive care for babies born to crack-addicted mothers in New York State alone would exceed one billion dollars by 1995. As a result, fiscal conservatives no longer strongly supported the pro-life position and the Republican Party was not wholly identified as pro-life. Kelly perceptively pointed out at that time that change would also come to the Democratic Party. The politically left of center cannot continue to ignore the class factors involved in the abortion decisions by poor women.

For these and other reasons the strong and almost absolute identification of the Republican and Democratic parties with the pro-life and pro-choice positions began to crack. In 1990 Lee Atwater, head of the Republican National Committee, called for a big-tent approach that would also embrace pro-choice Republicans.[24] The Democratic Party would not allow the pro-life Democratic governor of Pennsylvania, Robert Casey, to address the 1992 Democratic National Convention because he was going to speak on his position. But the Democratic National Committee strongly supported the victorious U.S. senate candidacy in Pennsylvania in 2006 of his pro-life son, Robert (Bob) Casey Jr., who addressed the 2008 convention.[25]

In the early 1990s, James R. Kelly developed his position based on the idea of truly free choice. He contended that it is impossible to overturn *Roe v. Wade*. From a broad pro-life perspective Kelly recognized the number of pro-life issues and also the need for the pro-life movement not to be seen as anti-woman. The pro-life position could cut down on the number of abortions by overcoming the poverty in which many women seeking abortion find themselves. However, pro-choice people should strongly support a truly voluntary choice made by the pregnant woman, and not have such a person be forced to have an abortion because of her poverty. Kelly concluded that it was entirely possible that such an approach could succeed.[26]

In 2004 Kelly publicly explained why as a pro-life Catholic he was voting for John Kerry, the pro-choice Democratic candidate. Kelly discusses solely his pro-life stance—not the many other issues on which he agrees with Kerry. Kelly's basic argument is that yes, George W. Bush is a pro-life candidate who promoted the ban on partial-birth abortion, but like other Republican presidents, would not deliver on his promises; however, a Kerry administration would support economic programs that would in reality reduce the number of abortions. Kelly writes as a sociologist interpreting available data. The Supreme Court is not likely to overturn *Roe v. Wade*, and fiscally conservative Republicans will not support funding for alternatives to abortion. He is unhappy that the power brokers of the Democratic Party have been intolerant of pro-life Democrats. Pro-life federal legislation, however, is successful not when it directly attacks abortion but when it emphasizes real choice and alternatives to abortion. On this issue one can find some consensus both in ecumenical terms and across political party lines.[27]

Some organizations have recently supported this basic approach. Catholics in Alliance for the Common Good is a nonpartisan, lay Catholic organization promoting greater awareness of Catholic social teaching through the media and work by Catholics and all people of goodwill for human dignity, social justice, and the common good in the public square. This organization wants to develop the necessary conditions for a culture that reverences the life and dignity of the human person at all stages—in opposition to the greed, materialism, and divisive politics that so often exist. Catholics in Alliance supports the consistent ethic of life, and released a study showing how changing socioeconomic factors can reduce abortion in the United States. The abortion rate among women below the poverty level is more than four times that among women above 300 percent of the poverty level. Elected officials can promote policies that reduce abortion: increase male employment, lower the poverty rate, provide funding for childcare for working women, and increase economic assistance to low-income families.[28]

Catholics United is a nonprofit, nonpartisan organization that promotes the message of justice and the common good at the heart of the Catholic social tradition through online advocacy and educational activities. This organization takes an approach similar to that of Catholics in Alliance.[29]

In 2008 Douglas Kmiec published a book justifying his support for Obama. Kmiec identifies himself, and is recognized by others, as a conservative Catholic who strongly supports the Church's ban on artificial contraception and a conservative Republican who worked in the Reagan administration. He tackles abortion head-on from the perspective of one fully committed to the magisterial Church teaching on the issue. His Catholic faith moves him to focus on new ways to reduce abortion practice in the United States. A first option is to work to overturn *Roe v. Wade,* but this has not been successful in the past, and probably will not be successful—and even if it were, states would be free to pass similar laws. A second option is to support the Obama program insisting on personal responsibility, a community seeing to it that a person is well informed, and presenting more help for poor women in this situation. He makes a prudential judgment that the second option has a more realistic chance of reducing the number of abortions in the United States.[30]

Growing consensus based on such an approach is evidenced by the positions of the two most significant leaders in the Democratic Party—Hillary Clinton and President Barack Obama. On the anniversary of *Roe v. Wade* in January 2005, Clinton gave a speech detailing her position on abortion. The front page of *The New York Times* read, "Clinton Seeking Shared Ground over Abortions." Clinton insisted that abortion has to be legal and safe, but abortion is a sad and even tragic choice for many women: "There is no reason why government cannot do more to educate and inform and provide assistance so that the choice guaranteed under our Constitution either does not ever have to be exercised or only in very rare circumstances."[31] Barack Obama has strongly supported the pro-choice position, but seeks to tone down the rhetoric on the abortion debate and find common ground. His top aides have been working with people on both sides of the issue to craft mutually agreeable policies to prevent unwanted pregnancies, promote adoptions, and support women who choose to keep their babies.[32]

Some proponents of a consistent ethic of life approach in the Catholic tradition seem to have found consensus across religious and political lines. This Catholic position rests on the presupposition that it is not possible or feasible to overturn *Roe v. Wade.* However, all antiabortion Catholics and most right-to-life Catholics (to borrow Kelly's categories) would object to this approach because it fails to address directly the protection of fetal life from the moment of conception, and it involves working with people who are pro-choice.

These three generic positions and the organizations and groups associated with them share the acceptance of the hierarchical Catholic moral teaching that the fetus from the moment of conception must be treated as a human person. Thus, they all consider themselves to be under a broad pro-life umbrella. However, Catholics for Choice (formerly called Catholics for a Free Choice) disagrees with and dissents from the moral teaching of the hierarchical magisterium. The website describes the organization's role as a voice for Catholics who believe that the Catholic tradition supports a woman's moral and legal right to follow her conscience in matters of sexuality and reproductive health. Catholics for Choice is not a grassroots organization; it works primarily in education, networking, research, and advocacy both in the Church and in broader society, and has an annual budget of three million dollars. Catholics for Choice looks forward to a world where abortion is safe, legal, and truly accessible. The Catholic hierarchy's powerful lobby plays a huge role in influencing public policy and affects everyone, Catholic or not, by limiting the availability of reproductive health care services worldwide. This organization sees itself as a most effective counterpoint to the very well financed and powerful Roman Catholic hierarchy. Catholics for Choice also believes that rights should be exercised in a responsible manner, which involves personal responsibility for pregnancy prevention and a societal commitment to provide education, health care, and economic security that will enable women to prevent pregnancy and have the children they want in a climate that welcomes all.[33]

However, Catholics for Choice strongly opposes Catholics in Alliance for the Common Good. Catholics in Alliance was created by a handful of Catholic Democrats who believe that Catholics would be unable to reject the instructions of their bishops. To the untrained eye, Catholics in Alliance is just another Catholic social justice organization, but a closer look shows its key aim is to limit the accessibility of legal abortion. Catholics in Alliance is willing to trade the pro-woman, pro-choice heritage of the Democratic Party for its mirage of Catholic voters so cowed by the Catholic hierarchy's position on abortion that they will vote Democratic.[34]

Lay Catholic involvement in the abortion issue has been stronger and more divisive than in any other area of the post–Vatican II U.S. Catholic Church. The different positions taken on the issue amply illustrate the catholic characteristic of the Church, and reflect different conceptions of the social mission of the Church. The antiabortion approach sees itself as being called to bear witness to the horror of abortion. The pro-life approach, as well as many elements of the consistent ethic of life approach, strives to work with others to reduce the number of abortions. However, these two groups differ because some in the consistent ethic of life approach claim that it is not feasible today to overturn *Roe v. Wade,* whereas the pro-life approach is committed to that goal. In addition, Catholics for Choice explicitly base their support of *Roe v. Wade* on their dissent from the Catholic hierarchical teaching on abortion. This could occur only in the post–Vatican II Church.

What are the relative strengths of these different approaches? The anti-abortion and pro-life positions have received the most publicity. In addition, they involve grassroots activists, whose groups by definition involve a comparatively small percentage of the total Catholic population. Consistent ethic of life is not a grassroots organization of activists but a position developed by Catholic theorists. Catholics for Choice is a comparatively small but well-organized and well-financed group that seeks and often finds a voice in the media.

For several years a group of respected Catholic sociologists have been polling Catholics on a number of issues concerning their faith. One question is whether Catholics look to Church leaders, themselves, or both as the proper locus for authority with regards to advocating choice concerning abortion. In 1987, 29 percent looked to Church leaders, 45 percent to themselves, and 22 percent to both. In 2005, 25 percent looked to Church leaders, 44 percent to themselves, and 30 percent to both. Their 2005 poll also found that only 44 percent said that the teachings opposing abortion were very important to them.[35] It is difficult to determine exactly how many Catholics would fit into each of the four categories of approaches described in this section, but clearly Catholics in this country are divided on how to approach the question of abortion law.

PEACE

The pre–Vatican II involvement of Catholics in the peace movement was treated in chapter 2; not surprisingly, there has continued to be organized involvement in this area after Vatican II. Two different historical causes also influenced Catholic attention to peace. The first is the Second Vatican Council; the second involves the situation in the United States.

Preliminary Considerations

The Pastoral Constitution on the Church in the Modern World deals with peace in chapter 5 of part 2. In light of the savagery of modern warfare the fathers of Vatican II are compelled to undertake an "evaluation of war with an entirely new attitude."[36] All must strain every muscle to work for a time when all war can be completely outlawed by international consent. The document definitely accepts just war principles, but these are interpreted in a somewhat restrictive sense. In addition, some elements stem from a more pacifist approach.

All are called to work for peace, which involves a change of heart and a change of structures, such as international agreements. But in our imperfect and sinful world the threat of war continues to hang over us. The strongest condemnation of the whole council explicitly applies the just war principle of noncombatant immunity: "Any act of war aimed indiscriminately at the destruction of entire cities or of extensive areas along with their population is a crime against God and humanity. It merits unequivocal and unhesitating condemnation" (294, n. 80).

Pacifism and nonviolence are legitimate option for individuals provided the common good is not diminished. Also, governments should make provisions for those who, owing to conscience, refuse to bear arms. No distinction is made here between conscientious objection to all wars and conscientious objection to a specific war (291, n. 78). The Pastoral Constitution also condemns the arms race as an utterly treacherous trap which affects the poor to an intolerable degree. The present balance of power brought about by nuclear deterrence is not a sure and true peace. The document calls on all to take steps toward disarmament, but explicitly does not call for unilateral nuclear disarmament (296, n. 82). A spirited discussion occurred at Vatican II on peace issues, and this discourse continued in the Catholic Church.

The second factor affecting Catholic social action on peace immediately after Vatican II was the historical situation in the United States—involving the Cold War, but especially the Vietnam War. Never before in U.S. history had there been such strong opposition to a particular war. The draft also contributed to strong youth opposition to the Vietnam War. In the beginning public opinion was in favor of the U.S. intervention, but by the late 1960s things were definitely changing. Protests took many different forms, and often involved nonviolent demonstrations. At times, however, violence erupted. The chaos at the Democratic National Convention in Chicago in 1968 and the killing of four antiwar protestors at Kent State University in 1970 raised the level of the protests. Many antiwar advocates also counseled potential draftees. Some young people left the United States rather than face the draft. Catholics on all levels became involved in the antiwar struggle and protest.[37]

Here, again, there were two different types of organized movements and protests involving lay Catholics and also priests and religious. The more radical approach engaged in various forms of public protest and civil disobedience. Many advocated nonviolent protest, but some made a distinction between violence against persons and violence against things. The more moderate approach aimed at changing U.S. policy and especially the position of the United States Catholic bishops. To proponents of this approach, protests and civil disobedience did not seem to be the best way to achieve this goal. However, there was also a significant difference between the social action of Catholics against abortion and against the Vietnam War. During the 1960s antiwar movement, Catholics were more conscious of a need to band together as Catholics. These 1968 approaches were chronologically closer to the Catholic lay involvement in the pre–Vatican II Church. The moderate approach was aimed precisely at changing the position of the U.S. bishops, so by definition it was a Catholic movement.

Different Approaches

One can distinguish four different organized efforts by Catholics to work for peace, but there exists some overlap among the different groups. All four had ties to the Catholic Worker Movement.[38] As mentioned, in the pre–Vatican II period the Catholic Worker was the most significant lay antiwar movement in the Catholic Church. The Catholic Worker Movement itself continued its nonviolent protests and activities, which in the mid-1960s took the form of burning draft cards. In 1963 Tom Cornell, then an associate editor of the *Catholic Worker*, burned his draft card. After Pope Paul's UN speech in 1965 ("War, never again") David Miller, a young Catholic Worker, burned his draft card as a political act. At a rally in November 1965 at the federal courthouse in New York City five men, including three Catholic Workers, burned their draft cards before 150,000 people. These actions were the beginning of the draft resistance movement, which ultimately involved the burning of more than 3,500 draft cards.[39] Unfortunately, on November 9, 1965, Roger LaPorte, a twenty-one-year-old member of the Catholic Worker Movement, burned himself to death before the UN building as a political protest against the war. James Forest, speaking for the Catholic Worker Movement, was shocked and perplexed by his death. If he had told them what he was trying to do they would have discouraged him, Forest remarked.[40]

In 1964, Daniel and Philip Berrigan asked Catholic Workers Forest, Tom Cornell, and Martin Corbin to work together to form a new peace group. The Catholic Peace Fellowship (CPF) had the support of the Fellowship of Reconciliation, an older religious peace group, but was a distinctive Catholic group in structure. Its stated aim was to affirm life and denounce war. Its educational mission was to build opposition to the Vietnam War, obtain medical relief for victims on all sides, and provide draft counseling. CPF also collaborated with other peace groups in demonstrations, marches, prayer vigils, and fasting, as well as involvement in forms of nonviolent direct action and resistance. Forest and Cornell were the primary leaders. In 1966, CPF called for U.S. bishops to condemn U.S. involvement in Vietnam. At its peak in 1974 CPF had a membership of three thousand and local chapters around the country, but by the end of the 1970s, CPF was in decline.[41]

Charles Meconis has identified a group of about two hundred people whom he calls the Catholic left. This did not constitute an organized association as such, but rather individuals and smaller groups who shared similar ideas and similar direct actions in opposition to the war. Their leaders were the Berrigan brothers, whose approach is discussed in chapter 4. They used highly symbolic actions by small cadres of dedicated activists that were publicized in the media. The action by and trial of the Catonsville Nine illustrates this approach. Such resistance and direct action differed from the nonviolent resistance of many traditional pacifists. By 1975, the "actions" of the Catholic left had waned for a number of different reasons.[42]

In 1962 Eileen Egan, a Catholic Worker member and close friend of Dorothy Day, reactivated an older group called PAX. To form international connections she affiliated PAX with the English PAX and slowly developed it into a lay group that also published a quarterly magazine. Its founders were all pacifists, but they were open to just war theorists and were generally opposed to nuclear weapons. Eileen Egan, Gordon Zahn (a World War II Catholic conscientious objector, longtime pacifist, and author of the first biography of Franz Jägerstätter, an Austrian conscientious objector executed by the Nazis in 1943), and James Douglass (author of books on peace and nonviolence, especially *The Nonviolent Cross*, and also an activist involved in civil disobedience) went to the Vatican Council in 1964 to lobby the bishops to oppose nuclear weapons. PAX also worked to change the position of the United States bishops on conscientious objection.[43]

In light of Vatican II, the role of religious groups and individuals in the civil rights and peace movements in this country, the agitation of the Catholic peace groups, and the growing disenchantment of many U.S. citizens with the Vietnam War, U.S. Catholic bishops slowly came to oppose the war. In 1966, 1967, and 1968, the bishops adhered to a position of conscientious support for the U.S. involvement in Vietnam. The November 1968 meeting produced the pastoral letter "Human Life in Our Day," which deals with the issues of artificial contraception and peace and war. The letter refers to the 1966 statement and describes it as a tentative judgment that on balance the U.S. presence in Vietnam was useful and justified. The 1968 letter never revoked the earlier judgment, but raised questions assessing the country's involvement: Have we already reached or passed the point at which the principle of proportionality becomes decisive? The letter opposes a blind nationalism, supports selective conscientious objection based on just war principles, and calls for the Selective Service to accommodate selective conscientious objectors. In 1971 the bishops finally came out against the war: "At this point in history it seems clear to us that whatever good we hope to achieve through continued involvement in this war is now outweighed by the destruction of human life and of moral values which it inflicts."[44] The Catholic Peace Movement, together with many other factors, thus had a role to play in changing the position of U.S. Catholic bishops.

Today, the largest and strongest Catholic peace organization is Pax Christi USA, which replaced PAX in 1972. Once again, the Catholic Worker in general and Eileen Egan and Gordon Zahn in particular played significant roles in its beginning.[45] In 1971, the English PAX merged with Pax Christi International, which was founded by French lay Catholics to work for peace and reconciliation between France and Germany after World War II. The movement spread throughout Europe and was supported by the Church.[46] In Europe, a bishop headed each national section, but Egan and Zahn wanted a lay organization. At the same time, however, they wanted contact with bishops, so they appointed auxiliary bishop Tom Gumbleton of Detroit as moderator. Later they added bishops Carroll Dozier of Memphis and Walter Sullivan of Richmond as moderators. At this early stage the movement saw itself as trying to influence both the hierarchy in the United States and the people in the pews, primarily through education toward peace and nonviolence. The movement focused on disarmament, amnesty, selective conscientious objection, peace education, and advocacy at the United Nations. They did not participate in civil disobedience.[47]

The movement continued to grow, especially when Mary Evelyn Jegen began as fulltime national coordinator in 1979. The organization encouraged the existence of local groups in parishes, published a magazine, and provided a press service that distributed to Catholic newspapers. The organization had significant influence on the U.S. bishops' 1983 pastoral letter on peace, but in general the members were disappointed because the bishops failed to condemn all use of nuclear weapons. As time went on the organization moved away from accepting a just war position and totally embraced pacifism, but also broadened itself by supporting the more radical Catholic resistance movement. Over the years more than one hundred Catholic bishops became members of the organization.[48]

Today, Pax Christi USA remains committed to nonviolence, rejecting war, preparations for war, and every form of violence and domination. Pax Christi USA commits itself to peace education and, with its bishop members, promotes the Gospel imperative of peacemaking as a priority for the U.S. Catholic Church. Its primary areas of concern include nonviolence and peace education, disarmament and reconciliation with justice, economic and interracial justice in the United States, and human rights and global restoration. Regional affiliates exist in many areas throughout the country.[49]

The 1983 U.S. bishops' pastoral letter, "The Challenge of Peace: God's Promise and Our Response," recognizes the long tradition in the Church of individuals embracing pacifism. The moral choice for the kingdom of God involves a commitment to work for peace, but the preservation of peace and the protection of human rights are to be accomplished in a world marked by sin. There is always a strong presumption in favor of peace, but limited self-defense cannot be denied to nations in our world. In the letter the bishops developed a just war theory for the guidance of states, concentrating on the Cold War debate over U.S. deterrence policy and opposing some aspects of U.S. policy. The bishops oppose counter-city weapons and the first use of even counterforce nuclear weapons but leave some ambiguity about retaliatory counterforce weapons. The letter recognizes a strictly conditioned moral acceptance of some limited counterforce deterrence but this can never be the basis for a true peace. However, the bishops do not call for unilateral nuclear disarmament. Owing especially to the public drafting process used by the bishops, the letter had a significant impact not only in the Catholic Church but also on public opinion in the United States.[50]

Peace and war are perennial issues in our society. The involvement of specifically Catholic groups in this area was strong immediately after Vatican II, and has waned in the later decades. There appear to be a number of causes for this—the lesser role played by the Church in the lives of many Catholics, the decreased credibility of the bishops, and the recognition of the importance of living and working in more pluralistic groups. The Church as a whole, its leaders, and its members should continue to respond to issues of peace and war, but many Catholics will probably work with broad-based pluralistic groups to bring about change in society rather than specifically Catholic groups.

CÉSAR CHÁVEZ AND THE FARMWORKERS

In the late 1960s and 1970s the issue of support for César Chávez and the farmworkers in California came to the fore. This issue had similarities with pre–Vatican II aspects of support for labor unions and even "taking care of our own," since the Hispanic farmworkers were at least nominally Catholic. However, there were other complicating factors in the mix together with a broad-based, ecumenical support for the farmworkers. A number of important actors were involved. Obviously Chávez and the union played the primary role, but they also received quite a bit of support from those who joined the boycotts of grapes and lettuce, from the AFL-CIO, and in the form of legislation protecting the rights of farmworkers. In this context the U.S. bishops also played a significant role.[51]

Chávez was a devout Catholic who was influenced by his family and in the 1950s by a Catholic priest Donald McDonnell. Fred Ross, an associate of Saul Alinsky, introduced Chávez to community organizing and the Community Service Organization that Chávez eventually headed until he began to work with farmworkers in 1962.[52] Chávez, Dolores Huerta, and others worked to establish a union for farmworkers. The United Farm Workers Organizing Committee was formed in 1966. Chávez targeted the Delano, California, area and the California table grape industry. The area had a large number of nonmigratory workers, which made it easier to organize. Chávez brought his Catholic faith into his union organizing work, and invoked the symbols and ritual of Catholicism. A banner of Our Lady of Guadalupe was present at most meetings and Catholic priests often blessed the group. Not all of Chávez's supporters were happy with his heavy emphasis on Catholicism.

Chávez and the California Grape Growers

The workers went on strike to support their cause. Chávez organized a 1966 march from Delano to Sacramento, which brought national media attention to his movement. Chávez was totally committed to nonviolence, fasted for the cause, and paid himself practically nothing. The union also became quite media savvy. Chávez announced the first boycott of California grapes in late 1965 and gradually extended it to all the growers involved in the Delano strike. In 1968 he made the boycott a central part of his strategy and sent representatives to major urban areas to gather public support. The boycott ultimately was quite successful. Many volunteers also came to support *La Causa.* The AFL-CIO and other unions backed the strike and even provided funding for the striking workers.

Many religious groups of all stripes also joined the boycott. In 1968 Chávez first appealed to the U.S. bishops to support the boycott. But the grape growers themselves were mostly Catholics and tried to influence local bishops against Chávez and the boycott—occasionally using financial threats. Msgr. George G. Higgins, a longtime member of the bishops' conference staff and specialist in labor relations, strongly supported the boycott. At the November 1968 meeting the bishops issued a statement recognizing the right of the farmworkers to organize and bargain collectively, affirmed the right to strike in certain conditions, and urged the government to protect the farmworkers under minimum-wage laws; however, they did not support the boycott.[53]

In 1969 Chávez again appealed to the bishops to support the boycott. George Meany and the AFL-CIO continued their active support of the farmworkers and Meany suggested to Cardinal John Dearden, president of the bishops' conference, the possibility that third-party intervention in the impasse between the farmworkers and the growers would be appropriate. Once again the November bishops' meeting did not endorse the boycott because of the opposition of some California bishops. However, the bishops established a seven-person Committee on Farm Labor to determine if anything could be done to mediate the dispute. The committee was to investigate the situation, take appropriate action, and if necessary make statements in the name of the entire U.S. hierarchy. Five bishops, including two from California, were appointed to the committee, and they elected auxiliary bishop Joseph Donnelly of Hartford as chair. Donnelly himself had worked for years mediating labor-management disputes.[54] Roger Mahony of the diocese of Fresno, later the Cardinal Archbishop of Los Angeles, was made secretary; George Higgins was appointed consultant to the committee. In reality most of the subsequent work was done by Donnelly, Mahony, and especially Higgins, but all bishops voted on what the committee would do and endorse.

Marco Prouty mentions five factors that contributed to the bishops' decision. The impasse could not be settled on its own. No other potential mediators were available. Many churches already supported the boycott. Most of the parties involved were Catholic. Finally, it would have been a colossal blunder to have turned down two requests from Chávez. There can be no doubt that Chávez forced the bishops to act. Two significant pro-grower bishops in California prevented the bishops from endorsing the boycott, and the bishops compromised by setting up mediation. In reality this approach became the best contribution the bishops could make in this case.[55]

It is not necessary to go into all the details of the negotiation process. The growers basically realized they had no other possibilities, and on July 29, 1970, with bishops playing the key mediating role, an agreement was reached. Bishop

Donnelly, asked to preside at a press conference called by Chávez, congratulated both sides, reiterated that the bishops mediated at the invitation of both sides, and were overjoyed that peace would now come to the valley. By the end of September 1970, the United Farm Workers (UFW) had agreements with 150 agricultural organizations representing 20,000 jobs. But an even bigger problem was already looming for the union.

Chávez and the Lettuce Growers

The scene immediately shifted to the Salinas Valley and lettuce growers. The Teamsters and thirty lettuce growers in the Salinas Valley signed contracts covering about five thousand workers. The growers obviously wanted nothing to do with Chávez and his union, so they were willing to work out sweetheart contracts with the Teamsters. The Teamsters feared that Chávez would take over representation of all those working in agriculture, canning, and marketing in California. Chávez and his supporters were surprised and caught off guard by this action. In 1967 the Teamsters agreed to give Chávez union jurisdiction over the workers in the field in return for recognizing the Teamsters' right to organize the canneries and other people who worked in the production and distribution of food. In all the new contracts with the Teamsters, the farmworkers themselves were never consulted.

A few months later, however, the Teamsters agreed to meet with Chávez under the mediation of the bishops to end the dispute. The negotiations seemed to be successful but no sooner was the agreement signed than the Teamsters went back on their word and said they would have to honor the contracts they had made with the lettuce growers. Chávez then called for a strike, which was quite successful. The Teamsters and their supporters used violent tactics against some of the strikers. A pro-grower judge in Monterey prohibited the UFW from using strikes and boycotts on the basis of the California Jurisdictional State Act. Chávez was jailed for twenty days for violating this order. Chávez then called for support from all corners, especially the religious groups, in his fight against the Teamsters. Once again George Meany and the AFL-CIO strongly supported Chávez.

Up until this point the bishops' committee insisted that they were neutral mediators in their public role, but things began to change. Higgins was irate at the Teamsters' action and had a number of sharp discussions with president Frank Fitzsimmons, whom he had known during his years in Washington. The Committee on Social Development of the bishops' conference—but not the entire body of bishops—supported a boycott of lettuce not harvested by the UFW. The chair of the committee, Bishop Raymond J. Gallagher of Lafayette, Indiana, wrote a letter to all U.S. bishops asking for support for the farmworkers at Labor Day masses.

The growers and their supporters drafted a proposition for the 1972 California election granting farmworkers the right to unionize but outlawing boycotts and severely restricting the right to strike. In September 1972 all the bishops of California, including those who had opposed the grape boycott in 1968 and 1969, came out against Proposition 22 and its restrictions on union activity. The voters defeated Proposition 22 by a 58–42 margin.

The growers and the Teamsters did not give up. Their supporters continued to put financial pressure on the local Catholic Church, especially the diocese of Fresno. When the UFW contract with the grape workers in Delano expired, the Teamsters came in and cut sweetheart contracts with the growers. For the members of the bishops' committee, this was the last straw; they wholeheartedly supported Chávez and his union. Bishop James Rausch, who was general secretary of the bishops' conference at this time, became a staunch advocate for Chávez. Higgins remained the primary contact and bridge between the bishops and Chávez, but there continued to be hesitancy among some bishops about what Higgins was doing. Higgins, Rausch, and their supporters arranged for Chávez to receive a private audience with Pope Paul VI in 1974.

Organized labor through the AFL-CIO and its president George Meany remained staunch advocates of Chávez and continued to provide financial help to the farmworkers. In 1975 Jerry Brown, a deeply committed supporter of the farmworkers, was elected governor of California and played a primary role in enacting the California Agricultural Labor Relations Act, which granted growers protection from strikes and boycotts until after the workers could vote for a union, but gave the union that was recognized the right to strike and boycott. There is no doubt that this legislation paved the way for victory for the farmworkers, who were now able to determine by secret ballot what union they wanted to join. Governor Brown appointed Msgr. Mahony, who played a major role in working for the legislation, the first chair of the board set up by the California Agricultural Relations Act.

The bishops' committee basically withdrew at this point, apparently thinking their goal had been achieved. Unfortunately in the late 1970s and afterward, the UFW lost much of its strength. Chávez was a forceful and charismatic leader of a social movement, but he was not a great labor union leader and organizer. The bishops' conference itself became more conservative and could do little or nothing about the deteriorating situation. A Republican governor who did not support the farmworkers replaced Jerry Brown. The victory of the Farm Workers Union was short lived.

Many Catholic laity, together with millions of other people, supported the boycott, and some also volunteered to help the farmworkers, but the institutional Church played a role that Chávez himself often acknowledged as being crucial. In the beginning the bishops saw their role as a neutral mediator. As the situation changed, the bishops became advocates for a particular position which they saw as a matter of social justice. However, the bishops acted through committee and not through the bishops' conference as a whole. This raises the question of when and how the whole Church and especially the bishops as leaders of the Church should take stands on controversial issues. In fact, the two issues of abortion and peace and war raise the same basic question. The next chapter deals with how the bishops should take stands on particular issues facing society while developing a more general picture of how the Church should carry out and structure its social mission.

Notes

1. Gerald Kelly, *Medico-Moral Problems* (St. Louis, Mo.: Catholic Hospital Association, 1957), 62–83.

2. Daniel Callahan, *Abortion: Law, Choice, and Morality* (New York: Macmillan, 1970), 9–10.

3. Michelle Dillon, "The Abortion Debate: Good for the Church and Good for American Society," in *American Catholics, American Culture: Tradition and Resistance*, vol. 2, *American Catholics in the Public Square*, ed. Margaret O'Brien Steinfels (Lanham, Md.: Rowman and Littlefield, 2004), 71–75.

4. Secretariat of Pro-Life Activities of the U.S. Conference of Catholic Bishops, www.usccb/org/prolife/intro.shtml.

5. James R. Kelly, "Learning and Teaching Consistency: Catholics and the Right to Life Movement," in *The Catholic Church and the Politics of Abortion*, ed. Timothy Byrnes and Mary C. Segers (Boulder, Colo.: Westview, 1992), 153.

6. Michael W. Cuneo, "Life Battles: The Rise of Catholic Militancy within the American Pro-Life Movement," in *Being Right: Conservative Catholics in America*, ed. Mary Jo Weaver and R. Scott Appleby (Bloomington: Indiana University Press, 1995), 270–99.

7. Cuneo, "Life Battles," 271.

8. National Right to Life Committee, www.nrlc.org/missionstatement.htm.

9. Kelly, "Learning and Teaching Consistency," 154–58.

10. Cuneo, "Life Battles," 274.

11. Cuneo, "Life Battles," 274–79.

12. Judie Brown, *It Is I Who Have Chosen You: An Autobiography* (Stafford, Va.: American Life League, 1992); Cuneo, "Life Battles," 279–82; Kelly, "Learning and Teaching Consistency," 159.

13. Pro-Life Action League, prolifeaction.org/about/; Joseph M. Scheidler, *99 Ways to Stop Abortion* (Westchester, Ill.: Crossway Books, 1985).

14. Cuneo, "Life Battles," 289–90.

15. Cuneo, "Life Battles," 298, n. 24.

16. Kelly, "Learning and Teaching Consistency," 158.

17. Randy Sly, "Randall Terry Arrested at Notre Dame," *Catholic Online,* May 1, 2009, www.catholic.org/politics/story.php?id=33423.

18. Operation Rescue, www.operationrescue.org/.

19. National Right to Life, "Abortion in the United States: Statistics and Trends," www .nrlc.org/abortion/Facts/abortionstats.html.

20. Kelly, "Learning and Teaching Consistency," 153.

21. Thomas A. Nairn, ed., *The Consistent Ethic of Life: Assessing Its Reception and Relevance* (Maryknoll, N.Y.: Orbis, 2008).

22. Cuneo, "Life Battles," 296.

23. Kelly, "Learning and Teaching Consistency," 161–63.

24. Dan Balz, "GOP Lurches toward New Consensus on Abortion: Atwater Seeks to Avoid Decision, Get Party through the 1990 Elections without Issue Hurting Party," *Washington Post,* January 22, 1990.

25. "Casey Tapped for Dem Convention," *ABC News,* August 13, 2008, blogs.abcnews .com/politicalradar/2008/08/casey-tapped-for.html.

26. James R. Kelly, "Abortion Politics: The Last Decades, the Next Three Decades, and the 1992 Elections," *America,* July 4–11, 1992, 8–12+; Kelly, "Pro-Life and Pro-Choice after Reagan-Bush," *America,* January 30, 1993, 11–15.

27. James R. Kelly, "A Catholic Votes for John Kerry," *America,* September 27, 2004, 13, 16–17.

28. Catholics in Alliance for the Common Good, www.catholicsinalliance.org.

29. Catholics United, www.catholics-united.org/.

30. Douglas W. Kmiec, *Can a Catholic Support Him? Asking the Big Question about Barack Obama* (New York: Overlook, 2008).

31. William Saletan, "Safe, Legal, and Never: Hillary Clinton's Anti-Abortion Strategy," *Slate,* January 26, 2005, www.slate.com/id/2112712/.

32. Laura Meckler, "Obama Confronts Abortion Debate," *The Wall Street Journal,* May 18, 2009, online.wsj.com/article/5B124257075593727628.html.

33. Catholics for Choice, www.catholicsforchoice.org; see also Mary C. Segers, "The Loyal Opposition: Catholics for a Free Choice," in *Catholic Church and Politics of Abortion,* ed. Byrnes and Segers, 169–84.

34. Catholics for Choice, "The Trouble with Catholics in Alliance for the Common Good," www.catholicsforchoice.org/documents/thetroublewithcacg.pdf.

35. William V. D'Antonio, James D. Davidson, Dean R. Hoge, and Mary L. Gautier, *American Catholics Today: New Realities of their Faith and Church* (Lanham, Md.: Rowman and Littlefield, 2007), 94–96.

36. Pastoral Constitution on the Church in the Modern World, n. 80, in *Documents of Vatican II,* ed. Walter J. Abbott (New York: Guild, 1966), 283. Subsequent references in the text will give the paragraph number from the Pastoral Constitution and the page number from Abbott.

37. On the history of Catholic peace movements and Vietnam, see Patricia McNeal, *Harder than War: Catholic Peacemaking in Twentieth-Century America* (New Brunswick, N.J.: Rutgers University Press, 1992), 131–72. McNeal has written a most authoritative history of the Catholic peace movements in the United States and I have heavily relied on her research in this section.

38. On the general influence of the Catholic Worker on U.S. Catholic pacifism, see Anne Klejment and Nancy L. Roberts, eds., *American Catholic Pacifism: The Influence of Dorothy Day and the Catholic Worker Movement* (Westport, Conn.: Praeger, 1996).

39. McNeal, *Harder than War*, 146–48.

40. Charles A. Meconis, *With Clumsy Grace: The American Catholic Left 1961–1975* (New York: Seabury, 1979), 13.

41. McNeal, *Harder than War*, 139–46.

42. Meconis, *With Clumsy Grace*, 142–66.

43. Gordon C. Zahn, *In Solitary Witness: The Life and Death of Franz Jägerstätter* (New York: Holt, Rinehart, and Winston, 1964); James W. Douglass, *The Nonviolent Cross: A Theology of Revolution and Peace* (New York: Macmillan, 1968); McNeal, *Harder than War*, 19–104, 140; for a detailed history of PAX by its founder, see Eileen Egan, "The Struggle of the Small Vehicle, PAX," in *American Catholic Pacifism*, ed. Klegment and Roberts, 123–52.

44. Todd D. Whitmore, "The Reception of Catholic Approaches to Peace and War in the United States," in *Modern Catholic Social Teaching: Commentaries and Interpretations*, ed. Kenneth R. Himes (Washington, D.C.: Georgetown University Press, 2005), 493–521.

45. McNeal, *Harder than War*, 230–38.

46. Etienne de Jonghe, "Pax Christi International: The Role and Perspectives of an International Catholic Peace Movement," *Cross Currents* 33 (Fall 1983): 323–29.

47. Gerard Vanderhaar, "Action for Peace in the U.S.A.: The Case of Pax Christi," *Pro Mundi Vita Studies* 3 (May 1988): 29–36.

48. McNeal, *Harder than War*, 235ff.

49. Pax Christi-USA, www.paxchristiusa.org/about_statement_purpose.asp.

50. For an analysis and criticism of the letter, see Whitmore, "The Reception of Catholic Approaches to Peace and War," 506–15.

51. There exists an abundant literature on Chávez and the farmworkers. For a biography, see Jacques E. Levy, *César Chávez: Autobiography of La Causa* (New York: Norton, 1975); also Susan Ferris and Ricardo Sandoval, *The Fight in the Fields: César Chávez and Farm Workers Movement* (New York: Harcourt Brace, 1997); Richard Griswold del Castillo and Richard A. Garcia, *César Chávez: A Triumph of Spirit* (Norman: University of Oklahoma Press, 1995). For the role of the U.S. bishops as developed in the following paragraphs, I am totally dependent on Marco G. Prouty, *César Chávez, the Catholic Bishops, and the Farmworkers' Struggle for Social Justice* (Tucson: University of Arizona Press, 2006).

52. Fred Ross, *Conquering Goliath: César Chávez at the Beginning* (Keene, Calif.: El Tailer Grafico, 1989).

53. For the best biography of Higgins, see John J. O'Brien, *George G. Higgins and the Quest for Worker Justice: The Evolution of Catholic Social Thought in America* (Lanham, Md.: Rowman & Littlefield, 2005). A discussion of Higgins and the farmworkers is on pp. 134–57.

54. George G. Higgins, "Tribute to Bishop Joseph F. Donnelly" in O'Brien, *George G. Higgins*, 238–39.

55. Prouty, *César Chávez*, 57–58.

7

Roles of the Church in Supporting
the Social Mission

What role should the Church and its members play in trying to achieve its social mission? This chapter presupposes all that has been said about the understanding of the Church and its social mission today as well as the sociological understanding of the Church and Catholics in United States culture and society. Particular instances of the social involvement of the Church at times have been quite contentious, as illustrated by the U.S. abortion law debate in the last few decades. Tensions arise when a particular position is said to be required of all those who belong to the Church, and one cannot be a good Catholic and disagree on a particular action. But in reality these contentious areas are comparatively few. In the vast majority of instances of working for the social mission of the Church, this problem does not arise, because it is not the whole Church that is acting but individuals in the Church or groups either of Catholics—or, more often today, of ecumenical and interfaith groups that do not purport to speak for the whole Church. The primary and most important work of the social mission of the Church is the work done by individuals alone or in association with others in their daily lives and in all aspects of their familial, social, political, economic, and cultural life. This chapter discusses first the most important and least contentious roles and later the more disputed roles the Church might play.

THE MOST IMPORTANT ROLE

As outlined in the preceding chapters, the most important role of the social mission of the Church is the formation, education, and motivation of all Catholics to work in their daily lives and activities for the common good of society.

Education, in the broadest sense of the term, constitutes the primary function of all Christian churches. The Church strives to form itself into a community of disciples of Jesus. This discipleship by its very nature should recognize that action on behalf of justice and the transformation of the world is a constitutive dimension of preaching the Gospel and of the Church's mission of redemption of the human race and liberation from oppression. Thus, the formation of all the members of the Church into a community of the disciples of Jesus constitutes the most important and fundamental role in developing the social mission of the Church.

I will consider three aspects of the formation and education of the Church community—the challenge, the areas in which the social mission takes place, and the means to carry out formation for the social mission. The challenge to make the social mission of the Church a constitutive dimension of the life of the Church and of all its baptized members is daunting. At best, this is an ongoing work that will never be totally successful. At present, the broader Catholic population is not as aware as they should be of the centrality of the social mission of the Church in their faith and life.

Challenge and Areas of Involvement

The Church has had modern social teaching coming from the popes and Vatican II since Leo XIII's famous encyclical *Rerum novarum* defended the rights of workers in 1891, and continuing through the 2009 encyclical *Caritas in veritate* by Pope Benedict XVI. However, Catholic social teaching has been called the Church's best-kept secret.[1] In the last few decades efforts have been made to make this teaching better known to Catholics in the pews, but many Catholics are still not familiar with it. When New York Catholic Al Smith ran for the presidency in 1928, someone asked him about the papal encyclicals. Smith's alleged answer was classic: "What the hell is an encyclical?"[2] To its great credit, Catholic social teaching does address many of the structural and institutional problems in our world. The Church continually faces the challenge of making this teaching better known to all Catholics. But the social mission of the Church also involves what individuals do in all aspects of their familial, social, cultural, and political lives. Individual Christians in their daily lives are called to work for the common good of society in their work, their play, their home, their neighborhood, their voluntary associations, their professional groups, and their role as citizens. As stated in chapter 4, structural change is only a part, albeit a significant part, of the total social mission of the Church.

Broader U.S. culture emphasizes an individualism that has little or no room for a social mission or the common good. As mentioned in chapter 4, Robert Bellah and his coauthors point out that individualism is now the primary language of most Americans. They see this individualism as supplanting biblical and classic communitarianism of Greece and Rome, which was more prevalent in the early part of our country's history. So strong is this individualism that it has influenced even the role of religion in U.S. life. Many Americans today see religion in terms of what it can do for them as individuals and not in terms of what they are called to do by God and the needs of neighbors near and far.[3]

To its credit, Catholicism in theory and practice has insisted on a communitarian approach that sees the individual believer in multiple relationships with God, neighbor, the earth, and the self. However there is no doubt that a vertical spirituality, with an emphasis on "me and Jesus," has often characterized many Catholics. Such an approach fails to recognize the social dimension of human existence and the basic Christian call for love of God and love of neighbor as being intrinsically connected.

The challenge to see the social mission of the Church and of the individual believer as a constitutive dimension of faith and Church is comparatively new, having come to the fore in Vatican II and afterward. Recall that before Vatican II the Catholic approach distinguished the divinizing and humanizing missions of the Church—the humanizing being less central and fundamental than the divinizing. Implementing the newer approach continues to be a challenge for the Church today.

It is erroneous, however, to think that there is no recognition of the centrality of the social mission of the believer and of the Church. William V. D'Antonio and fellow sociological authors report that Catholics in the United States see care for the poor as a basic component of their faith. Their 2005 survey asks, "As a Catholic, how important is each of the following twelve elements of Catholicism to you?" The responses of helping the poor and belief in the resurrection of Jesus from the dead tied for first place. Eighty-four percent of the respondents called these two aspects very important.[4] Still, there remains a challenge to broaden and deepen the consciousness of the importance of the social mission.

A full development of the content of the social mission of the Church is beyond the scope of this volume. My focus is on the areas in which people work for the social mission of the Church. Chapter 4 discusses the need to see the social mission in light of the principle of subsidiarity, which recognizes all areas that make up the social order. The federal, state, and local government should help individuals and smaller institutions and associations carry out their function, only intervening when and insofar as necessary to do what cannot be done on a lower level. Society thus begins with the individual; followed by the family; the neighborhood; and a whole host of professional, vocational, recreational, industrial, social, and political associations, institutions, and structures—which include the media, public and private educational institutions, professional groups, and business corporations.

The 1976 Call to Action sponsored by U.S. bishops spelled out various areas of working for the common good and justice such as church, family, neighborhood, ethnicity and race, personhood, nationhood, and humankind.[5] The Church cannot credibly claim to speak for justice in the world if it is not just itself. Catholic teaching has consistently emphasized the role of the family as the most basic and fundamental institution in society. The neighborhood is likewise most important for the development of individuals and families; and the Church must work to protect and promote supportive neighborhoods. Most people spend a great deal of their time in their work environment and what they do has an important contribution for the common good, but they must also work for just and equal work opportunity for all, which is so important for the good of society. Ethnicity and race highlight the pluralism within our society and call all to respect and promote diversity in all aspects of our lives. Race problems have been and continue to be very acute in U.S. society. Especially now, the question of immigration is most important.

The area of personhood involves the basic rights of all persons, especially the poor and the marginalized, to fully participate in the life of their communities and to develop their own personal resources. The area of nationhood focuses on the need for institutions and structures to assure the right of all to a minimally decent human existence and the importance of a peaceful society. The area of humankind focuses on what is today called globalization and the need for global justice and peace. There is recognition of the importance of the ecological environment and the need for the individuals to work to protect and improve the environment, as well as the need for policies and laws that guarantee such protection.

Means to Carry Out Education and Formation

How should the Church carry out its teaching, motivating, and formation roles? The movements discussed earlier carry out a social justice formation with regard to those that belong to the movement, but very few baptized Catholics are involved in these movements. The institutions already mentioned also have a role here. Catholic health care facilities aim to have all those who work in them carry out the social mission of the Church with regard to the sick and the poor. Catholic Charities staff and volunteers are motivated to share in the mission to the poor and the needy. In both Catholic health care facilities and Catholic Charities in action, others can see a witness to the social mission of the Church. However, the three most important instrumentalities in carrying out the social mission of the Church are bishops, schools, and parishes.

BISHOPS

In the Roman Catholic Church the bishops have an important teaching role, but all the baptized share in the teaching function of Jesus in and through their baptism. Bishops in the post–Vatican II period have taught the social mission of the Church in some significant ways, especially in the sponsorship of the Call to Action conference in 1976, two pastoral letters (on peace, war, and deterrence; and on the economy) in the 1980s, and documents stressing the important role that Catholic schools and parishes play in teaching the centrality of the social mission.

Under the leadership of Cardinal John Dearden the U.S. bishops planned an extensive program in connection with the U.S. bicentennial in 1976. The Call to Action process started early in 1975 and urged all Catholics to join in the widest possible sharing of assessments of how the American Catholic community could contribute to liberty and justice for all in our country on the occasion of the bicentennial. Discussions took place in individual parishes and in dioceses; six national and one international hearings were held. On the basis of these preliminary discussions the staff prepared working papers on the eight topics mentioned above. Finally, 1,300 delegates of the U.S. Catholic Church assembled in Detroit in October 1976. On the basis of the working papers, the delegates proposed recommendations and resolutions. The process was not perfect; media reports emphasized the areas in which the delegates made recommendations against existing Church teaching and practice; the long-term influence of the whole Call to Action process was probably not significant. The process, however, stimulated broad interest in the social mission and the participants had an unforgettable experience of Church.[6] Even though the bishops did not really implement a very large percentage of the recommendations, Cardinal Dearden deserves great credit for organizing the whole effort, thus emphasizing the centrality of the social mission. The bishops recognized that they as teachers needed to learn before they taught and so they called for the widest possible participation.

In the 1980s the U.S. bishops wrote two important letters on peace and the economy.[7] In the pre–Vatican II period, the bishops had addressed significant issues facing society but their documents never had the impact within society as a whole and within the Church of these two letters. The bishops made some concrete conclusions criticizing positions taken by the U.S. government, but the most significant aspect of the two letters was the process followed. The bishops consulted with experts from all areas, including government officials. They published their preliminary drafts and welcomed comments and criticism from all who wanted to express their opinion. These letters dealt primarily with structural change but made all Catholics and others aware of the social mission of the Church.

Call to Action and the two pastoral letters involved the whole Church. However, since the 1980s the bishops never again followed this process of broad public consultation within and beyond the Church. As a partial consequence, subsequent statements by the bishops have had minimal effect on American public life and the life of the Church—except on the issue of abortion, which is considered in depth in the next chapter.

Why was this broad consultative practice abandoned by the Catholic Church in the United States? The bishops later tried to write a pastoral letter on the role of women in the Church using a similar process, but ultimately they gave up. The primary problem was opposition between the official Vatican teaching and practice and the beliefs of many women in the United States. The Vatican also sharply curtailed the role of bishops' conferences throughout the world. Under the papacy of John Paul II the Church became more centralized, the local churches were downplayed. At the same time, the men appointed bishops in the United States were much more conservative than those appointed earlier in the post–Vatican II period. In addition, child sex abuse and its coverup greatly damaged the credibility of the bishops.[8]

The United States Conference of Catholic Bishops (USCCB) has a number of departments and programs that deal with the social mission of the Church at the national level—Justice, Peace, and Human Development, Campaign for Human Development, Faithful Citizenship, and Pastoral Care of Migrants, Refugees, and Travelers. Since 2001 five offices of the bishops' conference, together with other Catholic organizations, have sponsored an annual Catholic Social Ministry Gathering in Washington.[9] By definition their departments and programs work from the top down, but they stimulate, support, and encourage social ministry at the grassroots level.

Individual bishops have an oversight role in their own diocese, and in this way have a responsibility to make sure that the social mission of the Church is seen as an essential part of the total redemptive mission of the Church. Almost all dioceses have such social justice structures as Justice and Peace Offices, Campaign for Human Development, social ministry programs of Catholic Charities, the St. Vincent de Paul Society, and others. But these alone are not enough. The bishop must work with all entities within the diocese to make everyone aware of the essential reality of the social mission of the Church.

CATHOLIC SCHOOLS

Since the mid-nineteenth century, the primary means of education and formation in the Catholic Church in the United States has been Catholic schools. The bishops at the First Plenary Council of Baltimore (1852) urged every parish to build a parochial school. The Third Plenary Council of Baltimore (1884) went even further, decreeing that within two years parochial schools should be erected wherever they did not exist and that Catholic parents were bound to send their children to parochial schools. This decree was never totally fulfilled, but it gave great impetus to the growth of parochial schools. Catholic parochial schools came into existence and thrived because of the work of the various orders and congregations of religious women dedicated to teaching. Catholic elementary and high schools in the 1960s reached a peak enrollment of 5.5 million students. In 1964, 85 percent of the faculty in these institutions were vowed religious. Many factors have contributed to the decline in the number of Catholic schools since that time, but the decreased number of vowed religious as teachers and the resulting increasing cost are most significant.[10]

According to statistics assembled by the National Catholic Education Association in the 2008–9 school year, there were 6,028 Catholic elementary schools and 1,220 secondary schools. In that year, 31 new schools opened, while 162 consolidated or closed. These schools enrolled a total of 2,192,531 students. Minority enrollment was 29.3 percent of the total and non-Catholics constituted 14.9 percent of the student population. Ninety-six percent of the teaching staff were lay people, while only 4 percent were religious and clergy.[11]

U.S. bishops have insisted on the important role that Catholic schools play in the social mission of the Church. For example, in their 1972 document, "To Teach as Jesus Did," the bishops maintain, "Since the Christian vocation is a call to transform oneself and society with God's help, the educational efforts of the Church must encompass the twin purposes of personal sanctification and social reform in the light of Christian values."[12] This volume does not seek to explore in depth the role and future of Catholic elementary and high schools. The background given here should provide sufficient understanding of the very important role that Catholic schools can play in teaching and formation with regard to the social mission of the Church.

In 1995, three committees of the USCCB established a Task Force on Catholic Social Teaching and Catholic Education. The task force had the twofold role of assessing the quality of Catholic social teaching in Catholic education and of suggesting strategies to strengthen and broaden this teaching. The task force addressed four different educational areas—elementary and secondary schools; religious education, youth ministry, and adult education; higher education; and seminaries.[13] In 1998 the bishops issued a statement, "Sharing Catholic Social Teaching: Challenges and Directions." In this document, the bishops affirmed the work of the task force and highlighted several key themes it developed.[14] Catholic education across the board has tried to implement the proposals in these documents.

The frequency of articles on social justice and social mission in *Momentum*, the quarterly journal of the National Catholic Education Association (NCEA), indicates their importance. The principal means of carrying out this function in Catholic schools are courses in Catholic social teaching and in-service programs involving working for social justice in the community.[15]

Some schools go further and integrate the total curriculum with work for social justice in the community. This demands a substantial commitment by faculty, and involves the education of the faculty themselves in Catholic social teaching and the social mission of the Church, so that they can see applications to their own disciplines. Trustees and administrators must give the encouragement and financial resources necessary for such integration.[16]

The Catholic school has a very strong claim on the time, loyalty, and commitment of both students and parents. A Catholic school also can integrate both the in-service involvement and the curricular emphasis on social justice with the liturgical life of the students. In contrast, religious education programs for those not in Catholic schools meet at most once a week and are not structurally able to accomplish anything approaching what the Catholic school can. The fact that Catholic educators have made such a strong commitment to social justice and the social mission of the Church simply highlights the reality that the school is the most effective means of educating and forming Catholics to be involved in the social mission of the Church. But Catholic Schools reach only a limited number of school-age Catholics.

Catholic colleges and universities also have committed themselves to educate and form their students for involvement in the social mission of the Church. There are 201 Catholic colleges and universities in the United States today. Founded in 1899, the Association of Catholic Colleges and Universities (ACCU) promotes and strengthens the mission and characteristics of Catholic higher education in the United States and acts as its collective voice. The ACCU carries out its work through its publications: the semiannual *Current Issues in Higher Education*; its electronic newsletter, *Update Quarterly*; conferences; consultations; special programs; and structural relationships.[17]

ACCU has taken seriously the challenge to educate and form its students in social justice. In 2001, the organization held its First Annual Catholic Higher Education Peace and Justice Meeting. The tenth annual meeting at the University of San Diego in 2010 featured faculty, administrators, and service coordinators presenting their practice of integration of Catholic social teaching into the classroom, research, and service.[18] In 2009, the ACCU developed and proposed to its members "Catholic Social Teaching: A Vision Statement." This statement addresses the three areas of education and formation, research, and institutional culture, and seeks to incorporate Catholic social teaching across the curriculum. Community-based learning illuminated by social justice teaching provides a profound opportunity for students to connect their education to their lifetime commitment to the common good. Catholic social teaching should also provide the lens through which Catholic higher education views how well they have prepared graduates to see their careers as vocations in service of the common good.[19]

Today every Catholic college and university has courses in social justice and offers in-service and community-based learning opportunities in this area. In addition, there are many opportunities to volunteer for direct service, usually under the auspices of campus ministry. David J. O'Brien, the preeminent historian of public Catholicism in the United States, reports on some extensive programs in Catholic colleges and universities throughout the United States. There are new departments in peace studies and international studies, a variety of volunteer and service programs, and institutes and centers dealing with various social topics and issues. Ethics programs across the curriculum enable faculty in diverse disciplines to raise moral questions facing society. Small groups of faculty and students, often relating to the particular charism of the founding religious community, work to raise the visibility of social justice on campus.[20] However, the work of integrating social justice and the social mission of the Church into the total curriculum and life of institutions of Catholic higher education has just begun. There is much more to be done.[21]

Catholic secondary schools and colleges recognize the importance of in-service and community-based learning. Classes and practical involvement mutually reinforce one another. This corresponds to the contemporary theological emphasis on praxis. Praxis is not merely the application of theory to practice. Through praxis, we come to new insights and knowledge. Praxis brings together theory and practice as they mutually influence each other.[22]

PARISHES

The 1993 document by the U.S. bishops, "Communities of Salt and Light: Reflections on Parish Social Mission," is the first in which the bishops directly address the crucial role of parishes in the Church's social ministry.[23] The parish is the central place to carry out the social mission of the Church. This mission is not an extra dimension of parish life, but an integral, essential, and constitutive part of the parish. More and more social justice has moved from the fringes toward becoming an integral part of parish life, but in some parishes the social justice dimension is neglected, underdeveloped, or touches only a few parishioners. This mission needs to be woven into every aspect of parish life—worship, formation, and action.

The document puts heavy emphasis on Catholic social teaching and the need to change political and economic structures, but it recognizes the fundamental importance of the everyday choices and commitments made by believers acting as parents, workers, students, owners, investors, members of voluntary associations, advocates, citizens, and policymakers. National statements, diocesan structures, and parish councils are useful, but they can never replace what the faithful do in their daily lives. This document does not propose a model or a new national program, but rather a framework for integration, and a recognition that this framework must be fleshed out at the local parish level. Bishops and others can and should learn from the experience of parishes that have made the social mission an essential element of their lives. The challenge remains to make this document live in practice.

Some significant steps have been taken in parishes in the post–Vatican II Church with regard to the social mission of the Church. Most parishes have a justice and peace committee or something similar. Parish renewal programs, such as "Arise: Together in Christ" sponsored by Renew International, see the social mission of the Church as an important part of parish renewal.[24] Groups such as JustFaith also have programs to help individual parishes promote the social teaching and social mission of the Church.[25]

The biggest challenge facing the individual parish is to make the Sunday liturgy a significant teaching and formation instrument of the social mission of the Church. The homily has an important role to play, but anecdotal evidence indicates that homilies do not often treat social teaching or the social mission of the Church. Every parish needs to celebrate the Eucharistic liturgy so as to highlight its social aspects. The beautiful liturgy of Holy Thursday, with its ceremony of the washing of the feet, emphasizes the social mission of the Gospel and of the Church. But the Eucharist itself also has a social dimension. In celebrating the Eucharist we are trying to transform our Christian selves and become one with Jesus both in the glory, praise, and thanks we give to our gracious Father and Mother God and in the care, mercy, and forgiveness shown to neighbors—especially those to whom we are committed and those who are most in need. We who are invited to Jesus's table to share love and companionship in the breaking of the bread and the drinking of the wine are called to break our bread and share our wine with all others, especially the poor and needy.[26]

A few, but not many, parishes have also promoted the formation of small Christian communities, which were first developed in a Latin American context. These groups put special emphasis on the social mission of Church.[27] It is obvious that not all parishioners will belong to these small Christian communities, but their existence can be a leaven within the parish itself.

Parishes should promote the important role played by families. The family is a basic unit not only of secular society but also the domestic Church, and without doubt has the most significant and formative role to play in inculcating the meaning and importance of the social mission of the Church. Parents teach not only in a theoretical way but above all by example and involvement. Individuals who are involved in the social mission of the Church are also excellent examples of Christian endeavor.

Most Catholics have contact with the Church for one hour at the Sunday liturgy—and not every Sunday at that. Parishes need to make the social mission of the Church a priority and find creative ways to promote this mission. The task is daunting and most challenging, but without such education and formation the social mission of the Church will never become a constitutive dimension of the preaching of the Gospel and the mission of the Church.

OTHER ROLES

Christians are called to provide for the needs of others, and almsgiving has had a central role in the life of the Christian Church. From its very beginnings, the Catholic Church in the United States has fostered such almsgiving. The St. Vincent de Paul Society was founded in 1845 to provide for the needs of Catholics. The organization still exists primarily at the parish level, but also has regional offices and a National Council of the United States. The early conferences also sponsored homes for orphans and poor children. Today the National Council, in light of post–Vatican II developments, also engages in advocacy for the poor and support for public policies.[28] Catholic Charities was founded with the help of the St. Vincent de Paul Society, but now uses government funding to serve the needs of all people.

Catholic Relief Services is an organization founded by United States bishops to provide help for the poor internationally. Its original focus in the late 1950s and early 1960s was on the provision of food, clothing, and medicine. Today, in addition to emergency relief, Catholic Relief Services is involved in long-term development programming in agriculture, community health, educational help, HIV/AIDS care and prevention, micro-financing, and peace development. Catholic Relief Services has a staff of about five thousand worldwide and receives funding from an annual national collection taken up in Catholic dioceses as well as from government and private sources.[29]

Church as Enabler and Advocate

A third role of the Church is that of enabler and empowerer. This newer aspect of the Church's social mission came to the fore in the twentieth century. Instead of simply providing what the poor need, the newer approach sought to help the poor help themselves. A popular adage maintains that rather than give a fish to a poor person it is better to teach the person how to fish. The best example of this approach in the contemporary Catholic Church involves community organizations.

Community organization is a means of empowering poor people and the lower-middle class to determine their own futures. Such people often feel unable to do anything about their situation. Local communities are organized to become actively involved in changing their own situations by responding to their needs for better police protection, better education, greater job possibilities, and a better neighborhood environment. Goals are not proposed from above or from outside but rather are decided by the local community itself. A trained organizer begins by trying to form a local community and identify natural leaders within that community. The local community, not the organizer, runs the organization. The members of the organization are the neighborhood groups and institutions that support the organizing work. Since churches are very significant entities in neighborhoods, they often play a prominent role in sponsoring and supporting community organizations—especially because their members belong to the community—financially and by providing meeting places. Often the organization will use some confrontational and conflictual means in order to teach the community that it can take on the powers that be. The locally organized community needs the power to bring about such changes and obtain a seat at the table of those who are deciding what to do. Thus community organizations recognize the important role of power as well as conflict, but also see the need for consensus and cooperation.[30]

Chapter 2 points out that the Archdiocese of Chicago supported the work of Saul D. Alinsky, an agnostic Jew who became involved in community organizing in Chicago with the Back of the Yards organization in 1939. Alinsky realized that the most powerful forces in the neighborhood were the Catholic parishes and the labor unions, and he used these as the basis for a local organization. Alinsky's work in Chicago in the 1950s and 1960s was heavily supported both humanly and financially by the Catholic Church. Alinsky founded the Industrial Areas Foundation (IAF) to support his community organizing work and to train organizers to go into the field. The Industrial Areas Foundation has grown considerably and still exists in different parts of the country.[31]

John (Jack) Egan, who was appointed director of the Office of Urban Ministry in Chicago in 1958, supported Alinsky's work and viewed community organizing as the best means of carrying out the social mission of the Church in changing urban environments. A few years later, other Catholic dioceses also appointed priests to deal with urban problems. Egan was instrumental in bringing together Catholic priests involved in inner-city work (later the group included women religious and many lay people) into a single organization that began informally in 1967 and later was called the Catholic Committee on Urban Ministry (CCUM). It is fair to say that this organization started out as friends of Jack Egan who supported one another in their ministries, and involved primarily a set of relationships rather than a strict organizational structure. CCUM did work other than community organizing, but such was always the group's primary focus. Thus support for community organizing spread throughout the Catholic Church in the United States especially through the work of CCUM.[32]

The late 1960s were a time of crisis for U.S. cities. All the churches recognized the need to respond to the assassination of Martin Luther King and the subsequent riots and destruction. James Foreman was the author of the "Black Manifesto," calling on churches to make reparations for injustices against blacks during and since slavery. Some Protestant churches made substantial contributions. In April 1968, the Catholic bishops established an Urban Task Force to coordinate Catholic activities in this area and to propose courses of action. At their November 1969 annual meeting, the Catholic bishops voted for a resolution that identified two priority activities—education in the Catholic community to inculcate a more Christ-like attitude toward the poor and minority groups, and the establishment of a special poverty collection in response to the evident need for funds to be used by organized groups of white and minority poor to develop economic strength and political power in their communities.[33]

The Catholic Campaign for Human Development (CCHD) formed in November 1970. Its primary purpose was to provide seed money for various community organizations throughout the country. That month a national collection in Catholic churches raised 8.4 million dollars, which was then the largest collection in the U.S. Catholic Church history.[34] CCHD continues to exist and prosper. In 2007, over 12 million dollars were spent, with over 80 percent of the funds going to grants for community empowerment and economic development. CCHD invites grant proposals from all comers and decides to fund proposals for community organization and economic development in keeping with their priorities and criteria.[35]

Lawrence Engel has pointed out that the staff who contributed most to the conceptualization of the CCHD were all members of CCUM, protégés of Jack Egan, and strong supporters of Saul Alinsky. There are other types of community organizations not directly under the aegis of the Alinsky-founded Industrial Areas Foundation, but there can be no doubt that Saul Alinsky indirectly exerted the most influence on the CCHD program.[36]

CCHD has not been immune to controversy. Some very conservative Catholics have attacked CCHD for adhering to socialist approaches and for supporting positions and groups who oppose Catholic teachings. CCHD has responded that it is simply carrying out the Gospel message of Jesus and does not support partisan groups or any group or organization that engages in action not in accord with Church teaching. In 2008, CCHD cut off all funding to ACORN (the Association of Community Organizations for Reform Now) groups because of concerns about its financial accountability, transparency, governance, and organizational integrity as a result of a major embezzlement in the national organization and its coverup by leadership. In addition there have been accusations that some local ACORN groups are involved in partisan activities.[37]

CCHD was the most innovative approach to the social mission of the Church in the United States in the post–Vatican II period and is still vibrant today. This approach embodies the theoretical importance of the need for all citizens to participate actively in community and political life. Providing the poor and marginalized with help and service still has a role, but enabling and empowering is more significant in terms of its effects both on societal institutions and on the marginalized themselves. By definition the CCHD operates on a top-down basis, but through its annual collection in every parish and a strong educational program CCHD tries to involve the whole Catholic Church in its work.

Community organizing has not only affected the Church as a whole in the United States but it has also had a significant effect on the social mission of the parish. In IAF and other organizations the local parish itself is a member institution, and thus becomes an agent of social change by working with the umbrella community organization and the other churches, religious groups, and local communities belonging to the organization. This involvement of the parish and people in community organizations is truly transformative.[38] Involvement in community organization over the last forty years has been the most concrete sign of the Church's work at all levels to empower and enable poor and minority groups.

The Church in all its expressions has another important role, that of advocate for the poor. Contemporary Catholic theology insists on a preferential option for the poor which rests on the fundamental scriptural message of God's special predilection for the poor.[39] But the pervasive assumptions of individualism mean that many persons narrow their focus only on their own good and look disfavorably on the poor. The well-known American adage maintains that the poor should be able to pull themselves up by their bootstraps. Such an approach neglects the great influence of structures and institutions that affect all our lives. Unfortunately many people in our society do not share this preferential option, so it is incumbent on the Church to make it visible.

In the last few decades Catholic Charities and the Catholic Health Association have, in light of Vatican II, seen advocacy for the poor as an important part of their role. But again, families and individuals also must perform the same advocacy in their daily lives, actions, and conversations. Structural change is absolutely necessary, but so is the need to influence the general culture of public opinion. All Christians are called to carry out a prophetic role of speaking and acting in favor of the poor.

Church as Model

The Church is also challenged to be a role model. Catholic social teaching never mentioned this aspect of the social mission of the Church until the 1971

Synod of Bishops's *Justitia in mundo* pronounced, "While the Church is bound to give witness to justice, she recognizes that everyone who ventures to speak to people about justice must first be just in their eyes. Hence we must undertake an examination of the modes of acting and of the possessions and lifestyle found within the Church herself."[40] Note here that two elements ground this assertion. First, the Church itself is the sacrament or sign of the risen Christ in the world and hence must give witness to others of being the light of the world. The second reason is more ethical and practical—you have to practice what you preach.[41]

The document then proposes what might aptly be called an examination of conscience on all levels of the Church. The Church must protect and promote the rights of all within it. Those who work for the Church including priests and religious should receive a sufficient livelihood and social security in accord with the customs of their own region. Lay people should exercise the important functions of administering Church property, and all lay employees should have a system for promotion. Women should have appropriate responsibility for and participation in the life of the Church. Church employees and workers have a right to freedom of expression and to be heard by Church authorities in a spirit of dialogue and respect. Judicial procedures in the Church should recognize the right of the accused to a proper defense and to know her or his accusers.[42]

Faith demands of the Church a sparing use of money and material goods, even though it is not always easy to draw a line between what is needed for proper use and what is demanded by prophetic witness. The Church must always remain committed to the poor, and if it appears to be among the rich and powerful of this world, its credibility is diminished. All in the Church must examine their own lifestyles to see if they exemplify the sparing consumption that we preach to others. This document clearly and forcefully calls the Church and all individual Catholics to be the light of the world.[43] One very practical expression of the Church as model on a diocesan or parish level involves the giving of a percentage of every fund drive to help the poor.

The U.S. bishops' 1986 pastoral letter, "Economic Justice for All," takes up the challenge of the earlier document: "All the moral principles that govern the just operation of any economic endeavor apply to the Church and its institutions; indeed the Church should be exemplary." The pastoral letter selects five areas for special reflection: wages and salaries, rights of employees, investment and property, works of charity, and working for economic justice.[44]

A very significant practical issue concerns unions in Catholic institutions such as schools and hospitals. Catholic social teaching since *Rerum novarum*, the first modern document of Catholic social teaching, has insisted on the rights of workers to form unions and bargain collectively. In their 1986 pastoral letter on the economy, U.S. bishops treat this as a challenge for Catholic institutions: "All Church institutions must also fully recognize the rights of employees to organize and bargain collectively with the institution through whatever association or organization they freely choose."[45] This section focuses on Catholic hospitals, but unions of Catholic schoolteachers also continue to be controversial.

Catholic supporters of unions often accuse Catholic hospitals of hiring union-busting consultants and lawyers. Often Catholic hospitals use intimidation and threats with regard to disciplinary action and even loss of jobs. Many outsiders wonder how Catholic hospitals could be so in opposition to Catholic teaching. Many such hospitals have a layperson as CEO and are often part of a larger Catholic health care network. Very often the corporate model dominates in such institutions and unions are looked upon as a problem and an enemy. Also, some Catholics argue that in Catholic institutions Christian charity should prevail, and not the confrontational relationship between management and workers. In most cases, local bishops have been unable to do anything about unions in hospitals. However, in New York, the late Cardinal John O'Connor ordered four Catholic hospitals to hire back strikers they had fired and forced another Catholic hospital to stop hiring permanent replacement workers during another strike.[46]

A bitter battle took place between the Service Employees International Union (SEIU) and Catholic Healthcare West, one of the largest hospital systems in the Western United States. Finally, in 2001, the union and the health care system established a working agreement and a better relationship. However, tensions and fighting continued in most other places. The nearly six hundred Catholic hospitals employ about six hundred thousand workers, and it is believed that only 15 percent are currently union members.[47]

A significant breakthrough occurred in 2009. The U.S. Conference of Catholic Bishops, the Catholic Health Association, and the AFL-CIO and SEIU announced an agreement on a set of principles to ensure that hospital workers have a fair process by which to determine whether they want a union. The principles are not legally binding on individual hospitals or health care systems, but they have a strong moral force. One commentator called the settlement a "peace agreement." Catholic hospitals were to drop aggressive tactics in opposing unions, and the unions were not to run a public leverage campaign against the hospitals.[48]

The Church as model remains a challenge at all levels of institutional existence and in the lives of all its members. The prophetic role of the Church as sacrament means that it should show forth the reality of justice in its own life and a proper use of worldly material goods.

Social Mission Roles and Ecclesiological Tensions

The discussion of the role of the Church as enabler points out that tensions can arise when the people being helped and enabled do something opposed to Catholic teaching. This ecclesiological tension comes to the fore whenever some teaching or practice involving a specific public issue is proposed in the name of the Church as *the* Catholic teaching. The issue arises for all religious groups and Christian churches. The leader who speaks for the whole church might be the head of the church and denomination, or a leader of a local church such as the pastor or even the homilist. Can and should the pastor or the homilist speak for the whole church, and claim the teaching proposed on a particular public issue is the teaching to be followed by all members? In the 1960s Paul Ramsey raised this issue for Protestant churches in *Who Speaks for the Church?*[49]

In Catholic ecclesiology, the pope and bishops are official teachers of the Church. By analogy, however, what applies here applies also to the role of the pastor and homilist in claiming to speak for the whole Church. This section will address three questions: First, should the Church and its leaders speak out on particular social issues such as the morality of the wars in Vietnam, Iraq, or Afghanistan; or the best way to reform health care; or the decriminalization of marijuana? The second question concerns Church support for a particular political candidate for election; the third question deals with Church support for a particular political party.

Church Teaching on Specific Social, Political, and Economic Issues

One extreme maintains that the Church and its leaders have no competency to address political, economic, or legal issues; it must restrict itself only to religious teachings. The Church has no competency given to it by its founder to teach about the morality of particular wars, the political status of immigrants, the economic systems that exist in our world, international trade policies, or the death penalty. The proper pay for executives is an economic issue, not a religious one. The treatment of immigrants is a legal and political issue.

The Church and its leaders can speak only on the basis of Gospel and religious warrants and have nothing to say on these issues.

An opposite stance maintains that the Church can readily, quickly, and with great certitude know and speak out on what God is doing in the world. One wag is reported to have said that all one needs is the Bible in one hand and the *New York Times* in the other.

The position I defend is basically accepted in principle by all operating out of the Catholic tradition and Catholic ecclesiology, and is a middle ground between the two extremes. In my view, the first position is much too restrictive and ultimately greatly curtails and perhaps even denies the social mission of the Church. Whatever affects human persons, human communities, and the environment is by its very nature a human issue, a moral issue, and—for the believer—a religious issue. Human judgment is the ultimate, and in some ways universal, judgment that takes into consideration many different particularities—the psychological, the sociological, the economic, the political, the hygienic, the eugenic, and so on. Sometimes one of these aspects is very heavily involved in human decisions, but one can never reduce human judgment to just one of its particulars. What is true of human judgment is also true of Christian judgment. The Christian faith touches and embraces all aspects of human life. An ancient axiom maintains that nothing human is foreign to the Christian. After all, Christians believe that God is the Creator of all things.

The opposite position fails to recognize the importance of catholicity and mediation. Catholicity maintains that the Gospel and faith must touch all aspects of our existence. But faith and the Gospel are mediated in and through the human. Faith does not provide a shortcut, enabling one to avoid the human and all its complexity. Many years ago, a Catholic justice and peace group asked me to review their position on multinational corporations. Their brief statement had two paragraphs: The first paragraph paraphrased Matthew 25—when I was hungry, thirsty, naked, etc. The second paragraph concluded that multinational corporations are immoral. I responded that one might be able to make an ethical argument that multinational corporations are immoral. However, if one is going to disagree with the CEO of General Motors (those were the days when General Motors was a multinational corporation!) one had better have knowledge of economics and business and know something besides Matthew 25.

Chapter 3 develops in some depth how catholicity and mediation affect the possibility of arriving at certitude on concrete, specific issues—precisely because on such issues so many perspectives and circumstances are involved one cannot claim to arrive at a certitude that precludes other possible responses. Some issues are less complex. Murder, for example, is always wrong, but at times one cannot be certain that a particular killing was murder. If bishops as leaders in the Church speak out on specific, complex issues they must recognize that other members of the church can legitimately hold other positions.

The basic question is this: In the Catholic Church, can and should bishops speak out on specific societal issues such as immigration, health care reform, unemployment, and the use of military force? The fact of the matter is that Catholic bishops in the United States have spoken out on such issues, as have the leaders of many other Christian churches in this country. Thus the question becomes, How should they speak out? I propose three conditions. First, the bishops have to do their homework and learn all they can about these complex issues. Second, bishops must recognize that other members in the Church can legitimately disagree with their positions. Third, since the bishops cannot speak on all issues facing our society, they must determine which issues are most significant.

One can never forget that bishops are not the only teachers in the Church. All the baptized also share in the teaching role of Jesus. Precisely because bishops see their role as teaching what the whole Church should believe and do, they will not be as prophetic as others in the Church can and should be. *Lumen gentium* speaks of the prophetic role in the Church belonging to all the faithful. The Holy Spirit has distributed gifts and charisms to the people of God to carry out this prophetic role.[50] In the social realm we have seen many different ways in which individual prophets and movements have taught the whole Church by word and example what the social mission of the Church might involve. The bishops could, however, carry out their teaching role in a more prophetic way. At present they tend to see their teaching role as explaining what the teaching of the Church is. However, we recognize that teaching is more than giving answers. The good teacher today often prods students to think on their own—often by raising probing questions. The bishops could at times also adopt such a teaching method, thus challenging themselves and the members of the Church with the questions they raise.

The Nature of Civil Law

One of the specific questions that often arises pertains to what should be the proper law in a given situation, particularly as regards civil legislation on abortion, same-sex marriages, and stem cell research. The Catholic tradition has taken two different approaches to civil law—the older approach strongly influenced by Thomas Aquinas, and the newer approach developed in the Vatican II Declaration on Religious Freedom.

Thomas Aquinas understood civil law in light of natural law. Natural law is the participation of the eternal law in the rational creature. Civil law either replicates natural law (e.g., murder is a crime) or makes determined what the natural law leaves undetermined. Natural law says that automobile drivers should drive safely; the civil law determines speed limits. Human law is truly a law and obliges only to the extent that it is derived from natural law. What is opposed to natural law is not a law but the corruption of law. This relationship of natural law to civil law also serves as the basis for Aquinas's justification of civil disobedience to unjust laws.[51]

Aquinas, however, recognizes that morality and law are not identical. Civil law is ordered to the common good, and as such should not legislate all the acts of all the virtues, but only those that affect the common good. What does not affect the common good should not be a matter of law. In civil society, for example, there is no law against lying, but there is a law against perjury. There is a significant difference between private morality and public law. Aquinas takes a further step based on his realistic understanding of human nature: Human beings are not perfect, and human law should suppress the most grievous vices from which most people are able to abstain—especially those harmful to others—because such laws are necessary for the good of society.[52]

In another context Aquinas approves of Augustine's toleration of prostitution and opposition to a law against it. The thirteenth-century theologian grounds such tolerance in human society on the basis of how God himself has acted. God, who is all powerful and all good, sometimes allows evil to occur in order to bring about a greater good or avoid a greater evil. Civil law, modeled on God's actions, can thus tolerate a lesser evil such as prostitution in order to achieve a greater good or avoid a greater evil.[53] Before Vatican II such an approach justified the acceptance of religious freedom in civil society. The ideal was a union of church and state with a denial of religious freedom, but in a pluralistic society a Catholic could tolerate religious freedom in order to avoid greater evil.[54]

Vatican II did not address head-on the question of law and morality, but it addresses the question in the Declaration on Religious Freedom. In so doing, the document follows the theory proposed earlier by American Jesuit John Courtney Murray. The document, however, does not accept the whole of Murray's understanding of religious freedom. For Murray, religious freedom is not primarily a theological issue based on the freedom of the act of faith or a moral issue based on the freedom of conscience; religious freedom is formally a juridical and constitutional issue about the role of law in civil society that has foundations in theology, ethics, and public policy.[55] Paragraph 7 of the Declaration on Religious Freedom discusses the juridical question of the role of law with respect to religious freedom and all political freedoms. The basic principle is that the usages of society are to be the usages of freedom in their full range. This requires that the freedom of the person be respected as far as possible and curtailed only when and insofar as necessary.[56] John Courtney Murray, in his commentary on the document, insists that secular experts may consider this to be the most significant sentence in the entire Declaration. It is the basic principle of a free society, which is new to the Church but still in concord with the Catholic tradition. Freedom is the end and purpose of society and the political method par excellence whereby the other aims of society are to be achieved.[57]

Society, however, has the right to protect itself against abuses. The criterion determining the proper intervention of coercive law is the public order. Public order has a threefold content—an order of justice, of public peace, and of public morality.[58] The document and Murray's commentary on it do not illustrate any such interventions but it is not difficult to recognize how these criteria have functioned in American jurisprudence. If your religion calls for child sacrifice, civil authority on the basis of protecting justice in the form of basic human rights can and should prevent such sacrifice. If your religion calls for a two-hundred-piece band to parade around a neighborhood Sunday at 2 A.M., public peace is greatly disturbed. The criterion of public morality insists on its public aspect. One example of this in U.S. history was the Supreme Court's contentious decision to prohibit Mormons from practicing polygamy.[59]

The religious freedom approach and the Thomistic approach have two significant differences. The Thomistic approach begins with natural law, even though civil law is more restrictive. The religious freedom approach begins with the principle of a free society—as much freedom as possible and as little restraint as necessary. The criterion for the proper intervention of law also differs. In the Thomistic approach, the state intervenes for the common good, whereas in the religious freedom approach the state intervenes for public order. Public order is more limited than the common good. Murray's approach, accepted by the Declaration on Religious Freedom, distinguishes between public society and the state. Public society embraces those realities that affect public life in its manifold cultural, social, political, economic, and intellectual dimensions. The state is the narrower and smaller reality that alone can use the coercive force of law. The common good is the end of the broader public society and all who are engaged in it. Public order is the end of the state and is the criterion that justifies the intervention of the coercive force of law.[60]

In his 1995 encyclical *Evangelium vitae,* Pope John Paul II develops his understanding of civil law especially in his discussion of abortion law. Herein he uses the Thomistic approach: "The acknowledgement of an objective moral law which, as the 'natural law' written in the human heart, is the obligatory point of reference for civil law itself";[61] "The doctrine on the necessary conformity of civil law with the moral law is in continuity with the whole tradition of the Church" (n. 72). John Paul II cites this clear teaching of St. Thomas Aquinas, "Every law made by man can be called law insofar as it derives from the natural law. But if it is somehow opposed to the natural law, then it is not really a law but rather a corruption of the law" (n. 72). In keeping with his Thomistic approach John Paul II insists that the purpose of civil law "is that of securing the common good" (n. 71). His discussion of civil law in *Evangelium vitae* never mentions public order. It is quite clear that John Paul II strongly supports the Thomistic understanding of law and not the religious freedom approach. In other writings I have tried to explain some reasons that might be behind his adoption of the Thomistic approach.[62]

In my judgment the religious freedom approach is the proper one but it needs to be filled out with a recognition of the pragmatic and practical aspects of civil law. Civil law must be enforceable. If it cannot be enforced, it is bad law. Prohibition is one such example in U.S. history. Law must also be equitable. If, for example, the rich are able to contravene the law but not the poor, such a law cannot be good law. Also in the legislative process itself feasibility is a practical consideration. Sometimes it is impossible under certain circumstances to pass a law.

This section addresses from a theoretical perspective the issue of legislation as an example of a specific, concrete action. Chapter 8 deals in a practical way with the specific question of the U.S. bishops and their support for laws against abortion.

Support of Political Candidates and Parties

Should the Church or its leaders support a particular political candidate in an election? Although I explicitly address the Catholic Church, what is said here applies to other Christian churches and obviously to pastors or parish leaders speaking in the name of a local church. Ordinarily bishops and church leaders should not support particular political candidates. The previous section pointed out that on a particular issue there often is disagreement within the Church. A political candidate may take stands on all issues facing society, and it is impossible to expect agreement within the Church on all these issues. The freedom of the believer is definitely curtailed if the Church as a whole takes a stand in favor of a particular candidate. Like all of us, candidates have weaknesses, sinfulness, and foibles. The Church should not identify itself or the Gospel so completely with any human being.

Notice the weasel word "ordinarily" in the position taken above. There might be some exceptions to this principle. One may recall the opposition of some church leaders to the election of Adolf Hitler in Germany. Some Christian churches in South Africa said their members could not vote for a candidate who supported apartheid. In my judgment these actions were proper. Note, however, in these cases the church leaders were opposing a particular candidate, not endorsing one. From a logical perspective it is always easier to make a negative judgment that finds general agreement than a positive judgment. To judge something to be good it must be good from all essential perspectives, but something may be judged evil or bad if it is lacking only one essential item. Many people in the United States today would agree that the funding of political candidates running for office in this country needs to be changed. But those who agree that the present practice is not good would never be able to agree on what should be done. Bishops and Church leaders should not support political candidates explicitly in the name of the Church, but in very extreme situations may be justified in coming out against a particular candidate because of a position counter to the very fabric of society.

Churches in the United States, including the Catholic Church, have tax-exempt status but must abide by restrictions on political and legislative activities. Section 501(c)3 of the Internal Revenue Code of 1986 (as amended) includes two stipulations—no substantial part of the organization's activities may consist of carrying on propaganda or otherwise attempting to influence legislation; and the organization may not participate in political campaigning in opposition to, or on behalf of, any candidate for public office. The clear wording maintains that church support of or opposition to a political candidate could jeopardize the church's exemption from tax.[63] There have been a number of court cases maintaining that the Catholic Church should lose its tax-exempt status because of its involvement in antiabortion legislation. None of these cases has been successful. In 1999 the Federal Appeals Court in Manhattan dismissed a nine-year-old suit in which abortion rights advocates challenged the Church's tax-exempt status.[64] The United States Conference of Catholic Bishops is well aware of these issues and often advises people in the Church as to what can and cannot be done in light of the tax code.[65]

A final question concerns Church support for political parties. No respected voice in the U.S. Catholic Church proposes such involvement. The Catholic Church has consistently refused to support a particular political party. The situation in other countries is different. In Europe after World War II, the Catholic Church was strongly identified with Christian Democratic parties. However, it seems today that the Church would have been better off not identifying itself with a particular political party.[66]

This chapter discusses the various roles the Church and its members should play in working for the social mission of the Church as a constitutive dimension of the mission of the Church. Without doubt the most important and the least controversial role is that of educating and motivating all the people of God to recognize the importance of the social mission and to participate in it. Less important but still significant are the roles of the Church as provider, enabler, advocate, and model. Problems and controversies arise when the bishops speak for the whole Church. As a result, bishops should speak out on specific issues only under certain conditions; ordinarily should not support particular political candidates; and should never identify the Church with a particular political party. The next chapter discusses the controversial issue of the role of the bishops regarding abortion legislation.

NOTES

1. Edward P. DeBerri, James E. Hug, Peter J. Henriot, and Michael J. Schultheis, *Catholic Social Teaching: Our Best Kept Secret*, 4th ed. (Maryknoll, N.Y.: Orbis, 2003).

2. Thomas J. Shelly, "Vatican II and American Politics," *America*, October 13, 2003, 16.

3. Robert N. Bellah, Richard Madsen, William M. Sullivan, and Ann Swidler, *Habits of the Heart: Individualism and Commitment in American Life* (Berkeley: University of California Press, 1985), 219–49.

4. William V. D'Antonio, James D. Davidson, Dean R. Hoge, and Mary L. Gautier, *American Catholics Today: New Realities of Their Faith and Their Church* (Lanham, Md.: Rowman and Littlefield, 2007), 23–24.

5. Frank D. Manning, *A Call to Action: An Interpretive Summary and Guide* (Notre Dame, Ind.: Fides/Claretian, 1977).

6. Manning, *A Call to Action*, 1–7, 93–101.

7. U.S. Catholic Bishops, "The Challenge of Peace: God's Promise and Our Response," and "Economic Justice for All," in *Catholic Social Thought: A Documentary Heritage*, ed. David J. O'Brien and Thomas A. Shannon (Maryknoll, N.Y.: Orbis, 1992), 492–680. This volume contains the documents of Catholic Social Teaching from Leo XIII to John Paul II.

8. For a description of these changing realities by the chair of the committee that wrote the economic pastoral, see Rembert G. Weakland, *A Pilgrim in a Pilgrim Church: Memoirs of a Catholic Archbishop* (Grand Rapids, Mich.: William B. Eerdmans, 2009).

9. United States Conference of Catholic Bishops, "Catholic Social Ministry Gathering: Sponsors," www.ausccb.org/sdwp/socminsponsors.shtml.

10. For a history of Catholic schools in the United States, see Harold A. Buetow, *Of Singular Benefit: The Story of Catholic Education in the United States* (New York: Macmillan, 1970), and Buetow, *The Catholic School: Its Roots, Identity, and Future* (New York: Crossroad, 1988).

11. National Catholic Education Association, "United States Catholic Elementary and Secondary Schools, 2008–2009: The Annual Statistical Report on Schools, Enrollment, and Staffing," www.ncea.org/news/AnnualDataReport.asp.

12. National Conference of Catholic Bishops, *To Teach as Jesus Did* (Washington, D.C.: United States Catholic Conference, 1973), 3.

13. United States Conference of Catholic Bishops, "Task Force on Catholic Social Teaching and Catholic Education," at www.usccb.org/sdwp/projects/socialteaching/summary.shtml.

14. U.S. Bishops, "Sharing Catholic Teaching: Challenges and Directions," *Origins* (1998): 102–6.

15. See, for example, Mike Daley, "Naked Justice," *Momentum* 40 (April–May 2009): 42–43; Linda Hanson, "Integrating Catholic Social Teaching into the Elementary Classroom," *Momentum* 40 (February–March 2009): 44–46; Rick Pendergast, "Creating a School That Is Catholic in All That It Does: How to Integrate Catholic Social Teaching throughout the Curriculum," *Momentum* 39 (September–October 2008): 10–14.

16. In addition to references cited in the preceding note, see especially Michael P. Horan, "Justice Education as a Schoolwide Effort: Effective Religious Education in the Catholic School," in *Catholic Education: A Journal of Inquiry and Practice* 9 (December 2005): 215–29.

17. "About ACCU," www.accunet.org/i4a/pages/index.cfm?pageid=3330.

18. University of San Diego News Center, "USD Hosts ACCU Catholic Social Thought Conference," www.sandiego.edu/insideusd/?p=7763.

19. Association of Catholic Colleges and Universities, "Catholic Higher Education and Catholic Social Teaching," www.accunet.org/i4a/pages/index.cfm?pageid=3614.

20. David J. O'Brien, *From the Heart of the American Church: Catholic Higher Education in American Culture* (Maryknoll, N.Y.: Orbis, 1994), 191–93; also O'Brien, "The Option for the Poor in Undergraduate Education," in *Love of Learning, Desire for Justice: Undergraduate Education and Option for the Poor*, ed. William E. Reiser (Scranton, Pa.: University of Scranton Press, 1996), 31–41.

21. O'Brien, *From the Heart of the American Church*, 191–211; see also Monika K. Hellwig, "Catholic Social Teaching: An Inter-disciplinary Challenge to Catholic Universities," *Journal of Catholic Social Thought* 1 (2004): 7–16.

22. Marvin L. Krier Mich, *The Challenge and Spirituality of Catholic Social Teaching* (Louisville, Ky.: JustFaith, 2005), 5–6.

23. U.S. Bishops, "Communities of Salt and Light: Reflections on Parish Social Mission," *Origins* 23 (1993): 443–48; see also Peggy Prevoznik Heins, *Becoming a Community of Salt and Light: Formation for Parish Social Ministry* (Notre Dame, Ind.: Ave Maria, 2003).

24. Renew International, "Arise Together in Christ," www.renewintl.org/renew/home.nsf/vFiles/ARISE_trifold-English + jun0208.pdf.

25. JustFaith, www.justfaith.org.

26. For a very good exposition of the social mission of the Eucharist that is accessible to the general reader, see Patrick T. McCormick, *A Banqueteer's Guide to the All-Night Soup Kitchen of the Kingdom of God* (Collegeville, Minn.: Liturgical, 2004).

27. Thomas A. Kleissler, Margot A. LeBert, and Mary C. McGinness, *Small Christian Communities: A Vision of Hope for the 21st Century* (N.Y.: Paulist, 2004); Arthur R. Baranowski, with Kathleen M. O'Reilly and Carrie M. Piro, *Creating Small Faith Communities: A Plan for Restructuring the Parish and Renewing Catholic Life* (Cincinnati, Ohio: St. Anthony Messenger, 1988).

28. Society of St. Vincent de Paul, www.svdpusa.org.

29. Catholic Relief Services, www.csr.org.

30. Ross J. Gittell and Avis Vidal, *Community Organizing: Building Social Capital as a Development Strategy* (Thousand Oaks, Calif.: Sage, 1998).

31. On the development of the IAF after Alinsky, who died in 1972, see James B. Ball, "A Second Look at the Industrial Areas Foundation: Lessons for Catholic Social Thought and Ministry," *Horizons* 35 (2008): 273–76.

32. John J. Egan, Peggy Roach, and Philip J. Murnion, "Catholic Committee on Urban Ministry: Ministry to the Ministers," *Review of Religious Research* 20 (1979): 279–90; for a biography of Egan, see Margery Frisbie, *An Alley in Chicago: The Ministry of a City Priest* (Kansas City, Mo.: Sheed & Ward, 1991).

33. Lawrence J. Engel, "The Influence of Saul Alinsky on the Campaign for Human Development," *Theological Studies* 59 (1998): 648–58.

34. Engel, "The Influence of Saul Alinsky," 661.

35. United States Conference of Catholic Bishops, "2007 Annual Report of CCHD," www.usccb.org/cchd/2007_annual_report.pdf.

36. Engel, "Influence of Saul Alinsky," *Theological Studies* 59 (1998): 648–61.

37. United States Conference of Catholic Bishops, "Bishop Morin's Subcommittee on CCHD and ACORN," www.usccb.org/cchd/morin_acorn_report.shtm.

38. Ball, "A Second Look," *Horizons* 35 (2008): 285–94.

39. Daniel G. Groody, ed., *The Option for the Poor in Christian Theology* (Notre Dame, Ind.: University of Notre Dame Press, 2007).

40. 1971 Synod of Bishops, "Justice in the World," in *Catholic Social Thought*, ed. O'Brien and Shannon, 295.

41. Richard P. McBrien, *The Church: The Evolution of Catholicism* (New York: Harper-Collins, 2008), 254.

42. 1971 Synod of Bishops, "Justice in the World," 295.

43. 1971 Synod of Bishops, "Justice in the World," 295.

44. U.S. Catholic Bishops, "Economic Justice for All," nn. 347–50, in *Catholic Social Thought*, ed. O'Brien and Shannon, 659–60.

45. U.S. Catholic Bishops, "Economic Justice for All," n. 353, in *Catholic Social Thought*, ed. O'Brien and Shannon, 660.

46. George Higgins with William Bole, *Organized Labor and the Church: Reflections of a "Labor Priest"* (New York: Paulist, 1993), 109–30. Higgins also strongly supported the right of Catholic school teachers to join a union.

47. Tom Schindler, "Unionizing Catholic Hospitals," *National Catholic Reporter*, August 11, 2006, 3a.

48. "Labor Unions, Catholic Hospitals Reach Agreement," *National Catholic Reporter*, June 23, 2009, ncronline.org/news/justice/labor-unions-catholic-hospitals-reach-agreement.

49. Paul Ramsey, *Who Speaks for the Church?* (Nashville, Tenn.: Abingdon, 1966).

50. Constitution on the Church, n. 12, in *Documents of Vatican II*, ed. Walter M. Abbott (New York: Guild, 1966), 29–30.

51. Aquinas, *Ia IIae*, q.95, a.2.

52. Aquinas, *Ia IIae*, q.96, a.2.

53. Aquinas, *IIa IIae*, q.10, a.11.

54. See, for example, Joseph Clifford Fenton, "Toleration and the Church-State Controversy," *American Ecclesiastical Review* 130 (1954): 330–43.

55. John Courtney Murray, *The Problem of Religious Freedom* (Westminster, Md.: Newman, 1965), 19–21.

56. Declaration on Religious Freedom, n. 7, in *Documents of Vatican II*, 687.

57. John Courtney Murray, n. 20, Declaration on Religious Freedom, n. 7, in *Documents of Vatican II*, 686. The official footnotes in this edition are in italics. John Courtney Murray added the footnotes, which are in regular type.

58. Declaration on Religious Freedom, n. 7, in *Documents of Vatican II*, 686–87.

59. *Reynolds v. United States*, 98 U.S. 195 (1878).

60. Murray, *Problem of Religious Freedom*, 28–29.

61. Pope John Paul II, *Evangelium vitae*, n. 70, in *The Encyclicals of John Paul II*, ed. J. Michael Miller (Huntington, Ind.: Our Sunday Visitor, 2001), 736. Subsequent references to *Evangelium vitae* in the paragraph will include the paragraph number of the encyclical in the text (e.g., n. 70).

62. Charles E. Curran, *Catholic Social Teaching 1891–Present: A Historical, Theological, and Ethical Analysis* (Washington, D.C.: Georgetown University Press, 2002), 241–42.

63. Rutherford Institute, "The Rights of Churches and Political Involvement," www.rutherford.org/resources/Pamphlets/Rights_of_Churches.pdf.

64. William Glaberson, "Catholic Church Tax Exemption Is Upheld," *New York Times*, September 7, 1989, B3.

65. Mark Chopko, "Parishes and Political Activity," *Church* 24, no. 1 (Spring 2008): 12–17; Dierdre Dessingue Halloran and Kevin M. Carney, "Federal Tax Code Restrictions on Church Political Activity," *Catholic Lawyer* 38, no. 2 (1998): 105–32.

66. Carolyn M. Warner, *Confessions of an Interest Group: The Catholic Church and Political Parties in Europe* (Princeton, N.J.: Princeton University Press, 2000).

8

U.S. Bishops and Abortion Law

I n the late twentieth and early twenty-first centuries, U.S. bishops as a national body and as individual heads of dioceses have devoted more time, energy, and money to abortion than to any other single issue. The media has given great attention to the role of the U.S. bishops on the abortion issue. This chapter describes bishop involvement and offers analysis and criticism of their approach.

In fall 1968 the U.S. Catholic bishops published a pastoral letter, "Human Life in Our Day." In light of the developing discussion of and mounting pressure for relaxed abortion laws, one would have expected this document to treat the abortion issue. But this was not the case. The document discussed at length the issues of contraception, which came to the fore in Pope Paul VI's 1968 encyclical *Humanae vitae*, and the issues of war (especially in Vietnam) and deterrence. Only three short paragraphs were devoted to abortion. In two paragraphs the bishops cited the Pastoral Constitution on the Church in the Modern World. Thus, at this point, abortion was not a high priority for the bishops.[1]

The staff of the bishops' conference in Washington, especially Father T. McHugh, the director of the Family Life Bureau, recognized the importance of the abortion issue. McHugh, who founded the National Right to Life Committee and later became a bishop, continued to play a most significant role in mobilizing the bishops in their defense of the fetus.[2]

In 1969 the bishops issued a short "Statement on Abortion" in response to movement toward less restrictive abortion laws, in which they maintained that abortion was not just a Catholic issue. They also recognized the need for something more than law—a social responsibility to provide health care and sustenance for pregnant women and the need to work for cures for maternal diseases and fetal abnormality.[3] A 1970 statement again described the antiabortion position not just as a Catholic position but one rooted in the U.S. Bill of Rights and the UN Declaration on the Rights of the Child. Again, the bishops committed themselves to seek solutions to the problems that lead some women to consider abortion.[4] James R. Kelly has described this as a "social work" approach to abortion, which does not raise questions about structures of society that contribute to abortion but seeks to provide help for pregnant women.[5]

THE 1970S

The bishops' involvement changed dramatically after the Supreme Court's January 22, 1973, *Roe v. Wade* decision, which came quite close to allowing abortion on demand. Cardinal John Krol, president of the National Conference of Catholic Bishops, condemned the decision as an unspeakable tragedy that involved both bad logic and bad law. By chance the newly formed bishops' ad hoc Committee on Pro-Life Activities met for the first time the following day and issued a statement advising people not to follow its reasoning or conclusions, while recommending every legal possibility to challenge the decision.[6] In a November 1973 statement at their annual meeting the bishops expressed their emphatic support for a constitutional amendment to protect the unborn.[7]

The bishops insisted that they were not trying to thrust their religious beliefs down the throats of others. In testimony to a Senate Judiciary Sub-Committee in 1974 Cardinal Krol emphasized that the right to life is not an invention of any church but a basic human right that should undergird any civilized society. In addition the bishops have a right as American citizens to advocate positions they believe to be for the good of the country. The bishops did not frame abortion as a Catholic issue, but defended their moral and pastoral obligation and their constitutional right as Americans to defend the right to life of the unborn.[8]

At their November 1975 meeting the bishops adopted a "Pastoral Plan for Pro-Life Activities."[9] This document raises an issue that the bishops have continued to struggle with—the relationship of abortion to other human rights and social issues. Is abortion the only issue, the most important issue, or one among other issues? Throughout the bishops have emphasized they are not interested in single-issue politics and support a broad range of issues, but at a minimum they have given more emphasis and more weight to abortion. Such is the case in this document. Internal consistency requires that the program extend to other life issues; but it is unlikely that efforts to protect other rights will be ultimately successful if life itself is continually diminished in value. In reality the plan deals only with abortion.

The plan involves three major efforts: an educational and informational program directed to the general public and also to the Catholic community to heighten public opposition to permissive abortion; a pastoral effort to meet the needs of pregnant women; a public policy effort to change the laws on abortion, aimed at a constitutional amendment providing "protection for the unborn child to the maximum degree possible." This last phrase is interesting because it recognizes the pragmatic aspect of feasibility because of which it might not be possible to achieve all that the bishops think is necessary.

The program is to be implemented on all levels of the Church—a state coordinating committee, the diocese, and the parish. But for the first and only time the bishops call for "an identifiable, tightly-knit, and well-organized pro-life unit," focused on passing a constitutional amendment, in every congressional district. They hasten to add—probably so as not to jeopardize the tax-exempt status of the Catholic Church—that this agency should not be operated, controlled, or financed by the Church.

Some bishops and staff members of the bishops' conference feared that the emphasis on abortion and explicitly the call for organized political activity in each congressional district was making the Church look like a single-issue voice, and would overshadow Church teachings on many other issues involving human rights and social justice. Bishop James Rausch, the general secretary of the bishops' conference, and his staff developed a document that was ultimately issued by the Administrative Board of the United States Catholic Conference before the 1976 presidential election.[10] "Political Responsibility: Reflections on an Election Year" explains the role of the Church in the political order.[11] The Church does not confuse its role with that of government but sees its mission as advocating the critical values of human rights and social justice. The Church carries on Jesus's mission of applying Gospel values to the contemporary world; its concern for human rights and social justice should be comprehensive and consistent.

In focusing on the upcoming election the bishops state that they do not seek the formation of a religious voting bloc, nor to instruct persons on how they should vote by endorsing candidates. Voters should examine the positions of candidates on the full range of issues—as well as the person's integrity, philosophy, and performance. The bishops then propose in alphabetical order eight issues, and emphasize that they are not the concern of Catholics alone: abortion, the economy, education, food policy, housing, human rights and foreign policy, mass media, and military expenditure. They describe the right to life as a basic human right that should have the protection of law, and call for a constitutional amendment to restore the right to life to the unborn. Note that no priority is given to any one of these issues.

Tensions and divisions thus existed among the bishops. Some gave priority to abortion, whereas others argued for a comprehensive and consistent approach to social issues and human rights. These differences would come to the fore in subsequent presidential elections. Also, every four years the bishops continued to publish their document on political responsibility, but with significant changes and developments.

Divisions over the priority of abortion became very public in the 1976 election campaigns. Timothy Byrnes, who has written the most in-depth work on Catholic bishops and American politics with a special focus on abortion, points out that religious commitments alone did not determine how bishops acted.[12] Political factors—especially a changing Catholic electorate and a changing American political scene in which the Democratic New Deal coalition was changing and more formerly Democratic Catholic voters shifted to the Republican Party—greatly influenced how bishops acted. Both Gerald Ford and Jimmy Carter wanted to attract the Catholic vote and sought good relations with and even some support from Catholic bishops.

In 1976 Archbishop Joseph L. Bernardin was president of the National Conference of Catholic Bishops (NCCB), and in that capacity attacked the Democratic platform supporting abortion rights as irresponsible, deeply disturbing, and seriously objectionable. Bernardin, while deferring other issues to future discussion, praised Republican opposition to abortion. Single-issue politics seemed to be replacing the need to consider a multiplicity of issues in a consistent manner.

Some maneuvering then took place behind the scenes by some in the bishops' conference and some Democrats to smooth over the problem. Eventually Carter asked for a meeting with the bishops' leadership. After some hesitation Bernardin announced that the NCCB executive committee would be willing to meet separately with both presidential candidates.

Carter thought he could reach some accommodation with the bishops because he too was morally opposed to abortion, but he was wrong. In no way were the bishops budging, and they asked Carter to change his position. At a press conference after the meeting with Carter, Bernardin reported that after an extensive conversation on abortion the bishops continued to be "disappointed" with Carter's position on the issue. At a press conference after the meeting with Ford, Bernardin reported that the bishops were encouraged by

Ford's support for a constitutional amendment. The media concluded that the bishops tacitly or implicitly supported Ford. Bernardin insisted then and later that he had not meant to endorse Ford and that his comments were misunderstood. But in reality they had given the impression to many that abortion was the top issue. A few years later, however, Bernardin took the lead in developing what he called a consistent ethic of life embracing all the life issues.

THE 1980s

In October 1979, the administrative board of the USCC, in anticipation of the 1980 election, reissued the document on political responsibility. A few more points were added but all the material cited above in the 1976 document was repeated.[13] But in 1980 the bishops changed their tactics. There were no public responses to the Democratic and Republican platforms and no meetings with presidential candidates. Jerry Falwell had formed the Moral Majority to work for family values and politically conservative positions. Conservative politicians saw the new Religious Right as significant support for the Republican Party. The Catholic bishops had no direct role in forming the new Religious Right headed by fundamentalists and some conservative evangelical Protestants, but they had been the first religious group to support the right to life. The public media gave little attention to the bishops' opposition to abortion in the 1980 presidential election.[14]

Before 1981 U.S. bishops had called for a constitutional amendment to protect the unborn, but they never spelled out the exact wording of that amendment. In 1981 discussions centered on a number of possible amendments. Recall that the support for an amendment even in the 1975 Pro-Life Plan recognized the criterion of the feasibility of passing an amendment. In 1981 Archbishop John Roach, president of NCCB, and Cardinal Terence Cooke, chair of the Pro-Life Committee, testified before Congress in support of the Hatch Amendment. Other possible amendments basically proposed a repeal of the *Roe v. Wade* decision. The Hatch Amendment authorized the possibility of both congressional and state legislation restricting abortion, but it would not in itself ban abortion. Archbishop Roach in his testimony recognized that the possibility of passing the amendment was a factor in the bishops' support of it.[15] Some within the pro-life movement, including some Catholics, accused the bishops of giving into political expediency rather than fighting to repeal *Roe v. Wade*.[16]

In the early 1980s the bishops turned their attention to other social issues, first to peace, war, and deterrence, and then to the economy. They issued two pastoral letters on these issues that were critical of U.S. policy and received great attention in the public media.[17] However, in the 1980s abortion remained a highly visible issue. In 1984 the administrative board of USCC again issued their statement on political responsibility in anticipation of the election. The basic thrust of the document was the same as the previous one, but there were two changes in the parts that were quoted above. The 1984 document dropped the paragraph including the sentence that the Church's concern for social justice should be comprehensive and consistent. Under abortion the right to life was now described as "the most basic human right" rather than "a basic human right."[18]

The bigger picture, however, indicated many bishops were embracing a comprehensive and consistent approach to life issues. The main figure and leader of this movement was Cardinal Bernardin. Bernardin had been the first general secretary of the bishops' conference (1968–72), president of the conference (1974–77), and chair of the committee that wrote the pastoral letter on peace, war, and deterrence. In 1983 he became the chairman of the Committee for Pro-Life Activities with the intention of promoting a consistent ethic of life. At the end of 1983 Bernardin gave the Gannon Lecture at Fordham University, in which he first developed his approach to a consistent ethic of life. He gave nine subsequent lectures developing this idea over the next three years. In the Fordham lecture he asserted that war and abortion are not two discrete issues but are intimately connected. The principles of Catholic moral teaching are rooted in the dignity of the human person and the principles based on this anthropology apply across the board to all life issues. Of course, Bernardin was very conscious of what had occurred in 1976. The obvious intention was to prevent any politician or political party from hijacking the bishops' approach to life issues and using it to claim the Catholic vote for one party or another. Obviously the Catholic position on abortion was consonant with the position of the Republican Party, but many of the other issues of peace, the economy, and social justice were clearly in line with Democratic positions.[19]

The 1984 election, however, showed that Catholic bishops were still divided on this issue, and some influential bishops did not agree with Bernardin's approach. Walter Mondale, the Democratic presidential candidate, selected Geraldine Ferraro as his running mate, expecting that a Catholic woman from the Northeast would be a significant help in the election. In the beginning her selection seemed to spark the Democratic campaign, but that did not last long. Questions were raised about her husband's finances and also about her position as a Catholic in supporting the *Roe v. Wade* decision. Catholic bishops publicly challenged her position.[20]

Even before the Ferraro nomination, the issue of Catholic politicians and abortion had come to the public's attention. At a press conference on June 24, 1984, the newly installed Archbishop of New York, John J. O'Connor, said in the context of a question about Governor Mario Cuomo's support for abortion funding that in his personal opinion he could not see how a Catholic in conscience could vote for an individual favoring abortion. This set off a long public debate between the archbishop and the Catholic governor. On September 13 Governor Cuomo gave a public lecture at the University of Notre Dame defending his position as a Catholic on abortion legislation and funding.[21]

In September O'Connor also publicly criticized Geraldine Ferraro and Catholic politicians like her who said they were personally opposed to abortion but still supported public legislation permitting and even funding abortions. O'Connor and Ferraro continued their public dispute over the issues. The fact that all this occurred in New York City, the media capital of the world, made it a very public controversy. The New York controversy was not the only public controversy involving a prominent Catholic bishop and Catholic politicians who did not support laws against abortion. Archbishop Bernard Law of Boston, at a September 4, 1984, news conference, released to the press a statement by eighteen New England bishops calling abortion the critical issue of the moment and criticizing Catholic politicians who said they were morally opposed to abortion but would not make their personal moral positions into law. Later that month Law maintained that Congresswoman Ferraro, Senator Ted Kennedy of Massachusetts, and Governor Cuomo were wrong to argue that Catholic politicians could support free choice as a legal policy while personally opposing abortion.[22] Thus, the 1984 political campaign saw a public debate between very prominent Catholic bishops and some prominent Catholic politicians over the issue of legalized abortion.

On November 14, 1985, the bishops' conference revised the 1975 Pastoral Plan for Pro-Life Activities and reaffirmed its central message. The three-pronged program of education, pastoral care, and public policy remained. The pro-life effort in every congressional district dedicated to passage of a constitutional amendment protecting the unborn was basically the same as in the original but the original twelve objectives of the program were reduced to three in support of the effective legal protection of human life beginning at conception. The introductory material shows some tension between the primacy of abortion and a consistent ethic of life. The pastoral plan focuses on the threat to life arising from abortion, but this focus and the Church's commitment to a consistent ethic of life complement each other. One notices here the influence of Bernardin's emphasis on the consistent ethic of life. This consistent ethic of life does not diminish concern for abortion but recognizes that different life issues are linked in principle because they involve the intrinsic dignity of human life. Because these issues are interdependent, a society that permits abortion undermines respect for life in all other contexts. Among the many important issues involving the dignity of human life with which the Church is concerned, abortion necessarily plays a central role. As a consequence this document focuses only on abortion.[23]

The 1988 "Political Responsibility" statement from the Administrative Board of the USCC incorporates two significant changes. The paragraph describing what the bishops do and do not want to do repeats the intention not to seek the formation of a religious voting bloc, and not to instruct persons on how to vote by endorsing candidates. However, obviously in light of 1984 events, they add the phrase "or opposing candidates." They repeat their earlier position that voters should examine candidates on the full range of issues as well as personal integrity, philosophy, and performance, and go on to maintain that a consistent ethic of life should be the moral framework from which to address all issues in the political arena. They address a spectrum of issues seeking to protect human life and promote human dignity from the inception of life to the final moment.[24]

In the 1980s bishops spoke out publicly and forcefully on peace and the economy, proposing positions much more in keeping with those of the Democratic Party but still insistently calling for legal protection for the fetus. In the 1988 election the bishops in general and individual bishops (with the exception of Archbishop John Whealon of Hartford) did not make abortion a central topic in the public media. As Byrnes points out, neither Republicans nor Democrats appealed to the U.S. bishops, and the campaigns were run without much attention to social justice issues or to abortion. Thus, neither the bishops nor the political parties apparently wanted to be involved in public debate about the bishops' position on abortion. The fact that none of the candidates, especially on the Democratic ticket, was a pro-choice Catholic also influenced the bishops' media silence on the abortion issue.[25]

A unanimous 1989 resolution of the bishops on abortion signaled a shift away from the consistent ethic of life to the strong primacy of abortion: No Catholic can responsibly take a pro-choice stand when the choice in question involves the taking of innocent human life. The resolution calls on Catholics to vigorously implement all three parts of the Pastoral Plan republished in 1985. The bishops urge Catholic public officials to advance the goals of the Pastoral Plan in recognition of their responsibility to protect and promote the rights of the most defenseless among us.[26]

THE 1990S

In their statements on "Political Responsibility" for the 1992 and 1996 elections, the bishops repeat their intention not to form a religious voting bloc or to endorse or oppose candidates. They urge Catholics to consider candidates on the full range of issues in the light of a moral framework of a consistent ethic of life. Abortion, however, is described as the fundamental human rights issue of our day.[27]

The bishops' involvement in the 1992 and 1996 presidential elections on the issue of abortion received scant attention in the public media. There were no Catholics running for the presidency or vice presidency in either of the two major parties. Also, in 1996, the Republicans under Bob Dole advocated a big-tent approach to the issue of abortion.[28]

However, the bishops were very active in public in other areas. The bishops staged an unprecedented press conference and prayer service with all the American cardinals on the steps of the Capitol urging an override of President Clinton's veto of the bill banning partial-birth abortion.[29] Cardinal O'Connor did not invite President Clinton to the Al Smith dinner in 1996. Traditionally both presidential candidates are invited to this dinner, presided over by the Archbishop of New York and raising funds for charity. In 1996 the vice presidential candidates were invited instead.[30] In some dioceses, including Washington, D.C., postcards urging legislators to overturn Clinton's veto of the ban on partial-birth abortion were passed out in churches, then collected by ushers and mailed. In addition a number of bishops sent out instructions that Catholic institutions were not to honor pro-choice politicians or allow them to speak on Catholic premises.[31]

At their semiannual meeting in November 1998, the U.S. bishops overwhelmingly approved and issued "Living the Gospel of Life," urging Catholics to make the fight against abortion and euthanasia a priority in their public life. This was a somewhat lengthy and in-depth statement of their views that abortion and euthanasia are preeminent threats to human dignity because they directly attack life itself—the most fundamental human good, and the condition for all other rights (n. 5).[32] The cry for all other rights is illusory if the right to life, the most basic and fundamental right and the condition of all other personal rights, is not defended with maximum determination (n. 19).

The document explicitly mentions "the consistent ethic of life" but gives it a new interpretation that goes against the meaning originally proposed by Bernardin. The consistent ethic of life means that opposition to abortion and euthanasia does not excuse indifference to those who suffer from poverty, violence, and injustice. But being "right" in all these other areas—including racism, poverty, employment, education, housing, health care, and capital punishment—can never excuse a wrong choice regarding direct attacks on innocent human life. The failure to protect and defend life in its most vulnerable stages renders suspect any claim to "rightness" in other matters affecting the poorest and least powerful among us. Direct attack on innocent human life attacks the very foundation of the house, whose crossbeams and walls are the other rights. One cannot build a house of rights on sand but only on the strong foundation of the basic right to life of all (n. 23). The document frequently cites John Paul II's 1995 encyclical *Evangelium vitae*—the Gospel of Life. But the bishops take great pains to show that their position is not a sectarian one based only on religious beliefs, but is also based on reason, science, and fundamental American values enshrined in our culture and history (nn. 13–20).

As bishops and chief teachers in the church their pastoral ministry calls them to explain, persuade, correct, and admonish Catholic public officials who contradict the Gospel of Life through their actions and policies. A private call to conversion and change should obviously be the first step taken by the bishops with regard to these Catholic political leaders. Unfortunately, some Catholic officials might refuse to change, but the bishops always have the duty and responsibility to challenge such officials on these issues (n. 29). No public official claiming to be Catholic can responsibly advocate for or actively support direct attacks on innocent human life. The bishops recognize and cite Pope John Paul II to the effect that sometimes it is impossible to overturn or prevent passage of a law that allows or permits moral evil. In such cases a Catholic politician whose position in favor of life is well known could seek to limit the harm done by the law. But nothing justifies a public official's not defending life to the greatest extent possible (n. 32).

The document strongly objects to the arguments of some Catholic politicians that they personally oppose abortion but cannot force their religious views on others. First, beginning of human life is not a religious belief but a scientific fact. Second, the sanctity of human life is not only Catholic teaching but part of humanity's global inheritance. Third, no one would accept the argument that one is personally opposed to slavery or racism or sexism, but one cannot force one's personal view on society at large (n. 24).

What explains the demise of the consistent ethic of life and the acceptance of abortion as the primary and fundamental public policy issue for the bishops? First, Pope John Paul II frequently insisted on the need for laws that oppose abortion in many venues, especially his 1995 encyclical *Evangelium vitae*. The bishops' 1998 document is basically an application of *Evangelium vitae* to the

U.S. milieu. According to John Paul II, civil law must support and guarantee certain fundamental human rights which belong to all persons. First and foremost among these is the inviolable right to life of every innocent human being.[33] Laws that legitimize the direct killing of innocent human beings through abortion and euthanasia stand in complete opposition to the inviolable right to life proper to every individual, and thus deny the equality of everyone before the law. Civil law must be in conformity with moral law. A civil law opposed to natural law is not really a law but the corruption of law (nn. 72–73).

Evangelium vitae also directly refutes some of the arguments proposed in defense of laws permitting abortion—unenforceability, the danger of illegal and medically harmful abortions, human autonomy and freedom, that the life of the unborn is only a relative good, and the lack of a consensus on abortion in our society and the consequent need to follow the position of the majority of citizens (nn. 68–69). Behind all these tendencies lies the ethical relativism so prevalent in contemporary culture. Some maintain such relativism is an essential condition of democracy with the purpose of guaranteeing tolerance, mutual respect among people, and the acceptance of the decisions of the majority. But democracy is a system—a means to an end. Democracy's moral value is not automatic but depends on conformity to moral law. The values of democracy stand or fall by the values it embodies and promotes. The basis of these values is not just majority consensus but the objective law, which is natural law written on the human heart (n. 70).

Second, the composition of the bishops' conference and the type of men made bishops were changing. Cardinal Bernardin died in 1996 and his moderating leadership was absent in the conference. In a very true sense the consistent ethic of life died with him. Cardinals O'Connor of New York and Law of Boston had never really accepted the consistent ethic of life, and they now had more influence in the conference of bishops. In addition, John Paul II had appointed conservative bishops who were eager to pursue his ideas and put them into practice. The times, the individual bishops, and the bishops' conference had changed quite a bit since the 1980s.

Third, many strongly antiabortion Catholics have at times been critical of the bishops for being too timid on the abortion issue. Recall the negative reaction of some Catholics to the bishops' support of the Hatch Amendment, which would fall short of making all abortions illegal. Especially in the existing Church climate, individual bishops and the bishops as a whole did not want to be accused of being soft on abortion.

Fourth, the 1998 document focuses almost entirely on abortion (and to an extent on euthanasia), and this approach constitutes the perspective that the bishops took in writing it. A document focusing on voting for candidates in an election stems from a different horizon or perspective. In addressing Catholic voters, bishops do not want to create a religious voting bloc or to endorse or oppose particular candidates, lest they lose their tax-exempt status by engaging in partisan politics.[34] The perspective of addressing Catholic voters is more conducive to a consistent ethic of life approach.

THE 2000 AND 2004 ELECTIONS

In this context, the document on the 2000 elections from the bishops is enlightening. Despite the 1998 "Living the Gospel of Life," the 2000 document on voting repeats exactly what had been said previously about forming no religious voting bloc, neither endorsing nor opposing individual candidates, and using a consistent ethic of life framework to judge candidates on the full range of issues. The document does cite the 1998 "Living the Gospel of Life" on the issue of abortion and describes abortion and euthanasia as the preeminent threats to human life.[35]

The bishops' reactions to Catholic politicians supporting pro-choice legislation came up again in the 2000 presidential election but not to the same extent as in 1976 and 1984. Some influential bishops, including Cardinals Bernard Law of Boston and Edward Egan of New York, emphasized the centrality and importance of the abortion issue. Many people saw their declarations and actions (e.g., photo ops with the Republican candidate) as a sign of their support for the Republican candidate.[36]

In 2001, U.S. Bishops reissued the "Pastoral Plan for Pro-Life Activities" first published in 1975 and again in 1985. The theoretical portion of the new document frequently cites the 1998 "Living the Gospel of Life" and closely follows the primacy given to abortion and the taking of innocent human life, together with the newer understanding of the consistent ethic of life found in that document. Being "right" in other areas of social justice, poverty, and peace can never excuse direct attacks on innocent human life. The document reiterates that no public official, especially a faithful Catholic, can responsibly advocate for or actively support direct attacks on innocent human life. The practical pastoral program outlined is substantially the same as in earlier versions of this plan.[37]

The reaction of U.S. bishops individually and collectively to pro-choice political candidates reached another peak in connection with the 2004 presidential election. The fact that the Democratic candidate, John F. Kerry, was a "pro-choice Catholic senator" ensured the issue would get great publicity, but even before Kerry was nominated this issue came to the fore. Once again the Administrative Board of the USCCB issued their document on faithful citizenship and political responsibility, once again basically the same as the one released before the previous presidential election.[38]

Even before the reissuance of the statement on "Faithful Citizenship," the bishops had already begun to address a new aspect of the abortion question. Some bishops declared that pro-choice Catholic politicians should not receive communion and they should be refused communion if they present themselves. One bishop invoked canon law to restrict pro-choice Catholic politicians from receiving communion unless they publicly changed their position.[39] In September 2003, the bishops set up a "Task Force on Catholic Bishops and Catholic Politicians" headed by Cardinal Theodore McCarrick of Washington and made up of the chairmen of the bishops' public policy committees and the doctrinal committee. This was a blue-ribbon committee to discuss the relationship of bishops and Catholic politicians. The committee made an interim report to the bishops at their June 2004 meeting. The bishops then adopted—by a 183–6 vote—a statement on the issue: that killing an unborn child is intrinsically evil and to make such intrinsically evil actions legal is wrong. The bishops counsel Catholic politicians that consistently supporting abortion on demand risks making them cooperators in evil in a public manner. The Catholic community and Catholic institutions should not honor such politicians or provide them with a platform. The bishops commit themselves to continue to teach, to persuade, and to act in support of their principles in public life, and to maintain communication with public officials. With regard to the question of denying communion to pro-choice Catholic politicians, the bishops punt: "Given the wide range of circumstances involved in arriving at a prudential judgment on a matter of this seriousness, we recognize that such decisions rest with the individual bishop in accord with established canonical and pastoral principles." Individual bishops could thus legitimately come to different conclusions on this issue.[40] It is somewhat paradoxical that the bishops' conference recognized the prudential nature of the judgment that a bishop had to make about denying communion but did not recognize that prudential aspects might influence Catholic legislators to come to different positions on abortion legislation.

The bishops could not agree on a common policy, but the interim report of the task force itself did not advocate the denial of communion for Catholic politicians or Catholic voters in these circumstances. Not wishing to trivialize the Eucharist or make it into a partisan political battleground, they urge persuasion and not penalties.[41] Of the seventy bishops who responded to the task force's request for input, a three-to-one majority opposed refusing communion.[42] The weakness of the bishops' conference itself and the lack of consensus among the bishops were evident.

Two aspects of the task force's work deserve mention. In a letter to the chair of the task force, forty-eight Catholic Democratic congresspersons, some of whom had a pro-life voting record, firmly opposed bishops' denial of communion on the basis of a voting record.[43] In making his report to the bishops, Cardinal McCarrick also pointed out that he had communicated on a number of occasions with Cardinal Joseph Ratzinger, then head of the Congregation for the Doctrine of the Faith, and that the cardinal left to the U.S. bishops prudential judgment on denying communion to pro-choice Catholic politicians. Someone leaked to the press the six principles that Ratzinger had sent to McCarrick indicating that one could and should on some occasions deny communion to such politicians. Some Catholic conservatives claimed that McCarrick had misled the bishops about Ratzinger's position. McCarrick responded that he had a number of exchanges with Ratzinger and stood by his original statement about Ratzinger's positions. On July 9 at McCarrick's behest, Ratzinger sent a letter stating that the bishops' statement in Denver was "very much in harmony" with his position.[44]

Differences of opinion persisted after the June 2004 bishops' meeting. Three bishops of the five dioceses in the metropolitan jurisdiction of Atlanta said that politicians who consistently support pro-abortion legislation should not be admitted to communion. But the bishop of Raleigh, North Carolina—one of the five dioceses in the Atlanta metropolitan jurisdiction—insisted there is a longstanding practice of not making a public judgment about the state of those who present themselves to receive communion.[45]

The task force continued its work after the 2004 election, including further dialogue with politicians especially in Congress. In February 2006 fifty-five Catholic Democratic congresspersons issued a "Statement of Principles" expressing their commitment to the principles of Catholic social teaching. The signatories are committed to reducing the number of unwanted pregnancies and to encouraging that pregnancies be carried to term. They agree about the undesirability of abortion and do not celebrate its practice, but they say nothing about support for pro-choice legislation. The task force officially ceased to function on June 15, 2006, insisting that there is no substitute for the local bishop's prudential judgment.[46]

THE 2008 ELECTION

In the last decade of the twentieth century and the first decade of the twenty-first, the trajectory of the U.S. bishops' position has moved to make abortion the primary and most important social issue facing voters. Their document preparing voters for the 2008 presidential election, "Forming Consciences for Faithful Citizenship," differs markedly both in length and in substance from the previous documents that had been issued every four years since 1976.[47] In the Catholic tradition intrinsically evil acts are always opposed to the authentic good of persons and must always be rejected and opposed—never tolerated or condoned. The intentional taking of human life—as in abortion and euthanasia—is an intrinsically evil act, and a legal system that violates the basic right to life is fundamentally flawed (8, n. 22).

This document again appeals to the consistent ethic of life, which, if rightly understood, provides a framework for a principled Catholic involvement in political life (12, n. 40). But it defines the consistent ethic of life in accord with the 1998 "Living the Gospel of Life" and thus differs from the earlier statements. The consistent ethic of life eliminates the two extremes of treating all issues as morally equivalent and also the extreme of reducing the Catholic approach to only one or two issues (12, n. 40): "The direct and intentional destruction of innocent human life . . . is always wrong and is not just one issue among many. It must always be opposed" (9, n. 28). But one cannot ignore other threats to human life and dignity—racism and discrimination, the death penalty, unjust wars, torture, poverty, health care, and immigration all involve serious moral challenges. In these areas prudential judgments are needed to apply specific principles to particular issues. The applications of principles and prudential judgments made by the bishops do not have the same moral authority as statements of universal moral teachings, but Catholics should still listen carefully to them (10–11, n. 33). These issues all involve prudential judgments and the specific acts involved are not intrinsically evil, as in the case of direct abortion or euthanasia.

There is some tension in the document. The bishops insist that Catholics are not single-issue voters. A candidate's position on a single issue is not sufficient to guarantee a voter's support. Yet a candidate's position on a single issue that involves an intrinsic evil, such as support for illegal abortion or racism, may legitimately lead a voter to reject a candidate (13, n. 42). In other words, it is legitimate but not necessary for a Catholic to vote against a candidate who does not work to overcome existing abortion laws.

The bishops employ some casuistry in their document. The Catholic voter cannot vote for a candidate who favors an intrinsic evil if the voter's intention is to support that position. But a Catholic who rejects a candidate's unacceptable position may decide to vote for that candidate for "other morally grave reasons" (11, nn. 34–35).

The 2008 election saw in an ever more intensive way the approaches of Catholic bishops that had been taken in the last four presidential elections. First, a number of Catholic bishops publicly mentioned that abortion was the most important issue in the campaign. Rocco Palmo wrote in the October 25, 2008, *Tablet* that some 50 of the nation's 197 active bishops publicly mentioned abortion as the key issue on which voters should determine their votes. Archbishop Charles Chaput of Denver called Barack Obama "the most committed abortion-rights presidential candidate of either party since the *Roe v. Wade* decision."[48] Chaput himself wrote a book on the role of Catholics in political life.[49] The Catholic News Agency—in a November 17, 2008, article—quoted the American Cardinal James Francis Stafford, head of the Vatican's Apostolic Penitentiary, criticizing Obama's rhetoric on abortion as "aggressive, disruptive, and apocalyptic." Obama had campaigned "on an extremist anti-life platform."[50]

Second, the issue of barring pro-choice Catholic politicians from receiving communion also came up regarding Democratic candidate for vice president, Joseph Biden, who is a Catholic. Biden was born and raised in Scranton, Pennsylvania. Bishop Joseph F. Martino of Scranton publicly stated that Biden and other Catholic politicians who support the culture of death should not receive communion. However, Bishop W. Francis Malooly, of Biden's home diocese of Wilmington, Delaware, said he would not ask Biden to refrain from receiving communion because he does not want to politicize the Eucharist; he would prefer to talk to Biden and try to convince him to change his position.[51]

Third, there were public statements by the chairmen of the bishops' Committees on Pro-Life and Doctrine disagreeing with the public statements of two Catholic politicians on abortion. On the August 24, 2008, *Meet the Press*, Nancy Pelosi, the Democratic Speaker of the House of Representatives, described herself as an ardent Catholic who had studied the abortion issue, and concluded that the doctors of the church such as St. Augustine have not been able to determine when human life begins, and that should not affect the woman's right to choose. Cardinal Justin Rigali and Bishop William Lori, in their capacity as chairs of two important bishops' committees, publicly responded that from the first century the church had condemned abortion. There were disputes about later animation in the Middle Ages, but modern scientific knowledge of life beginning with the union of sperm and egg makes the older biological theory obsolete. In keeping with this modern understanding, the church teaches that from the time of conception (fertilization), each member of the human species must be given the full respect due to a human person. Later Pelosi's spokesperson issued a statement quoting Augustine but adding that the Catholic teaching is clear that life begins at conception. However, many Catholics do not subscribe to that view.[52]

Note that Pelosi was correct on the debates about later animation but incorrectly implied that the Catholic tradition had allowed abortions for this reason. The two bishops, however, failed to recognize that many disagree on the scientific judgment concerning the beginning of personal life, and somewhat overstated the Catholic position. In their judgment, contemporary biological knowledge might have made the older position about delayed animation obsolete, but there is still a philosophical argument in favor of delayed animation. Catholic teaching even today recognizes the existence of some theoretical doubt about when human life begins. The two bishops implicitly recognized this fact when they stated that from conception the being "must be given the full respect due to a human person." They did not say that it is definitely a human person.

Senator Biden appeared on *Meet the Press* on September 7, 2008, and was asked about abortion. He replied that he accepted on faith the Catholic teaching that human life begins at conception and that Catholics and others who hold that position should not be required to subsidize abortion with their taxes. But, he said, his position on the beginning of human life is a personal and private matter of faith that he could not impose on others. Cardinal Rigali and Bishop Lori responded that Biden correctly expressed Catholic teaching, but strongly disagreed that this position is personal and private and should not be imposed on others.[53]

In January 2009 the U.S. Catholic bishops publicly committed themselves to work constructively with the new Obama administration, but issued a tough challenge on life issues. The bishops will work to protect the lives of the most vulnerable and weakest members of the human family, especially unborn children, and will oppose any attempts to expand abortion.[54] The University of Notre Dame invited President Obama to give the May 2009 graduation address. Over eighty bishops, including Cardinal Francis George of Chicago, the president of the conference of bishops, publicly disapproved of Notre Dame's action.[55]

What effect did the public positions of the bishops have on Catholic voters? According to an article published in the November 7, 2008, issue of the *Washington Times*, Catholics voted for Obama over McCain by a nine-point margin (54 percent versus 45 percent) which was a turnaround from the 2004 election when Catholic voters supported Bush by a five-point margin (52 percent to 47 percent).[56]

The position of Catholic bishops on the legal and public policy aspects of abortion has galvanized over the years. In the 1980s especially, many bishops defended a consistent ethic of life, recognizing a number of life issues that did not take priority over another. Today the bishops clearly say that abortion, which is intrinsically wrong, is the primary political and social issue. Other threats to human life and dignity (e.g., poverty, violence, and injustice) all involve serious moral issues, but they are not of primary importance and involve prudential judgments, so Catholics cannot claim certainty on these issues. The consistent ethic of life is now interpreted to recognize the primacy of abortion but also the need to respond to other challenges. On the basis of this understanding, the bishops have developed a casuistry for Catholic politician and voter behavior.

ANALYSIS AND CRITICISM

The U.S. bishops' present position on abortion involves many different facets. This section limits itself to defending the position that the bishops have claimed too much certitude in their position on abortion law and have failed to recognize that other Catholics may legitimately hold other positions. The last chapter maintains bishops could, and at times should, speak out on specific policy issues but they must recognize that on such complex issues they cannot claim certitude, and that other Catholics may disagree with them. But the bishops themselves maintain that such is not the case for abortion because it deals with a matter of principle and an intrinsically evil act—not just a prudential judgment. My claim is that the issue of abortion law does involve prudential judgments and hence Catholics can take positions different from that of the bishops.

Speculative Doubt

From the perspective of the hierarchical moral teaching on abortion there is more doubt and uncertainty than the bishops have publicly recognized. Is the fetus a human person? In traditional terminology the question is this: When is the soul infused into the body? Gerald Kelly, a well respected pre–Vatican II theologian who strongly upheld all the teachings of the hierarchical magisterium on medical ethics, notes that in answering the question one must distinguish the realm of the speculative from the realm of the practical. In the sphere of the speculative there are two theories, each backed by representative Catholic philosophers and theologians. Thomas Aquinas is the best known theologian to defend delayed animation, which was the commonly held theory for a very long time, but was to some extent abandoned. According to Kelly (1958) many philosophers still hold this position. The view that the soul is infused at the moment of fertilization also has many supporters. Catholics are still free to speculate about this. But in the practical order we must follow the safer course of action and always treat a fertilized ovum at any stage of development as a human person.[57]

Kelly supports his position by citing the 1951 address of Pope Pius XII: "Whatever foundation there may be for the distinction between these various phases of the development of life that is born or still unborn, in profane and ecclesiastical law, and as regards certain civil and penal consequences, all these cases involve a grave and unlawful attack upon the inviolability of human life." Kelly comments that the words of the pope do not condemn the speculative position that the rational soul is not infused at the moment of fertilization, although they seem to favor the opposite view.[58]

The 1974 Declaration on Procured Abortion by the Congregation for the Doctrine of the Faith explicitly acknowledges speculative doubt, and purposely leaves aside the question of the moment when the spiritual soul is infused: "There is not a unanimous tradition on this point and authors are as yet in disagreement." This is a philosophical problem. It suffices that the presence of the soul be probable because one cannot take the risk of killing a human person.[59] In *Evangelium vitae*, John Paul II recognizes the speculative doubt. From the standpoint of moral obligation the mere probability that a human person is involved would suffice to justify an absolutely clear prohibition of an attack aimed at killing the embryo. The magisterium has not committed itself on the philosophical question of when the soul is infused, but has taught that the result of human procreation from the first moment of its existence must be regarded and treated as a person.[60]

Three practical consequences follow from this speculative discussion in Catholic theology. First, Catholics have to be careful not to apodictically claim that abortion, even of an early embryo, is murder. In its own understanding the Catholic tradition cannot be certain about that judgment. Second, some Catholics disagree with the hierarchical teaching on abortion precisely because they do not believe that the fetus, especially in the early stages of development, is a truly human person. Some respected U.S. Catholic theologians—such as Lisa Cahill of Boston College, Margaret Farley, emerita of Yale, Christine Gudorf of Florida International, Daniel Maguire of Marquette, Jean Porter of Notre Dame, and Thomas Shannon, emeritus of Worcester Polytechnic Institute—maintain in practice that the early fetus is not a human person.[61] Cahill's position is quite nuanced. She does not hold that a human person is present from fertilization but she still insists that the early embryo and fetus have significant value and worth. She worries that some who hold similar positions of delayed animation do not give enough value to the fetus before animation occurs.[62] This is not the place to treat in an in-depth manner discussion of when the soul is infused or the question of when a truly individual human person begins to exist; and many Catholic theologians do not differ that much from the hierarchical teaching. Third, recognition of the difficulty of claiming certitude about when personal life begins calls for respect for those who disagree with hierarchical Catholic teaching. They are not necessarily hard-hearted people or ethical relativists.

Different Understandings of Law

Chapter 7 discusses the Thomistic and the religious freedom approaches to the role of law in the Catholic tradition today. There is no doubt that U.S. bishops have based their position on abortion law on the Thomistic approach; direct abortion is morally wrong not on the basis of distinctive Catholic theology but on that of natural law and human reason. Civil law must condemn abortion precisely because civil law can never approve or allow what the natural law condemns.

The religious freedom approach does not begin with natural law but with the recognition that the freedom of the person must be respected as far as possible and curtailed only when and insofar as necessary. In light of this, the pro-choice position is not the same as the pro-abortion position. The bishops' too ready identification of pro-choice as pro-abortion is somewhat consonant with the Thomistic approach to civil law, but it cannot be made on the basis of the religious freedom approach.

Antidrug laws help illustrate the difference. The Thomistic approach would argue that hard drugs are harmful to the person and to society as based on human reason and natural law; consequently, civil law must make the use and sale of such drugs a criminal offense. But some theorists, including well-known political conservative and Catholic William F. Buckley, argued in favor of the decriminalization of drugs. Decriminalization would create fewer problems than present laws prohibiting drugs. Buckley was not in favor of drug use, but decriminalization would be a lesser evil than the present war on drugs.[63] Buckley did not use the religious freedom approach to law in his discussion, but one could make the argument for decriminalization on that basis.

To support the freedom of a person does not necessarily involve the approval of what the person does with that freedom. The best theological illustration of this is that God has given us our freedom, which also occasions our sin. But God is not pro-sin! Although some people are pro-choice precisely because they are proabortion, conceptually pro-choice and proabortion are not the same thing; many pro-choice people object to being called proabortion. Many see abortion as tragic but still respect the freedom of the woman to make the decision.

The best practical example of the difference between pro-choice and pro-abortion is the positions of James R. Kelly and Douglas Kmiec described in chapter 6.[64] The two Catholics support the pro-choice position precisely because they are opposed to abortion, and make the prudential judgment that it is not feasible to change *Roe v. Wade*. A truly pro-choice position gives every woman what she needs to make a truly free choice, and would strive to over-come the conditions of poverty that prevent some poor women from having and raising a child. A pro-choice position would actually cut down on the number of abortions that take place in our country.

The religious freedom approach to law recognizes the difference between being pro-choice and proabortion, but this approach can still be used to justify a law prohibiting abortion. Accordingly, law must intervene to protect and promote the public order, which includes an order of justice. Justice requires that the law protect the right to life of all human beings. The fetus is the most vulnerable and defenseless of human beings—all the more reason the law should protect it. However, it is possible for someone who holds that the fetus is a truly human person to use the religious freedom approach to argue against trying to overturn *Roe v. Wade*. We live in a pluralistic society that is sharply divided on the issue of abortion law, and in light of this one should follow the presumption in favor of the freedom of the individual. Catholics can apply the religious freedom approach to come to different conclusions about abortion laws, but neither side can claim absolute certitude for its position. Both are legitimate Catholic positions.

Feasibility, Intrinsic Evil, and Advocacy

Law in a democratic society needs to be based on consensus. Lawmaking is not a clean and orderly process: an old adage maintains that the two things one should not see made are sausage and laws! The consensus on which law is based often requires compromise on the part of different groups of citizens and legislators. At times an individual must make a judgment on whether half a loaf is better than none. Feasibility is a significant consideration in determining what to do with respect to law.

The feasibility argument is applicable to both the religious freedom approach and the Thomistic approach. It involves a prudential judgment: Is it possible to overturn *Roe v. Wade*? Recall that the 1975 Pastoral Plan for Pro-Life Activities acknowledges a feasibility criterion in its call for protection for the unborn child to the maximum degree possible.[65] The president of the bishops' conference in 1981 testified before Congress in support of the Hatch Amendment that did not attempt to repeal *Roe v. Wade* but would remit the question of abortion to Congress and the states, and mentioned that the possibility of passing the Hatch Amendment was reason to support it.[66] Today there is strong evidence of the impossibility of passing a constitutional amendment repealing *Roe v. Wade*. Even if one could pass an amendment leaving abortion legislation up to the states, most large states would probably support something quite similar to the position of *Roe v. Wade*.

The U.S. bishops introduced a new argument in their position on abortion law in the first decade of the twenty-first century. The bishops had always recognized that prudential judgments or the application of principles are areas in which there can be no certitude about one's position and hence there must be room for different positions within the Church. When bishops teach in these areas their positions do not carry the same authority as those on principles or universal Church teaching. Now they seek to demonstrate that their position on abortion laws does not involve the prudential judgments that are involved in specific policy issues such as the justice of a particular war, housing, health care, immigration, and other such issues. Abortion is different precisely because abortion involves an intrinsically evil act—one that is always and everywhere wrong: "There are some things we must never do, as individuals or as a society, because they are always incompatible with love of God and neighbor. Such actions are so deeply flawed that they are always opposed to the authentic good of persons. These are called 'intrinsically evil' actions. They must always be rejected and opposed and must never be supported or condoned. A prime example is the intentional taking of innocent human life, as in abortion and euthanasia."[67] This is a poor argument.

Pope Pius XI condemns artificial contraception for spouses as intrinsically evil: "But no reason, however grave, may be put forward by which anything intrinsically against nature may become conformable to nature and morally good. Since, therefore, the conjugal act is destined primarily by nature for the begetting of children, those who in exercising it deliberately frustrate its natural power and purpose sin against nature and commit a deed which is shameful and intrinsically vicious."[68] Hieronymus Noldin, a German Jesuit whose text-book was often used in the pre-Vatican II seminaries in the United States, notes that artificial contraception for spouses is prohibited by the natural law and is intrinsically evil.[69] By the force of their own arguments about intrinsic evil, the bishops then logically would have to hold that a society must never accept artificial contraception for spouses since it is intrinsically evil. The concept of intrinsic evil does not help the bishops make a stronger case for abortion law. Note that the Catholic tradition considers many actions—such as lying or masturbation—to be intrinsically evil. Intrinsic evil in the Catholic tradition refers to moral actions, but morality and law are not the same.

Earlier this chapter pointed out internal Church reasons that helped to explain why the U.S. bishops changed their approach and with great certitude made abortion their primary social and political focus. Another partial explanation for these developments stems from the context in which the bishops have exercised their teaching function. The bishops have not only been teachers but also strong advocates—abortion being a very significant issue in the culture wars.[70]

In the midst of partisan support for competing approaches, there is not much room for nuance or recognition of gray areas. Teaching and advocacy are two quite different realities. Partisan involvement by definition is not interested in nuance. The very fact that the abortion debate has been carried out in the broader context of partisan politics only increases the problem. In the future, the bishops should be aware that advocacy or partisanship might interfere with a proper understanding of their role as teachers in the Church.

This chapter focuses narrowly on showing that the bishops have claimed too great a certitude for their position on abortion law and have not recognized the role of prudential judgments in this area. There was no attempt to discuss all aspects of the abortion issue. In conclusion, the bishops in their teaching role can and should continue to speak out against abortion, and in the light of their moral teaching even propose positions with regard to abortion law but with a number of conditions. First, in keeping with the principle of subsidiarity, the bishops should recognize, as they themselves have said in the past, that laws against abortion are not the only way to defend and protect the life of the unborn. Education, support for pregnant women, and change in structures that might make abortion more appealing can have a significant effect. Second, bishops should not treat abortion law as the primary social issue; other important social issues of poverty, equality, discrimination, ecology, peace, and all forms of justice have not been given the importance they deserve. A consistent ethic of life maintains there is a connection between all the life issues. Third, when the bishops do speak on abortion law, they must not claim theirs is the only legitimate position within the Church. The truly catholic Church has room for different positions on abortion law. Fourth, politicians and voters who disagree with the bishops should not be threatened with excommunication or denial of Eucharistic communion. These conditions provide the parameters within which all the other aspects of the bishops' positions should be developed.

NOTES

1. *Human Life in Our Day: A Collective Pastoral Letter of the American Hierarchy* (Washington D.C.: United States Catholic Conference, 1968), 27–28.

2. Timothy A. Byrnes, *Catholic Bishops in American Politics* (Princeton, N.J.: Princeton University Press, 1991), 57–59, 68–69.

3. National Conference of Catholic Bishops, "Statement on Abortion, April 17, 1969," in *Quest for Justice: A Compendium of Statements of the United States Catholic Bishops on the Political and Social Order 1966–1980*, ed. J. Brian Benestad and Francis J. Butler (Washington, D.C.: United States Catholic Conference, 1981), 146–48.

4. National Conference of Catholic Bishops, "Statement on Abortion," 148–49.

5. James R. Kelly, "Learning Consistency: Catholicism and Abortion," in *The Church in the Nineties: Its Legacy, Its Future*, ed. Pierre M. Hegy (Collegeville, Minn.: Liturgical, 1993), 88.

6. Byrnes, *Catholic Bishops in American Politics*, 57.

7. National Conference of Catholic Bishops, "Resolution on the Pro-Life Consitutional Amendment," in *Quest for Justice*, ed. Benestad and Butler, 157–58.

8. Michael W. Cuneo, "Life Battles: The Rise of Catholic Militancy within the American Pro-Life Movement," in *Being Right: Conservative Catholics in America*, ed. Mary Jo Weaver and R. Scott Appleby (Bloomington: Indiana University Press, 1995), 277.

9. National Conference of Catholic Bishops, "Pastoral Plan for Pro-Life Activities," in *Quest for Justice*, ed. Benestad and Butler, 159–69.

10. Byrnes, *Catholic Bishops in American Politics*, 69.

11. Administrative Board, United States Catholic Conference, "Political Responsibility: Reflections on an Election Year," in *Quest for Justice*, ed. Benestad and Butler, 14–21.

12. Byrnes, *Catholic Bishops in American Politics*, 65–81. I depend heavily on Byrnes in describing this period from the 1970s to 1988, especially in the following paragraphs.

13. Administrative Board, United States Catholic Conference, "Political Responsibility: Choices for the 1980s," in *Quest for Justice*, ed. Benestad and Butler, 2–13.

14. Byrnes, *Catholic Bishops in American Politics*, 86–91.

15. "Bishops Support Hatch Amendment, Capitol Hill Testimony," *Origins* 11 (1981): 359ff.

16. Cuneo, "Life Battles," 283.

17. Byrnes, *Catholic Bishops in American Politics*, 92–131.

18. Administrative Board, United States Catholic Conference, "Political Responsibility: Choices for the 1980s," in *Pastoral Letters of the United States Catholic Bishops, 1983–1988*, ed. Hugh J. Nolan (Washington, D.C.: United States Catholic Conference, 1989), 5:95–108.

19. Byrnes, *Catholic Bishops in American Politics*, 114–15. For a further elaboration and discussion of the consistent ethic of life, see Joseph Cardinal Bernardin et al., *Consistent Ethic of Life*, ed. Thomas G. Fuechtmann (Kansas City, Mo.: Sheed and Ward, 1988); Joseph Bernardin, *The Seamless Garment: Writings on the Consistent Ethic of Life*, ed. Thomas A. Nairn (Maryknoll, N.Y.: Orbis, 2008); Thomas A. Nairn, ed., *The Consistent Ethic of Life: Assessing Its Reception and Relevance* (Maryknoll, N.Y.: Orbis, 2008).

20. Byrnes, *Catholic Bishops in American Politics*, 116–26.

21. Richard P. McBrien, *Caesar's Coin: Religion and Politics in America* (New York: Macmillan, 1987), 136–40, 151–55.

22. McBrien, *Caesar's Coin*, 145–58.

23. National Conference of Catholic Bishops, "Pastoral Plan for Pro-Life Activities," 200–202.

24. Administrative Board, United States Catholic Conference, "Political Responsibility: Choices for the Future," in *Pastoral Letters*, 5:526–30.

25. Byrnes, *Catholic Bishops in American Politics*, 131–35.

26. National Conference of Catholic Bishops, "Resolution on Abortion," in *Pastoral Letters and Statements of the United States Catholic Bishops, 1989–1997*, ed. Patrick W. Carey (Washington D.C.: United States Catholic Conference, 1998), 6:197–203.

27. Administrative Board, United States Catholic Conference, "Political Responsibility: Revitalizing American Democracy," *Origins* 21 (1991): 317–18; Administrative Board, United States Catholic Conference, *Political Responsibility: Proclaiming the Gospel of Life, Protecting the Least among Us, and Pursuing the Common Good* (Washington, D.C.: United States Catholic Conference, 1995), 12–14.

28. James R. Kelly, "Abortion Politics: The Last Decades, the Next Three Decades, and the 1992 Elections," *America*, July 4–11, 1992, 8–12.

29. James T. McHugh, "Catholics and the 1996 Election," *First Things*, February 17, 1997, 17.

30. "Partial-Birth Abortion Veto Complicates Al Smith Dinner," *National Catholic Register*, September 1, 1996, 4.

31. Thomas J. Reese, "Catholic Voters: Pulled in Two Directions," *America*, November 2, 1996, 7.

32. United States Conference of Catholic Bishops, "Living the Gospel of Life," www.usccb.org/prolife/gospel.shtml. The text will give the paragraph numbers of this document (e.g., n. 5).

33. Pope John Paul II, *Evangelium vitae*, n. 71, in *The Encyclicals of John Paul II*, ed. J. Michael Miller (Huntington, Ind.: Our Sunday Visitor, 2001), 737. The text will give the paragraph number for subsequent references to this document.

34. Charles Capetanakis, "Abortion Rights Mobilization and Religious Tax-Exemptions," *Catholic Lawyer* 34 (1991): 169–93.

35. Administrative Board, United States Catholic Conference, "Faithful Citizenship: Civic Responsibility for a New Millennium," *Origins* 29 (1999): 312–14.

36. Joseph L. Conn, "The Bishops' Biased Blessing," *Church and State* 53 (December 2000): 254–57.

37. National Conference of Catholic Bishops, "Pastoral Plan for Pro-Life Activities: A Campaign in Support of Life," www.usccb.org/prolife/pastoralplan.shtml.

38. Administrative Board, United States Catholic Conference, "Faithful Citizenship: Civic Responsibility for a New Millennium," *Origins* 29 (2003): 325–26.

39. William J. Levada, "Reflections on Catholics in Political Life and the Reception of Holy Communion," *Origins* 34 (2004): 102.

40. United States Catholic Bishops, "Catholics in Political Life," *Origins* 34 (2004): 97–99.

41. Theodore McCarrick, "Interim Reflections of the Task Force," *Origins* 34 (2004): 108.

42. William H. Keeler, "Summary of Consultations," *Origins* 34 (2004): 106.

43. U.S. Congresspersons, "On Denying Communion as a Sanction: Letter to a Cardinal," *Origins* 34 (2004): 35ff.

44. Cardinals Ratzinger and McCarrick, "Vatican, U.S. Bishops: On Catholics in Political Life," *Origins* 34 (2004): 133–34.

45. Atlanta, Charleston, and Charlotte Bishops, "A Manifest Lack of Proper Disposition for Holy Communion," *Origins* 34 (2004): 188–89; Bishop Joseph F. Gossman, "The State of Soul of Those Presenting Themselves for Communion," *Origins* 34 (2004): 189–90.

46. Theodore McCarrick, "Final Report: Bishops and Catholic Politicians," *Origins* 36 (2006): 97–100.

47. United States Conference of Catholic Bishops, *Forming Consciences for Faithful Citizenship: A Call to Political Responsibility from the Catholic Bishops of the United States* (Washington, D.C.: United States Conference of Catholic Bishops, 2007). Reference to this document in the text will include the paragraph number and the page number of this document, e.g. (n. 22, p. 8). This document is also available at www.usccb.org/bishops/FCStatement.pdf.

48. Rocco Palmo, "Church in World," *Tablet*, October 25, 2008, www.thetablet.co.uk/article12189.

49. Charles J. Chaput, *Render unto Caesar: Serving the Nation by Living Our Catholic Beliefs in Political Life* (New York: Doubleday, 2008).

50. "Cardinal Stafford Criticizes Obama as 'Aggressive, Disruptive, and Apocalyptic,'" *Catholic News Agency*, November 12, 2008, www.catholicnewsagency.com/new.php?n = 14355.

51. Steven Ertelt, "Joe Biden's Catholic Bishop Won't Deny Communion over Pro-Abortion Views," LifeNews.com, www.lifenews.com/state3635.html.

52. "Bishops Say Pelosi Misrepresented Abortion Teaching in TV Interview," *Catholic News Service*, August 27, 2008, www.catholicnews.com/data/stories/cns/0804350.html.

53. USCCB News Release, "Bishops Respond to Senator Biden's Statement regarding Church Teaching on Abortion," September 9, 2008, www.usccb.org/comm/archives/2008/08-129.shtml.

54. James Roberts and Timothy Lavin, "US Bishops Pledge to Fight Obama on Life Issues," *Tablet*, January 24, 2009, www.thetablet.co.uk/article/12590.

55. "List of Bishops Opposing the Notre Dame Invitation and Award to President Obama," www.lifesitenews.com/ldn/2009/max/09060607.html.

56. "Catholic Voters Heavily Favored Obama, Analysis Shows," *Washington Times*, November 7, 2008, www.washingtontimes.com/news/2008/nov/07/catholic-voters-heavily-favored-obama-analysis-sho/; see also Lisa Sowle Cahill, "Religion and Politics: U.S.A.," *Theological Studies* 70 (2009): 186–91.

57. Gerald Kelly, *Medico-Moral Problems*, (St. Louis, Mo.: Catholic Hospital Association, 1958), 66–67.

58. Kelly, *Medico-Moral Problems*, 67.

59. Sacred Congregation for the Doctrine of the Faith, "Declaration on Procured Abortion," in *Medical Ethics: Sources of Catholic Teachings*, ed. Kevin D. O'Rourke and Philip Boyle (St. Louis, Mo.: Catholic Health Association, 1989), 39n19.

60. Pope John Paul II, *Evangelium vitae*, n. 60, in *The Encyclicals of John Paul II*, 727.

61. For my description of the positions of U.S. Catholic moral theologians on the question of the status of the personal life of the fetus, see Charles E. Curran, *Catholic Moral Theology in the United States: A History* (Washington, D.C.: Georgetown University Press, 2008), 232–37.

62. Lisa Sowle Cahill, *Theological Bioethics: Participation, Justice, and Change* (Washington, D.C.: Georgetown University Press, 2005), 229–35.

63. William F. Buckley, Jr., "The War on Drugs Is Lost," *National Review*, February 12, 1996, 35–38.

64. James R. Kelley, "A Catholic Votes for John Kerry," *America*, September 27, 2004, 13, 16–17; Douglas W. Kmiec, *Can a Catholic Support Him? Asking the Big Question about Barack Obama* (New York: Overlook, 2008).

65. National Conference of Catholic Bishops, "Pastoral Plan for Pro-Life Activities," 164.

66. "Bishops Support Hatch Amendment: Capitol Hill Testimony," *Origins* 11 (1981): 359ff.

67. United States Conference of Catholic Bishops, *Forming Consciences for Faithful Citizenship*, 7–8.

68. Pope Pius XI, *Casti connubii*, in *The Papal Encyclicals 1903–1939*, ed. Claudia Carlen (Wilmington, N.C.: McGrath, 1981), 399.

69. H. Noldin, *Summa Theologiae Moralis: Complementum de Castitate*, 36th ed., ed. Godefridus Heinzel (Innsbruck: Rauch, 1958), 66 n. 72.

70. James Davison Hunter, *Culture Wars: The Struggle to Define America* (New York: Basic, 1991).

CONCLUSIONS

Looking Backward and Forward

Three significant factors have influenced the understanding and structuring of the social mission of the U.S. Catholic Church. The first is the theological understanding of the Church and its social mission. Here Vatican II theology has posited an approach that culminated in a recognition that action on behalf of justice and the transformation of the world is a constitutive dimension of the preaching of the Gospel and the mission of the Church. This newer approach raised questions about the specific roles of the hierarchy—clergy, religious, and the laity—that occasioned some controversy in the post–Vatican II Church. Today all recognize that social mission is an essential part of the reality of the Church.

Second, the sociological situation of the Church in the United States also greatly influences its social mission. The immigrant Church's primary concern was to provide for its own people and—in light of discrimination and prejudice against Catholics—to show that the immigrant Catholics were good Americans and not a threat to the nation. The immigrant Church played a very significant social role in the lives of urban Catholics, who lived in mostly Catholic neighborhoods. As time went on, the number of immigrants decreased significantly and the first generation of immigrants and their children increasingly assimilated into U.S. culture. In post–World War II culture Catholics as a whole entered into the middle class and the mainstream of U.S. society. Many more Catholics obtained a college education and frequently moved to the suburbs. The Church and especially the local parish no longer played as prominent a role in their lives as before. The changing relationship of Catholics to U.S. society, together with Vatican II's theological developments, resulted in U.S. Catholics no longer understanding their role in the world in accordance with

Catholic action, which had been prominent in the pre–Vatican II Church. Catholics more often than not worked with others in trying to bring about a more just society.

A better-educated Catholic laity appreciated the emphasis on freedom, responsibility, and conscience in the post–Vatican II Church. The 1968 papal encyclical *Humanae vitae* led many Catholics to question the role of authority in the Church.[1] As a result of the sociological and theological developments, the Catholic Church in the United States was much more heterogenous than it had been in the pre–Vatican II period.

Third, the historical situation and developments in U.S. culture and social life also influenced the mission of the Church. At the time of Vatican II (1962–65) no one could have guessed that abortion law would become such a contentious issue in our society. The plight of the farmworkers under the leadership of César Chávez posed a unique opportunity for the Church. Catholics worked together with many others by joining boycotts in support of the union and the bishops played a substantive role in supporting the UFW—first as mediators but ultimately as strong partisans.

The characteristic of catholicity has played the most central theoretical role in the understanding and structuring of the social mission of the Church. First, catholicity grounds the need for and importance of the social mission of the Church in its insistence that the mission of the Church embraces all things. God created all that is. Redemption affects not only human beings but all of creation. Consequently the redemptive mission of the Church must touch all reality. The social mission is not something ancillary to the mission of the Church but itself is an essential aspect of that one mission.

Second, catholicity in a certain sense grounds the principle of subsidiarity, which indicates all the different areas in which the social mission takes place. There has been a tendency to identify the social mission of the Church with Catholic social teaching, which is the teaching of modern popes and the hierarchy primarily on political and economic issues. These are significant issues, but they are not all there is to the social mission of the Church. In fact, the social mission of the Church involves lay people in all the aspects of their lives. Families, neighborhoods, work environments, and various professional, social, and recreational associations are called to carry on the social mission of the Church and work for a better and more just society. As citizens at the local, state, and federal levels, the laity work for structural change as well.

The issue of racism amply illustrates that social mission involves more than just changing structures. The civil rights movement, to its great credit, brought about significant change in law and public policy with regard to racism and other forms of discrimination. Before Vatican II the Catholic Interracial Councils tried to bring Catholics together to overcome racial division, segregation, and discrimination. Like most of the forms of Catholic action, this involved an elite and did not really encompass the mass of Catholics, but at least it was an attempt to address the problem. After Vatican II these councils largely ceased to exist. Once policies and laws were changed people thought there was no more to be done in the area of racism, but this is totally false. Despite the election of Barack Obama, racism is still an unfortunate feature of U.S. society. Recently, white Christians and Catholics have been challenged to recognize their own white privilege. Even today whites and blacks are treated very differently: white drivers are pulled over by police officers proportionally far less often than black drivers; white males have a much longer lifespan than black males; and white people continue to have many financial and educational advantages. Whites are challenged to recognize white privilege and strive to work for greater fairness in this area.[2]

To overcome attitudes of racial superiority, discrimination, and white privilege, a concerted effort is required on all levels, beginning with the family. Parents need to inculcate the proper racial and ethnic attitudes in their children. Neighborhoods, workplaces, and professional, social, and recreational associations present innumerable opportunities to practice respect for others regardless of the color of their skin, their sex, or their ethnic background. Proper attitudes that are formed in the home and other environments must lead to other actions challenging the racism that continues to exist in U.S. social life. The problem of racism and the ways in which Christians are called to struggle against racism serves as an excellent reminder that the social mission of the Church involves more than changing political and economic structures.

Third, catholicity, recognizing the inclusive nature of the Church and the need for diversity as well as unity in the Church, shapes how and when leaders can speak for the whole Church and what is the obligatory force of their teaching and actions. The U.S. bishops dealt with this issue in two 1980s pastoral letters on peace and the economy. Implicitly the bishops also recognized this issue when they struggled to determine their proper role concerning César Chávez's UFW. Recall that they moved from a policy of neutral mediation to one of active support for the farmworkers.

The issue for which this aspect of catholicity came to the fore is abortion law. In this area the bishops failed to recognize the legitimacy of positions that differed from their own. Both internal Church factors and the complications stemming from their strong advocacy role in the midst of deep political polarization help to explain their failure to appreciate and recognize the catholicity and inclusiveness of the Church.

184 — Conclusions

Fourth, catholicity's emphasis on an inclusive "both-and" approach also contributed to a proper understanding of the social mission of the Church. I have already mentioned the need to work for both structural change and to transform the many milieux in which the baptized live their daily lives. In addition there have been discussions and debates over whether lay people should have a role in the internal life of the Church, or a role in transforming the temporal order. Again, the answer is "both-and." Vatican II called for a greater participation of all the baptized in the liturgy and internal life and ministry of the Church. External conditions such as the decreasing number of priests and religious women and men, as well as the problems associated with child sex abuse and its coverup, have contributed to the growing involvement of lay people in the internal life of the Church. But by definition the baptized who live in the world must be committed to striving for a just society.

Fifth, catholicity recognizes a role for both unity and diversity in the Church, and this is true also of the social mission of the Church carried on by individuals. Two different approaches can be described as the witness approach and the effectiveness approach. The witness approach emphasizes the need to stand up for a particular issue and especially to protest against those who deny it. Such an approach is not primarily concerned with building consensus, which is the focus of the effectiveness approach. The different tactics of the anti-abortion approach and the pro-life approach as described in chapter 6 exemplify these two different approaches. Opposition to the Vietnam War revealed the same two approaches at work. The Catholic Resistance followed the witness approach, whereas many other Catholics adopted the effectiveness approach in trying to bring about national consensus against the war.

The witness approach by its very nature is prone to engage in civil disobedience and perhaps even some limited use of force. This is not the place to develop an in-depth analysis of such civil disobedience and the use of some force. However, the justification for such means cannot be mere agreement with the position in support of which civil disobedience or force is being used. In the United States the "right" has historically used such tactics in the abortion issue, whereas the "left" has used similar tactics on the war issue. Justification for or opposition to such means must apply to all such tactics no matter what cause is being supported.

Sixth, catholicity recognizes a significant difference between Catholic morality and legality as such. If Catholic morality is presented and seen primarily in terms of legality, it is somewhat distorted.

Catholicity recognizes that we are sinful human beings who often fall short. All of us recognize our sins and faults and the need for forgiveness. Penance is one of the seven sacraments of the Church, precisely because of God's mercy and forgiveness of sinners. The Catholic Church lives with the tension of positing moral obligations for all but recognizing that all will fall short in some way. For those who are truly sorry, forgiveness is always available. At the beginning of every Eucharistic celebration, Catholics confess their sinfulness to God and one another and ask for forgiveness. Moral theologians have always pointed out there is a difference between what the priest says in the pulpit and in the sacrament of penance.

Forgiveness is also possible for those who have had an abortion. Project Rachel is the name of the Catholic Church's healing ministry to those who have been involved in abortion. Project Rachel programs exist in 140 Catholic dioceses in the United States. Women who have had an abortion often have many questions: Can God ever forgive me? Can my child? Can I forgive myself? Will my pain ever go away? Is healing possible? The answer to all these questions is, of course, YES. Project Rachel operates as a network of professional counselors and priests trained to provide spiritual and psychological care following an abortion. Some programs also include support groups and retreats.[3]

Law is a blunt instrument that does not recognize the possibility of forgiveness. When so much emphasis is put on the legal aspect of abortion, it distorts the full understanding of Catholic morality, with its recognition of the tension between the moral call to all and the possibility of forgiveness for all of us sinners.

This study makes clear that the primary challenge facing the Church is to make Catholics understand that action on behalf of justice and the transformation of the world is a constitutive dimension of the mission of the Church. In the light of this challenge the primary responsibility of the whole Church is the formation and education of Catholics to carry out this mission. In theory it is easy to recognize the primacy of this challenge. The more practical and difficult question is how to carry out this daunting task. This book has made some suggestions, but the response to this challenge requires the commitment, creativity, and the informed initiative of all in the Church.

The most important aspect of educating and forming Catholics to carry out the social mission of the Church is not controversial. The most controversial aspect of the social mission of the Church has been the statements and actions of the bishops as leaders of the Church on what is required of all Catholics. This book reflects this paradox, and devotes many more pages to the abortion law discussion than to any other topic. But in closing, it is important to note that what is the most controversial is of minor importance compared to the primary need to educate and form Catholics to take their part in the social mission of the Church as a constitutive dimension of what it means to be Catholic.

LOOKING FORWARD

Predictions about the future are always very difficult to make. The vicissitudes of history are such that while some things will remain basically the same others will change dramatically. However, we should have learned something from history that will at least help us to address the future.

One can be quite certain that the major challenges of the past and the present will persist in the future. How can the Church make all the baptized recognize in theory and in practice that the social mission of the Church is a constitutive part of what it means to be Catholic? This issue by its very nature should have the highest priority. Here the educational role of the Church in its many dimensions must be encouraged to try to meet the challenge. The Church and its members have yet to realize that the Church can have the most participative and lively liturgies, magnificent choirs, good preaching, life-giving education, and still not be Church if no one is living out the social mission.

The three factors that have most influenced the understanding and structure of the social mission of the Church in the past will continue to be most influential. These factors do not depend on changing historical situations but rather they call attention to the importance of historical circumstances. The perspective adopted in this book hopes that the first factor, the theological understanding of the Church and its social mission, will not change dramatically, but will deepen and develop. The second factor, the sociological situation of the Church in the United States, will certainly change dramatically. At present there are already significant changes occurring that will perdure and even grow in the future. The Pew Research Center in 2009 reported that almost one-third (31.4 percent) of those who were raised Catholic are no longer Catholic. One in ten adults in the United States is a former Catholic. These are astounding statistics and indicate a very significant loss of membership. Over half of those who left were dissatisfied with Catholic teachings on morality (birth control, divorce, homosexuality, and abortion) and the role of women.[4]

Many Catholic parents today have had some, and maybe even all, of their adult children leave the Catholic Church. This trend will continue if the Catholic Church does nothing to modify the teachings mentioned above. These teachings by definition do not belong to the core of Catholic faith, but the leaders of the Church have been adamant in their refusal to change them. Catholic dioceses throughout the country are amalgamating or closing parishes. The Diocese of Rochester, New York, recently reported that attendance at weekend Eucharistic liturgies declined from 110,000 in 2000 to less than 90,000 in 2008.[5] To the amazement of many, the U.S. Catholic Church and its leadership have not even considered the problem of Catholics leaving the Church, let alone done something about it.

There is an even bigger change on the horizon. At present about one-third of all Catholics in the United States are Hispanic and the Latino/a population will continue to grow for decades.[6] Sometime in the future the majority of Catholics in this country will be Hispanic, and without doubt this change will have a significant impact on the Church and its social mission. Will the social mission take on some of the same characteristics of the immigrant Catholic Church in the nineteenth and early twentieth centuries?

Analogous to the sociological position of the Church in the United States is the broader relationship of the Church in the United States to the Church universal. For many centuries the Catholic Church has been primarily a Western and somewhat northern Church, but the Church is not as vital in these areas as it once was. Now and in the future Church growth will take place in the Southern Hemisphere. This change in center of gravity will definitely affect the understanding of the social mission of the U.S. Church.

A third factor is that historical developments in the United States and the world will have considerable ramifications for the future social mission of the Church. New issues and problems will come to the fore, but there will be a continuing need to address issues that have concerned the Church for some time. Poverty, equality, and justice are perennial issues, but they take on different forms and faces in different circumstances. It is safe to say that ecological issues will become even more significant in the future. It is only in the last few decades that we have become conscious of how our lifestyles have negatively affected the earth and its atmosphere. The problem will become even more acute as global industrialization and its concomitant pollution rises. Increased globalization will affect ecology and most other issues facing society in the future.

One can safely conclude that there will be no shortage of problems to face. Specific issues usually call for some type of public regulation or policy, but one should not forget that they often also include aspects that can be addressed by individuals. The individual person, for example, can do much to overcome the ecological devastation that is occurring in our world. In addition, one must be careful not to equate the total social mission of the Church with responses to controverted societal issues.

Chapter 7 discusses the various roles that the Church should play in carrying out its social mission. Once again, these roles do not have much material content and hence may be applied to quite disparate circumstances. Recall that these roles are educating and forming Catholics in the social mission; providing for, advocating for, and empowering those in need; the recognition that the Church must itself be a model for other institutions in society; and addressing specific complex issues facing society.

The most divisive issue at present has been abortion law. The public policy issues of same-sex marriage and stem cell research raise some of the same concerns. More such issues will undoubtedly arise in the future; one hopes that the bishops will recognize the danger of claiming too great a certitude on issues of law and public policy.

The one great continuity between the past and the future and the most important aspect of the social mission of the Church is the call for the Church to educate and form all its members to acknowledge in theory and practice that the social mission is a constitutive and essential dimension of what it means to be a Catholic Christian.

NOTES

1. Andrew M. Greeley, William C. McCready, and Kathleen McCourt, *Catholic Schools in a Declining Church* (Kansas City, Mo.: Sheed & Ward, 1976), 35, 103–54.

2. Laurie M. Cassidy and Alex Mikulich, eds., *Interrupting White Privilege: Catholic Theologians Break the Silence* (Maryknoll, N.Y.: Orbis, 2007); Jon Nilson, *Hearing Past the Pain: Why White Catholic Theologians Need Black Theology* (N.Y.: Paulist, 2007).

3. Project Rachel, www.hopeafterabortion.com.

4. The Pew Forum on Public Life, "Faith in Flux," at pewresearch.org/pubs/1204/religion-changes-affiliations-survey.

5. "Thinning Flocks Spur Closings," *Catholic Courier*, October 2009, 1A, 6A–7A.

6. USCCB Department of Communications, "Hispanic Catholics in the United States," www.usccb.org/comm.backgrounders/hispanic.html.

INDEX